Scamps Scoundrels & Heroes

The Post War Exploits of Civil War Veterans from
Washington County, Pennsylvania

Jim Douglas

Plum Run Press

ACKNOWLEDGEMENTS

A special thank you to those who have supported my work for the past eight years. A few stand out for various reasons. Thanks to Jessica Denny for the great pictures of the fabulous Sweetapple family. What a treasure you have there. And also to Jan Price for the awesome Paul family images. They are a pleasure to see, a treasure in their own right, and are a great addition to this book.

A big Thank You to Captain John Mort of Company G, 11th Pennsylvania Volunteer Infantry. John did a great job providing encouragement, just at the right time. I could always go to John and find answers. He understands and has been there, and is as tough as they come. When others stabbed me in the back, he stood side by side with me, with great advice, and ready to take on all comers, all the way. There is no quit in him. He is the personification of Major Happer. Captain, you really need to be promoted to Major.

And special thanks to my son Jason for providing some high quality pictures of the author for various purposes, and for his second set of eyes on several areas of question. And also to my son Jim for picking up the slack around the house when I went down with a knee injury. He has filled in for me very nicely in every capacity for a long time, and is still doing so, taking the load off without being asked, so I can recover. I can always count on Jim. He's my rock.

Last, but not least is my wife, Personal Assistant, Chief of Staff, Bringer of Coffee, and first line Punctuation Editor who makes sure I don't have too many run on sentences, and always a double-space after every period. She listens patiently every day while I talk (and complain) incessantly about the latest writing problem and all with minimal eye rolls! What a gal she is.

Thank you to everyone who cheered me on all along the way. Especially those such as Linda Greene and the others who "liked" all the colorized images and other stuff I posted on social media as trial runs. Thanks everyone for your support, it's greatly appreciated and a lot of help!

My motto is and has always been: Tell the truth, tell it straight, and tell it all.

J. D.

Contents

This book is dedicated to the mothers and fathers who agonized through unending days and nights, wondering if their boys were alright. Waiting for word that they were fine and doing well tramping along in the choking dust on one of a thousand country roads on the way to battle in some faraway place that would soon be etched in the history books forever.

For the brothers and sisters who were so proud of their brother, or the children who watched their father go off to war, because it was the right thing to do. For the wives who silently wept every night after the children were asleep, hoping against hope that their husband was well and would come home safely to them once again.

For all those who waited impatiently for a letter from some place they never heard of from their loved one, saying he was alive and missed them all so terribly. And for the many thousands who received another kind of letter, with the worst news on earth.

For all the children of the men who made it home, who sat on their father's knee by the fireplace and breathlessly listened to to the stories of what it was like in the War of the Rebellion. For the grandchildren who did the same, years later with grandpa, then grew up and went off to fight in another war, kin some other place, but for the same reason.

And for all those today who remember their ancestors who fought at one battlefield or another. Those who keep their memory in their hearts and refuse to let it fade away to dust. For those today who stand at the parade when the flag marches by, carried proudly by Civil War re-enactors who live the life in the hopes that these men would not be forgotten, and once again renew the honor and dignity that those long departed veterans bought with their life's blood and sacrifice.

For all those reasons and many more, I humbly dedicate this work so that these veterans and their stories will never fade away. That their actions, their heroism, and their devotion will forever be remembered.

We shall always remember them.

J. D.

My very dear Sarah,

The indications are very strong that we shall move in a few days-perhaps tomorrow. Lest I should not be able to write again, I feel impelled to write a few lines that may fall under your eye when I am no more.

I have no misgivings about, or lack of confidence in the cause in which I am engaged, and my courage does not halt or falter. I know how strongly American Civilization now leans on the triumph of the Government, and how great a debt we owe to those who went before us through the blood and suffering of the Revolution. And I am willing-perfectly willing-to lay down all the joys in this life, to help maintain this Government, and to pay that debt.

Sarah, my love for you is deathless. It seems to bind me with mighty cables that nothing but Omnipotence could break; and yet my love of country comes over me like a strong wind and bears me irresistibly on with all these chains to the battlefield.

The memories of the blissful moments I have spent with you come creeping over me, and I feel most grateful to God and to you that I have enjoyed them for so long. How hard it is for me to give them up and burn to ashes the hopes of future years, when, God willing, we might still have lived and loved together, and seen our sons grown up to honorable manhood around us. I have, I know, but few and small claims upon Divine Providence, but something whispers to me-perhaps it is the wafted prayer of my little Edgar, that I shall return to my loved ones unharmed. If I do not my dear Sarah, never forget how much I love you, and that when my last breath escapes me on the battlefield, it will whisper your name. Forgive my many faults, and the many pains I have caused you. How thoughtless and foolish I have often times been! How gladly would I wash out with my tears every little spot upon your happiness.

But, oh Sarah! If the dead can come back to this earth and flit unseen around those they loved, I shall always be near you; in the gladdest days and in the darkest nights...always, always. And if there be a soft breeze upon your cheek, it shall be my breath, and as the cool air fans your throbbing temple, it shall be my spirit passing by. Sarah, do not mourn me dead; think I am gone and wait for me, for we shall meet again.

(Sullivan Ballou was killed a week later at the battle of Bull Run)

PROLOGUE

It is late January as I write this and it is a cold, dark, miserable evening and it's snowing heavily. Inside I have a roaring fire going in the fireplace and a handful of my neighborhood friends are starting to drift by, as they know what I do on these kinds of nights. Nothing planned, it just happens. A warm fire, good friends, and tasty drinks are the order of the evening.

I keep the lights low, and let the fire light the way. I sit back and let the conversation just happen on it's own as I know it will come down to funny stories and some tall tales along with some good-natured kidding to bring a laugh and a smile to us all. This is what keeps me going in the seemingly endless dreary days of Winter.

Oh, another knock on the door, wonder who it is? No matter, they are welcome here this night. Excuse me while I answer the door. Hello! Welcome, stomp the snow off your boots and throw your coat on a peg. Have a seat by the fire and warm yourself, while I pour another round. There are stories to be told, and you, are among friends.

J. D.

CHAPTER ONE

The Achesons

The woods were filled with the acrid gray and white smoke of the battle. As the 140th Pennsylvania Volunteer Infantry double-quicked to the wood's edge, they came upon a large field of wheat. Through the smoke, they could see men in blue being pushed back toward them.

On the right of the line, they advance at an oblique across the northwest part of the field toward the tree line ahead. They were met with a great volley of smoke and fire and their nearby Brigade commander S. K. Zook was shot out of the saddle.

The regiment went forward, then across the field, taking heavy casualties all the way, but sweeping the enemy from the field. Halting at the stone wall at the western edge of the field, the men clambered over and continued their advance into a rocky woods just to the north of Stony Hill. Company C came into close quarters with elements of the 3rd South Carolina Infantry. They were confronted with a blaze of fire so severe that they could no longer advance. The Company commander, Colonel Roberts, fell mortally wounded. The ranking Captain, young David Acheson, assumed the command and was preparing to lead his men forward when his friend First Lieutenant Isaac

Vance from Amity, PA, was severely wounded, his left hand shattered. As Captain Acheson was attending to his friend, he was shot through his chest. As the Union line fell back, Acheson was being carried rearward when he was hit again in the chest area. The South Carolinians overwhelmed the field and the intense fire forced his men to leave Captain Acheson on the battlefield among the dead and wounded.

He was only twenty-one years old on this day, July 2nd, 1863. The place is a small bucolic town in south central Pennsylvania called Gettysburg. An attempted retrieval of Captain Acheson's remains was made by his good friend and classmate, First Lt. George Laughlin, and Captain John Ewing, both of the 155th Pennsylvania the next day, but had to be abandoned due to heavy Rebel sharpshooter fire. It wasn't until rainy July 5th that his body was recovered by his friends and interred in a shallow grave on the Weikert farm. One of the men carved the letters D A on a large rock to mark the location. Acheson's first cousin, A. Todd Baird, and schoolmate, James Blaine Wilson, had the gruesome task of retrieving the captain's body ten days after the battle. Wilson uprooted a geranium from a nearby garden to take home to the fallen man's father, Washington County Judge A.W. Acheson.

Acheson's Rock

Wilson then sat atop the "rude coffin lined with zinc" in a wagon that carried the party through the night in a steady rain from Gettysburg to Harrisburg. A train likely carried the crew to Pittsburgh, where another wagon finished the trip to Washington, PA. Captain Acheson was buried on July 15th, 1863, at Washington Cemetery in Washington, PA. Five years later a member of Company C revisited the battlefield site, deepened the carved initials, and added "140 PV." This inscription can still be seen today in the Gettysburg National Military Park.

Of the thirty-eight men present for duty in Company C that afternoon, at the end of the day, seven had been killed, twenty-two wounded, and three missing and presumed captured.

David Acheson was born in 1841, one of nine children to prominent Washington attorney and judge, Alexander W. Acheson, and his wife Jane Wishart. Incidentally, three of David's brothers also served in the Union army during the war, including Sandy Acheson who was a Sergeant in Company C. We'll get to them a little later.

Judge Acheson was very well-liked by all for many years. His passing in 1890 was felt by all. Here's a part of his obituary:

Judge Acheson

"Judge Acheson was born in Philadelphia, July 15, 1809; was graduated at Washington College in 1827; admitted to the bar in 1832 and was married in 1836 to Jane Wishart. He was three times District Attorney of Washington and in 1866 was elected President Judge of the Beaver-Washington district. He was noted on the bench for the strength and clearness of his judicial opinions and especially for his rulings in liquor cases.

Judge Acheson retired from active practice on the first of last October, after 57 years of devotion to the profession. He was a man of great ability and learning. No man in the country was more universally loved and respected."

Judge Acheson's home would be purchased a few years later by Major A. G. Happer to serve as the first Washington Hospital. More on that later.

It's interesting to note that David's father was as mentioned a prominent judge for many years, and David's uncle, Marcus Wilson Acheson (June 7, 1828 - June 21, 1906) was nominated by President Rutherford B. Hayes on January 6, 1880, to a seat on the United States District Court for the Western District of Pennsylvania. He was confirmed by the United States Senate on January 14, 1880. He was nominated by President Benjamin Harrison on January 23, 1891, to a seat on the United States Circuit Courts for the Third Circuit, and was confirmed by the Senate on February 3, 1891. He was also assigned by operation of law to additional and concurrent service on the United States Court of Appeals for the Third Circuit on June 16, 1891, which he served until his passing in 1906.

David Acheson grew up on the family farm and enrolled in Washington College in 1860. He decided to leave college and recruit a company of men from

Washington, many from Washington College. He recruited "many of the best and brightest young men of the town and its environs." This became Company C of the 140th Pennsylvania Volunteer Infantry. Acheson was elected Captain and two of his friends, Charles Linton and Isaac Vance were chosen Second Lieutenant and First Lieutenant respectively.

The 140th Pennsylvania Infantry was recruited in the counties of Washington, Greene, Mercer, and Beaver. They were mustered onto service at Camp Curtin/Harrisburg for three years. On September 10, it left the state for Parkton, Maryland, where it guarded the North Central Railroad. In December after the battle of Fredericksburg, it joined the army and was assigned to the 3rd Brigade, 1st Division, 2nd Corps. They were encamped at Falmouth where they received brand new Springfield rifles. The Regiment marched for Chancellorsville where they saw real action and had forty-four

Judge Marcus W. Acheson

killed, wounded, or missing. They then returned to Falmouth. When General Lee's Confederate army invaded Pennsylvania, they marched through Maryland and on into Pennsylvania and the rest is history.

Mention should be made of the interesting story of Captain George Laughlin, 1842-1908. He was born in Pittsburgh, the son of James and Ann Laughlin. James Laughlin founded the Pittsburgh Trust Company in 1852 and served as its President for the rest of his life.

In 1862, the company was reorganized into the First National Bank. He also formed a partnership with Mr. Frank Jones sometime around 1855. That became the American Iron Works, the second largest iron works in the

US. As the business grew, it became Jones & Laughlins, then later Jones and Laughlin Steel. He also started a blast furnace company called Laughlin & Company.

His three sons, including George Laughlin, were instrumental in those companies for many years. George Laughlin was educated in private schools in Pittsburgh and attended Washington College (later Washington and Jefferson) where he left in his junior year to muster into the Union army as a private. He soon received a commission to Second Lieutenant in Company E of the 155th Pennsylvania Vol. Infantry. He served throughout the war until Appomattox, being promoted to Captain, then to Brevet Major. In the last year of the war he served on the staff of Major

James Laughlin

General Charles Griffin who was in command of the 5th Army Corps. General Griffin was one of three commanders designated by General Grant to arrange the details of the surrender of General Lee's army and Captain Laughlin accompanied him as his aid de camp, and was, therefore, witness to the meeting between General Grant and General Lee at the McLean house at Appomattox, Virginia.

Lto R. George Laughlin, Alexander Sweeney, David Acheson

Major Laughlin returned home to join his brothers in the Jones & Laughlin Steel Company where he served as Treasurer and Vice-Chairman of the board until 1900.

He remained a Director & Board member until his death. He also was a founder and a Director of the Keystone National Bank of Pittsburgh, and bank President from 1899 until his death.

If that wasn't enough, he was a founder of the Pittsburgh Trust Company and served as a Director. He was married on November 16, 1865, to Isabell B. McKennan of Washington, PA, daughter of Judge William McKennan of the United States Circuit Court.

George and Isabelle's children were as follows: William M. died in childhood; Irwin B.

Major Laughlin

born April 16, 1871, was educated at St. Paul's School in Concord New Hampshire, and graduated from Yale University in 1893. He joined the firm of J&L Steel and worked his way up to Treasurer where he served until 1904 when he left to serve in the U S Diplomatic Corps. He worked all over the world in several posts including charge' d'affaires of the American Legation in Athens, Greece.

George M. Laughlin Jr. was born February 25, 1873, educated at St. Pauls, and then on to Yale University. He then joined J&L Steel.

Thomas K. Laughlin was born on March 16 1875 and was educated at St. Pauls in Concord New Hampshire, and like his brother attended Shefield Scientific School at Yale University, where he graduated in the class of 1897. He became a Director and Assistant Treasurer at J&L Steel and a Director at the Keystone National Bank. Thomas Laughlin committed suicide by gunshot on March 11, 1910. Major Laughlin and Isabelle had a daughter as well, Pauline Gertrude, however sadly she died at the young age of eight.

Major Laughlin was a member of the Duquesne, Pittsburgh, and Union Clubs, and the Pittsburgh Golf Club.

He also held memberships in the National Arts Club of New York City, the Manufacturer's Club of Philadelphia, the Grand Army of the Republic, the Loyal

Legion, and the Sons of the Revolution. Major George McCully Laughlin passed away on December 11, 1908, of Pleurisy. He is buried in Allegheny Cemetery, in Pittsburgh.

Pictured in 1940, the Laughlin mansion on Woodland Road in Pittsburgh was built in 1887 by George Laughlin. Pittsburgh banker Andrew Mellon bought the house in 1917 and added a swimming pool, bowling alley, tennis courts, breakfast room, and gardens. The red brick Tudor-style home also contains many pieces of carved stone, wood paneling, bay windows, and a marble solarium. It was

The Laughlin Mansion

donated by Paul and Mary Mellon to what became Carnegie Mellon University in 1940.

Captain David Acheson's eldest brother, John Wishart Acheson, was born in Washington PA, in 1837. At the age of twenty, he graduated from Washington College and began teaching Latin at his alma mater while he developed his interest in the piano. When the war broke out in 1861, he enlisted for three months in the 12th Pennsylvania Volunteer Infantry.

John W. Acheson

After his term expired, he mustered into Company A of the 85th Pennsylvania Vol. Infantry. Quickly advancing up the ranks, he was promoted to First Lieutenant on August 2, 1862. Feeling his progress was being blocked, he mustered out on February 29, 1864. He then transferred to the U.S. Volunteers Adjutant General Department and was commissioned Captain. He joined the staff of Brig. General Absalom Baird (who was also from Washington PA) commanded the 3rd Division, XIV Corps serving as Assistant Adjutant General. Serving in Sherman's army during the Atlanta campaign, Captain Acheson was wounded on September 1st at the battle of Jonesboro. For his service, he was brevetted to the rank of Major. At the war's end, he was given orders to return home to await further orders.

Joseph M. Acheson

At this point, he expressed an interest to become a doctor, so he studied under Dr. Thomas McKennan in Washington, PA. He then attended the University of Pennsylvania where he graduated on March 13, 1868. He opened a practice in Washington where he was very successful for a time. However, he developed a severe addiction to alcohol and passed away on May 1, 1872, at the age of 35.

Joseph M. Acheson was born in Washington PA, on March 22, 1848. While only a boy of 16, he enlisted in Knapp's Independent Battery on May 19, 1864. Of slight build, he contracted malaria and was discharged on September 15, 1864. He entered Washington College and graduated in the class of 1868. He studied law under his father, Judge Alexander Acheson, and passed the bar in Pittsburgh in 1871.

At some point, he traveled to Fairfield, Iowa, where he married Miss Alice T. Campbell, daughter of Judge Edward Campbell on November 27, 1873. He practiced law there until his untimely death on October 21, 1886. He was only 38 years old. They had a daughter, Mrs. Bessie George who lived in Chicago.

Time now for a short aside. I must mention here another Acheson.

He didn't serve in the Civil War but he did serve his country admirably for many years. I'm talking about Earnest F. Acheson, brother to David, John, Joseph, and Sandy. Born, of course, in Washington, PA, on September 19,

E. F. Acheson

1855. He was educated in the local schools until enrolling in Washington College in 1875. After graduating, he studied law and passed the bar in 1877.

He practiced law until 1879 when he bought the weekly newspaper, the Washington Reporter. He served as its editor, as well, until 1884 when he decided to enter politics. He ran for and won a seat as a delegate for the Republican National Convention, and served in that position in 1884.

In 1882, he married Miss Jane Bushfield Stewart and they had five children. Phoebe was born in 1884, Alexander was born in 1885, Elizabeth was born in 1889, Janet was born in 1892, and Martha was born in 1896.

A quick review of the guests at the wedding reveals a who's who of Washington.

Congressman E. F. Acheson

Along with all the Achesons, McKennans, etc., tucked in there neatly is Mr. and Mrs. Major A. G. Happer. (We will get to him later in this book.)

Earnest returned to his newspaper pursuits and started a daily edition of the Washington Weekly Observer. He was chosen as Recording Secretary of the National Editorial Association and also served as a Trustee at Washington College from 1894 until 1917.

Also in 1894, he ran for and was elected to a seat in the United States Congress, serving Pennsylvania's 24th District in the House of Representatives from 1895 until 1909.

E. F. Acheson Front Row Center

This guy was the very definition of multitasking. In May 1907, at the invitation of the Legislature of Hawaii, a party of U. S. Congressmen and others visited the Territory. Rep. Acheson is shown seated in the image taken outside the Royal Hawaiian Hotel. He again returned to the newspaper where he served until his retirement in 1912, also working as a Director in the Pittsburgh Life and Trust Company.

After a lifetime of relentless business pursuits and public service, his health began to fail. On May 16, 1917, he passed away from pneumonia and nervous prostration at his home on East Maiden Street in Washington, Pennsylvania, at the age of 51. His wife, Jane, passed away less than one year later.

US Congressional Delegation

Outside the Royal Hawaiian Hotel

The final Acheson brother to talk about is Alexander "Sandy" Acheson. Born on October 12, 1842, he entered the Civil War at age 19 as a Private in the 13th Pennsylvania Volunteer Infantry for three months of service. Upon discharge, he returned to school for a while before reenlisting in

Company C of the 140th Pennsylvania Volunteer Infantry. He was sick and in the hospital during the battle of Gettysburg, but he was first promoted to Sergeant, and eventually to Captain by May of 1864, he was leading his company into the Confederate works at Spotsylvania and was said to have been the first Union officer to reach the top of the center of the enemy works before he was shot in the face.

He survived and while recuperating in Philadelphia, in June of 1864, he married Miss Sarah Morgan Cooke of Washington, PA. She

Alexander "Sandy" Acheson

was related to the famous Col. Morgan of Revolutionary War fame. She was also related to the wife of Major A. G. Happer, Matilda Morgan Watson Happer. By the way, Miss Cook was the daughter of John L. Cook, whose former home is now the clubhouse of the Washington Golf and Country Club. We'll get into the Morgan stuff later. Captain Acheson was serving as Aide de Camp of General Nelson Miles when the war ended.

Sandy returned to Washington, PA, and was awarded an honorary degree from Washington and Jefferson College. He then went on to study medicine under Dr. Thomas McKennan and received his MD from the University of Pennsylvania in 1867. He established his medical practice in Philadelphia in 1872 but soon decided to close that up and move to Texas.

They ended up in a then lonely, dusty railroad stop called Denison, Texas. There was not much there at the time and very few, if any, people actually lived there.

Dr. Alexander Acheson

Acheson Home in Denison Texas ca. 1895

In fact, the Achesons were considered the founders of the city. He was the first physician and opened a practice there, of course. Apparently, he wrangled a meeting with railroad magnate Jay Gould and convinced him to run the tracks of his Texas and Pacific Railway through Denison. Well, the little whistle-stop soon grew into an actual town, and the people elected Sandy as Mayor. He served four terms.

Along the way, he and Sarah had five children. Catherine "Kate" 1866- 1871, Jean Wishart 1868-1923, Helen Beatty 1873-1874, Alexander Wilson 1876-1880, and Alice Lucy 1883-1945.

Sandy was the Texas Republican nominee for Governor in 1906, but he lost that one.

Next up in 1916, he ran for the US Senate and lost again. Maybe the third time is the charm, but it wasn't to be in 1920 either. He

*The Former Acheson Home Today.
Denison Texas*

ran for the US House of Representatives and lost yet again. He did serve as the City Physician for the City of Denison from 1923 to 1929. He also sat on the board of directors for both the State National Bank and the Denison and Suburban Railway. He was a member in good standing of the Knights of Pythias and the Elks, and an honorary member of the Veterans of Foreign Wars, along with various state and national medical organizations.

His wife Sarah wasn't exactly a stay at home mom herself. She was very active in the Women's Christian Temperance Union, serving as President of the Denison Chapter from 1883 until 1888, and President of the State Chapter from 1888 until 1891. She helped organize and was the first President, of the Denison Equal Rights Association. In 1893, the Texas Equal Rights Organization was formed and Sarah became the Vice President. She wasn't done yet either. She became the Superintendent of Educational Opportunities for Women and Children in 1894. Sarah passed away on January 16, 1899, she was only fifty-four.

Dr. Alexander Acheson

Dr. Acheson himself lived for another thir-ty-five years, practicing medicine and being involved in civic affairs. He got to see his daughter Alice grow up and get married to Frank Sproul, who she later divorced. They had three children, two girls, and a boy, all still alive as of this writing.

Sarah Acheson

But no one can defeat Father Time, and time, along with heart trouble caught up with Sandy on September 7th, 1934. He was nine-ty-two. In his final and testament will he wrote the following. *"I am utterly opposed to extrav-agant and expensive funerals, which are more for show than anything else, and it is my desire that my funeral be inexpensive without flowers."*

The Acheson family has certainly seen more than their share of both triumph and tragedy over the decades. One of the old and premier families of Washington County, PA, they have done more than their share to help build and maintain the thriving community that they were so much a part of. Their legacy remains vibrant even today. We shall always remember them.

Women's Christian Temperance Union ca 1896

The original Acheson home was purchased in 1897 by a small group led by Major A. G. Happer to be the first hospital for Washington PA. The hospital and associated facilities today have grown into The Washington Health System.

CHAPTER TWO

John McNutt, Alexander Anderson, James Sibert

I was originally hoping to be able to tell the full life story of John McNutt, but after protracted digging, there just wasn't much available on him. I wasn't about to leave him out altogether, so here is what I could find.

Not all that much is known about John McNutt except he was born in 1844 on the family farm in Chartiers Township in Washington County, PA. His father was William A. McNutt (1822-1881) and his mother was Nancy McMillan Weaver (1823-1893). John was one of nine children: Mary (1847- 1850), Elizabeth (1849-1922), William (1851-1878), Rachael (1854-1909),

Mary E. (1857-1938), Joseph (1860-1925), George (1862-1958), and Catherine (1866-1947).

He enlisted in the Union Army at the age of 16 and was mustered into Company G of

Private John McNutt

the 140th Pennsylvania Vol. Infantry on August 22, 1862, as a Private. John served until July 2, 1863, when according to the regimental history of the 140th PA, they "arrived at Gettysburg on the morning of July 2, 1863, and lost heavily in the fierce fighting at the Wheatfield. Its total losses during the battle were 241, more than half its effective strength."

Among the number who fell for their country that day was the young Private Mc-Nutt. He died the next day. He is buried in the National Cemetery in Gettysburg, PA in the Pennsylvania plot in grave F-25. There is also a marker to his memory back home in the Chartiers Hill Cemetery. Johnny McNutt was only 19. We shall always remember him.

Alexander Anderson

Alexander T. Anderson was born on his father's farm on May 1, 1846, in West Union, West Virginia, (then Virginia) on the state line near West Alexander, PA. The son of James Anderson of County Clare, Ireland, and Rhoda Thomas of Washington, PA.

When the Civil War broke out, he was too young to enlist, but at seventeen in 1861, he lit out to Wheeling, (Virginia) West Virginia, and enlisted in Company B of the 1st West Virginia Cavalry.

He took part in the fighting in the Shenandoah Valley and the Winchester area then was sent with the guard of a wagon train to Washington D. C. Anderson was then sent to General Grant's headquarters at City Point, Vir-

Alexander Anderson

ginia, where he contracted typhoid fever and spent the remainder of the war in a hospital.

After his discharge, he returned to his father's farm and went back to that work. The next year, his father died and young Alex continued working the farm with his mother and four sisters, Mary Jane, Rhoda, Jane and Lydia. He then moved to Taylorstown, West Virginia, where he owned and operated a general store for nine years until he moved once again to Washington, PA.

He there owned and operated a real estate business with offices in the Washington Trust Building. On July 13, 1882, Alexander Anderson married Miss Emily Wilson of Taylorstown, PA. He then went to work building a home at 47 North Avenue in Washington, where they lived for the rest of their days.

He had joined the William F. Templeton Post 120 of the G. A. R. when he first came to Washington, and served as the Commander of that post for several years. He was Commander when the post surrendered its charter on July 9, 1935. Only four members remained.

Anderson served two terms as the Commander of the Department of Pennsylvania. He also held the post of Vice National Commander in Chief of the G.A.R. He became the National Commander in Chief upon the passing of Commander John R. Andrew. The only resident of Washington to ever hold that office. At that time, there was only one other Civil War veteran remaining in Washington, PA his name was George Harshman, who adminis-

The Former Anderson Home Today

tered the oath of office at his home in July 1940 in Washington. Alexander presided at the 74th annual encampment of the G.A.R. held in Springfield, Illinois, in September of 1940.

Anderson was admitted to the hospital on September 2, 1944, where his health gradually declined until September 15, 1944, when he passed quietly away of old age at 98 years. He was the last remaining Civil War veteran in Washington County, and the records of the G.A.R. show he was one of four remaining in the state of Pennsylvania.

Services were held at the Richie and Piatt Funeral Home and flags on numerous buildings were flown at half mast. Condolences were received from Pennsylvania Governor Edward Martin. Members of the American Legion and Daughters of Union Veterans formed a guard of honor. Legionnaires were the pallbearers and formed the firing squad at the cemetery. The G.A.R. Burial ritual was read by County Commissioner John N. O'Neil.

We shall always remember him.

James Sibert

James Sibert was born in Greene County, PA, on June 30, 1833, but was only three months old when his parents, farmers Isaac and Phebe Sibert moved to Amwell Township in Washington County. Three of the five children born to Isaac and Phebe lived to maturity: James, George, and Nancy.

Jim grew up in Amwell and attended the local schools while working on the family farm, as most kids did then. He also learned the carpenter trade and was interested in raising Merino sheep. Washington County, PA, was at one time the sheep raising capital of the world. On August 22, 1862, James enlisted for service in Company D of the 140th Pennsylvania Volunteer Infantry.

James Sibert

Unfortunately, in early 1863, he had become so ill that he was mustered out on February 24 of that year.

It took a year and a half for him to recover his health, but he did return to his normal occupation. James Sibert married Miss Elizabeth Dalrymple and they had ten children together before Elizabeth passed away in 1879. James didn't give up easily and married once again to Miss Eliza Jane Zimmerman. They only had eight children all told. Elizabeth died in 1903.

Jim Sibert was well respected and liked by those who knew him. He was a member in good standing of the W. F. Templeton Post 120 of the G.A.R. as well. He suffered a Cerebral Hemorrhage on August 22nd, 1918 and passed away at the age of 85. He is buried in the Amity Cemetery. Although he didn't serve the entirety of the Civil War, he enlisted and served all he could, and did his best. We shall always remember him.

Jim Sibert

CHAPTER THREE

Hugh P. Boon

Captain Hugh Boon was born on July 24, 1834, on the family farm in Chartiers Township, Washington County, Pennsylvania. He descends from one of the oldest families in Washington County.

The son of James M. and Margaret Miller Boon, who farmed along the old Steubenville Road, as it was known then.

James and his two brothers, William and John, served in the War of 1812. James was a Corporal in Captain Graham's Company, Second Regiment, First Brigade, Pennsylvania Militia, under the command of Lt. Colonel Adam Richie at York, PA. The Company served from September 2, 1814, to March 2, 1815.

Hugh was one of seven brothers: John, William, Samuel, Richard, James, and Thomas, who served in the Union Army with Company A of the 100th Pennsylvania Vol. Infantry, the "Roundheads." He also had three sisters: Nancy, Johanna, and Margaret.

After being educated in the local schools, Hugh worked the farm and also

Captain Hugh Boon

was a clerk in a grocery store on North Main Street in Washington. When the Civil War broke out, Boon enlisted in Company E of the 12th Pennsylvania Vol. Infantry. According to the War Department, he then was mustered in as a Second Lieutenant on September 19, 1861, to serve three years in the 1st West Virginia Cavalry. He was promoted to First Lieutenant on January 18, 1863, and again promoted to Captain on September 1, 1863. His description was as follows: 5 feet 9 1/2 inches tall, with a fair complexion, dark hair, and blue eyes.

Near Port Republic, Virginia, in early June 1862, while engaged with the enemy, Lieutenant Boon was injured by an exploding enemy shell that impaired the hearing in his left ear. This hearing loss plagued him for the rest of his days. But as we will soon see, there was more to come.

1st West Virginia (Union) Cavalry Flag

While engaged in a nasty fight near Wytheville, Virginia, in 1864, on May 10, as part of Averill's raid on the Virginia and Tennessee railroad, Captain Boon received gunshot wounds in the neck and shoulder, barely missing his spinal column. He was taken to a field hospital near Lewisburg, West Virginia, where he was treated. Captain Boon survived the wounds and returned to duty commanding the Company.

After the fall of Richmond, Confederate General Robert E. Lee's Army of Northern Virginia marched westward in an attempt to break contact with the Union forces. Their ultimate goal was to join up with General Joseph Johnston's Army in North Carolina. Leading Lee's columns was his First and Third Corps commanded by General James Longstreet. He was followed by General Richard Anderson's Corps, and the Reserve Corps led by General Richard Ewell. Following all that was the army supply train and the Second Corps led by General John B. Gordon. They marched through the night of April 5.

The morning of April 6 dawned rainy and miserable. And it was about to get a lot worse for Lee's army. Union General Phil Sheridan's Cavalry rode parallel to Lee's army launching hit and run raids on the column.

Ewell and Anderson's troops stopped at Holt's Corner to try to slow the attacks and buy some time. This created a large gap between Confederate forces.

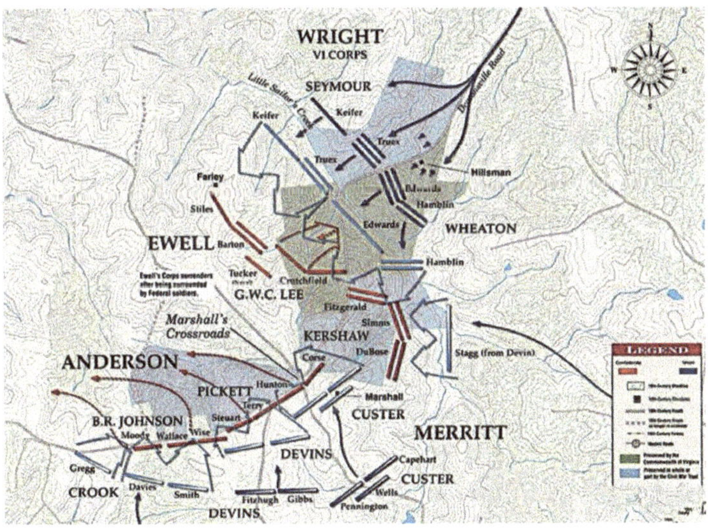

General Custer exploited that gap and stormed his cavalry right through the breech. General Gordon's Corps was diverted to the north to try to link back up with the main column. He made a series of stands on the high ground to allow the supply train to escape. When the wagons became bottlenecked at the Double Bridges over Sailor's Creek, that allowed the Union infantry to catch up. Just before dark, the Federal force attacked Gordon's men, who were driven across the creek, but darkness ended the fighting on that part of the field.

Historical View of Sailor's Creek

To their south, Ewell and Anderson's troops dug in between Little Sailor's Creek and Marshall's Crossroads. Union commander Wright shelled the Confederates for 30 minutes, then advanced across the creek. Ewell's men launched a devastating volley that staggered Wright's men and they retreated across the creek. Confederate General Crutchfield launched a counter-attack which resulted in brutal hand to hand combat and Crutchfield was killed.

Federals were now advancing back across and attacking Ewell's men once again. After yet another brutal fight, the Confederates began to surrender. Over at Marshall's Crossroads, things were no better for the Rebels.

Union General Merritt's cavalry attacked both Confederate flanks, while General Custer sent cavalry assaults against General Pickett's division. Custer's troopers broke through and the Confederates began retreating and surrendering. General Lee watching from a hill some distance away exclaimed, "My God, has the army dissolved?" General Lee would surrender his army three days later.

According to First Sergeant Frank Cunningham of Company H 1st W Va Cavalry, *"For six days we had been pounding at the Rebels and for six days they had been pounding at us. On the afternoon of April 6, we again came up with them in a strong position on the thickly wooded banks of Sailor's Creek. They were behind rude fortifications and the thick growth of underbrush kept their numbers concealed from us. We didn't know how many Rebels were in those ditches until we charged."*

Over where Captain Boon's Company B was located, they could see in the distance the Confederates along the creek bank hastily building breastworks.

Some of Boon's men were saying, *"See the Johnnies down there?"* and *"Why doesn't the bugle sound the charge?"* The Captain replied, *"Boys, you'll be hearing that bugle soon enough."*

Not long after that, the command came, *"Mount, right dress, forward march."* The Company advanced and was placed on the far right of the Regiment. When about a quarter of a mile from the enemy, that bugle sounded the charge and off they went at the gallop. When their line reached the Rebel lines, Boon noticed a Battalion of the Tenth Georgia Infantry off to their right. Instinctively, Captain Boon wheeled his men out of line and charged the Georgians directly. The Captain contin-

General George Custer

ues, *"In the clash that followed, I cut down the color bearer and captured the colors of the Tenth Georgia Infantry."* Later, Captain Boon was a little apprehensive about his attack saying afterward *"I admit I felt scared when I realized what I had done. Had I failed in checking and routing the Rebel Battalion, I should in all probability have been cashiered and dishonorably dismissed the service for leaving the line of battle."* He needn't have worried. His actions had been witnessed by a superior officer who judged that Captain Boon had acted correctly.

Less than a month later, on May 3, 1865, the President of the United States, in the name of Congress, Captain Hugh Patterson Boon of Company B 1st West Virginia Cavalry United States Army, was awarded the Congressional Medal of Honor for extraordinary heroism and the capture of that Confederate flag on April 6, 1865, in action at Deatonsville (Sailor's Creek) Virginia.

Four other men of the 1st W Va. Cavalry were awarded the Congressional Medal of Honor for actions in this battle: Sergeant Francis Cunningham of Company

H, Sergeant William Houlton - Company unknown, Corporal Emisire Shahan of Company A, and Private Daniel A. Woods of Company K.

By April 8, the Regiment had made its way to Appomattox Station, Virginia, where the next day they were present at the surrender of General Robert E. Lee and his Army of Northern Virginia. Following that, they marched to Danville, Virginia, and then on to Washington, DC, where they participated in the Grand Review on May 23.

Captain Boon mustered out with his Regiment on July 8, 1865. The war was over.

When Boon returned home to Washington, PA, he went right back into the grocery business at his store on North Main Street for some time. He then gave up the store and returned to the farm, though, and was married on October 25, 1866, to Miss Hannah J. Cook. They only had one child, Martha J. "Mattie" Boon, was born in 1869. She grew up to marry J. Wilbert Wallace (1874-1931), of the Dunbar and Wallace Lumber Company.

They had one child, a son, Wilbert Boon Wallace born February 14, 1901, and died in November 1975. Mattie passed away on February 14, 1901, during childbirth. Wilbert Boon Wallace married Margaret O Colhran, and they had a daughter, Marjorie Mae Wallace (1932-1986).

Upon leaving the farm for good, due to the lasting effects of his wartime injuries, on August 15t 1879, Captain Boon received an invalid pension due to those injuries. Captain Boon worked as a clerk in E. G. Cundall's store and the M. Sharp Company. He then worked for many years in the men's furnishings department at A. B. Caldwell's store, where he was universally liked and admired.

Medal of Honor

He built a home on Jefferson Avenue, where he lived out the rest of his days. He continued working at Caldwell's store until a few weeks before he passed away. He could no longer climb the hill between his home and the store. Finally, on January 14, 1908, Captain Hugh P. Boon passed away at his home, aged 73 years. He was a member of G.A.R. W. F. Templeton Post 120 and a member of the Third Presbyterian Church. The house that Captain Boon built no longer stands. A sandwich shop now occupies the ground where it once stood.

On May 12, 2001, a monument was placed at the entrance to the Washington Cemetery. One of seven such monuments erected in tribute to Washington County's Civil War Medal of Honor recipients. It was part of a project undertaken by Mr. Edward Snarey, who performed exhaustive research into the family history of each of the seven men so honored. Shown below is an image of the monument laid in tribute to Captain Hugh Patterson Boon. We shall always remember him.

CHAPTER FOUR

Fleming Cunningham, Andrew McDonald, James B. Gibson

Fleming Cunningham

Fleming Cunningham was born to John Cunningham (1804-1874) and his wife, Elisabeth, (1806-1881+ on March 5, 1842, in Monongahela, Pennsylvania.

We don't know much about him other than he mustered into Company F of the 155th Pennsylvania Vol. Infantry on August 22nd, 1862.

As far as can be determined, he served in all the engagements in which his Regiment was present, including Little Round Top at the Battle of Gettysburg on July 2, 1863. His name appears with his Regiment and Company on the bronze tablet affixed to the Pennsylvania monument there.

He was promoted to Corporal on January 12, 1865, and mustered out with his Company on June 2nd, 1865.

Fleming Cunningham

After the war he worked as a glass blower in New Eagle and was married to Miss Mary Ann Dittmar and they had four children: Mary, Dominic, Robert, and Henry.

Sometime before 1879, he was married a second time to Miss Nancy A. ?? They had two children: John. and Elizabeth Jane. Corporal Fleming Cunningham passed away on February 2, 1915. We shall always remember him.

Former Cunningham Home
Today South 23rd Street
Pittsburgh, PA.

Andrew McDonald

Andrew McDonald was born on the ancestral farm on April 20, 1840. The son of John and Mary Tish McDonald, and the grandson of Andrew and Mary Hair McDonald, who came to America from Scotland and settled on four hundred acres of land in the beautiful Shenandoah Valley of Virginia.

He was a slaveholder there until 1799 when he sold his estate and bought a two hundred acre farm in Washington County, PA, where they raised eight children. He was a farmer, stock raiser and opened a distillery, and became one of the prominent members of the community. His son John, who is the father of

Andrew McDonald

our subject, was born on the Virginia farm, and often told of the long trip by wagon to Washington County on the Braddock Trail. At the age of fifty, he married Mary Tish who was from Fredericktown along the Monongahela River. In fact, on the night of her birth, her father accidentally drowned in that river. John passed away at the age of sixty four, but Mary lived another forty-four years. They had nine children over the years: Andrew, the eldest, then Mary, Nancy Jane, Gabriel, Edith, John, Hiram, and Matilda.

Andrew McDonald was just fourteen years old when his father died, so the responsibilities of running the farm were his to deal with. To his credit, he managed the farm well until the start of the Civil War.

On October 13, 1862, he mustered into Company E of the 22nd Pennsylvania Cavalry better known as the Ringgold Cavalry. On January 1, 1864, he was promoted to Corporal. He served clear until the end of the war and was discharged on May 10, 1865. He then returned home to life on the farm.

Monongahela Cemetery, GAR Section

Just about a year later, on May 17, 1866, he was married to Miss Isabell Whitfield of Carroll Township. Her parents were Nicholas and Fannie Whitfield, who owned a mill on Mingo Creek. The Mcdonald's had eight children: Fannie, Laura, John, George, Edward, Andrew, and Joseph.

In addition to being a farmer, stock raiser, and distiller, Andrew was also prominent in local politics. He served over forty years in almost every elected office available, including many years as Justice of the Peace. He was a member of the Fairview Presbyterian Church, where he taught Sunday School. After a month long illness, Squire McDonald

passed away at his home on August 25, 1917, aged seventy-seven years. We shall always remember him.

James B. Gibson

Captain James B. Gibson was born on March 1, 1839, on the family farm in Carroll Township, Washington County, PA. He was the son of James (1797-1865) and Maria Figley Gibson (1802-1898), a grandson of Colonel James Gibson. Colonel Gibson is interesting in that he served in the Revolutionary War in the Second Virginia Regiment, where he lost an arm. He later led a Regiment to Pittsburgh, then to the Washington County area, during the Whiskey Rebellion. His son, James Jr., arrived in Washington County and settled in what is now Carroll Township.

Captain James B. Gibson

He and Maria had five children: James B; Josephine, Elizabeth, Jacob, and Mary. He was reared on the farm until October 13, 1862, when James B. Gibson mustered as a Private into Company E of the 22nd Pennsylvania Cavalry. (Notice how many of these men enlisted in the fall, after the harvest was done.) He saw his first action at Stump's Mills and soon after made Orderly Sergeant, then First Sergeant was promoted to Second Lieutenant on April 1, 1863.

Lydia Isabella "Belle" Thomas

In July of that year, he was wounded severely at the battle of Leesburg Virginia, then wounded again the next year on July 25 at Martins- burg, West Virginia. He was commissioned as a Captain on March 29, 1865, and mustered out of service on June 8 of that year.

Carl E. Gibson

After the war, he returned to the farm where he remained until 1869 when he ran and won the election as County Treasurer. He moved to Washington during his term in office, the first Democrat to hold that office in forty years.

Following his term as Treasurer, in 1872 he married Miss Lydia Isabella (Belle) Thomas (1844-1939). They had four children: Harry who died at age seven, Carlos (Carl), James, and Cora May.

Carl married Miss Mary Lamont with whom they had three children: Mary, Lois, and Ruth. Mary passed away and he married a Miss Wycough. They had two daughters: Ethel and Elizabeth. Carl later became the City Solicitor for Washington, PA.

Daughter Ruth married a Mr. Martin Yost in 1921. They lived in Allentown, PA, where they had three children, two are still living at this writing. The other, a son named Carl Gibson Yost (1929-2003), served in the US Air Force and served in the Korean War and Viet Nam. He lived in Montgomery, Alabama, where he passed away at the age of seventy-three. Thank you for your service, Mr. Yost.

James D. (1876-1930) lived on the farm in Carroll Township, first married a Miss Sampson. Following her death, he married her cousin, Sara Samson (1879-1967), with whom he had five children: Lucretia (1902-1903), LuLu Mae (1904-1929), Clyde (1905-?), and two others who are still living.

James' daughter, Cora May (1879-1936), married a Frank Jones (1875- 1907) with whom she had six children: Edgar, Robert (1907-?), Helen (1901- 1909), Frank Jr. (1905-1972), and two more who may be still living.

Captain Gibson retired from active farm life, his farm being managed by his son James.

Carl's Daughter Mary L. Taken January 18, 1914

James D. Gibson and Sarah Jane Sampson

He bought a home in Monongahela, PA in 1902, but ran for, and won, a seat on the Board of Commissioners of Washington County, where he served one term. He then ran for State Senator but was not successful.

At the close of his term as treasurer, he purchased a farm of 170 acres in Fallowfield Township, and four years later bought and moved to a farm of 130 acres in Carroll Township, where he resided until 1902 when he moved to Monongahela City, where he lived in retirement. His farm in Carroll Township was operated

Cora May Gibson December 1896

by his son Donald, and he kept a large number of cattle on the farm in Fallowfield Township.

Captain Gibson was a stockholder in the Monongahela Trust Company, the Bellwood Gas Company, and the Monongahela Water Company.

He was a member in good standing in the G.A .R. At Starkweather Post 60, and the First Presbyterian Church as well. In 1927, he took part in the Memorial Day celebration at the Soldier's Circle.

On August 20th, 1928, after a lengthy illness, Captain Gibson passed away at his home in Monongahela at the ripe old age of 91. His wife Belle joined him on February 3rd, 1939 at the age of 94. They rest side by side in the Monongahela cemetery. We shall always remember them.

The Former James Gibson Home in Monongahela, PA

Bell with Ruth Gibson

Chapter Five

Enos L. Christman

Now here's a story that is an incredible journey with several levels and any one of them would make a great tale of adventure. This man Enos Christman and his amazing family led lives that were packed full of action, travel, heartache, war and sorrow, triumph, and success. There is something for everyone here.

Enos L. Christman was born in Vincent Township, Chester County, Pennsylvania, on December 27, 1828, the eldest son of George and Sarah Christman. George passed away in 1843 when Enos was only fifteen years old. Leaving his younger brothers Jefferson and William to help their mother work the farm, Enos, in the summer of 1844 went to work for his uncle Jacob Beerbower as a clerk in his store in Lancaster County.

In the fall of that year, he returned home and went to school until February 10, 1845, when he was apprenticed into the printer's occupation

Enos Christman

with Mr. Henry Evans who owned the Village Record in West Chester, PA. He worked and learned there for four years until in 1849 gold fever broke out all over the country. Mr. Evans released Enos from his remaining apprenticeship and advanced him the sum of $400. Enos also left his betrothed, Miss Ellen Ann Martin Apple, who promised to wait for his return, to try his luck in the gold fields of California. Enos and Ellen wrote letters the entire three years he was gone. Those letters were made into a book called "One Man's Gold The Letters and Journal of a 49er".

The sea voyage to California lasted for two hundred and twenty two days. It was a miserable undertaking even for those days. The ship was barely seaworthy and they had problems the entire time they were at sea.

Ellen Apple Christman

They were forced to put into Valparaiso, Chile for repairs, before continuing to San Francisco, California.

Upon landing and getting settled in, Enos wrote to Ellen the following letter, from Happy Valley, near San Francisco, on St. Valentine's Day, February 14th, 1850.

"Before I started and bid farewell to as good friends as ever lived, I counted the cost. I had strong and honorable motives for encountering the terrors of Cape Horn and the dangers of a long sea voyage and here, just on my arrival in the land of promise, would be a poor place indeed to regret the undertaking. No danger must be met halfway, every difficulty should be met with manly fortitude, and my intention is to meet them in such a manner that I need never be ashamed.

I now boldly turn my face toward the celebrated Sierra Nevada. What we may there have to encounter, I cannot anticipate; perhaps we shall have to engage with the native Indian in some sanguinary and bloody conflict, or be hugged to death by the fierce and savage grizzly bear. But whatever may be my fate - should the worst come and I be fated to leave my bones to whiten on the bleak plains of this golden land, I can never forget the image that has been present to my mind's eye for so long a time."

Enos in addition to his letters, kept a journal as well. His first entry is worth sharing herein. It shows the happy anticipation of his new endeavor and the wonder at the uncertainty of the outcome he now must face.

"Friday, February 15, 1850 — Tuesday, February 12th, we were landed with our baggage on the beach at a place called Happy Valley, about a mile east of the city, where we soon cleared a place and put up our tent and removed our trunks and bedding into it. We then cooked our supper of tea and fried bread, and although this meal was quite

humble and prepared by our own hands, I never partook of any that I enjoyed more, not even the best cured fowl.

Being determined to have as lively a time of it as circumstances would permit, we soon after introduced the violin and enjoyed ourselves in the giddy mazes of a real Spanish fandango for an hour or two. About nine o'clock we arranged our trunks and placed our beds upon them. Two of our party had to lie upon the ground, but Atkins and I had trunks enough to form a platform for our beds. We then turned in without a single weapon by us, they all being locked up in our trunks, feeling quite as secure as when surrounded by thick and massive walls, and enjoyed as good a night's repose."

It wasn't all fun and games in those gold diggings. There were great dangers constantly from both man and beast. The following short stories in Enos's own words illustrate that fact quite well.

"Wednesday, April 17, 1850. Yesterday afternoon a bloody tragedy was enacted in the town, resulting in the death of a young man named Marcey, of Massachusetts. A man named Messick accused Marcey of robbing him of seven hundred dollars while on a drunken frolic together last winter, and it is said had sworn to shoot Marcey the first time he saw him. He had armed himself early in the morning with a double barrelled shot gun heavily charged with buckshot, and lay in wait until the afternoon, expecting Marcey to pass that way.

By and by Marcey made his appearance, only armed with a sheath knife and revolver, as is usual in this country, and an altercation took place, in which Marcey endeavored to clear himself of the charges brought against him. He was about going away when Messick cocked both barrels of his gun and asked the other if he was armed, and he replied that he was and that he would fight him in a fair fight but he would not fight in that way. Messick then told him to defend himself, to which he replied that he might fire if he would.

At this he fired one barrel which the other received principally in the right arm, and instantly turned with his back towards the man with the gun, who seeing that the other did not fall, immediately fired the other barrel which took effect through the lungs and heart. Marcey fell, uttered a few words, and was a corpse in a few minutes. Messick, with a companion, left at once for parts unknown. The deceased has a number of mules and for some time had been engaged in the packing trade. Of him, all speak favorably."

August 11, 1850. "Sonora is the county seat of Tuolumne County, about two hundred and twenty-five miles southeast of San Francisco. The country round about is very hilly and mountainous, being forty miles from the main range of the Sierra Nevada. Many of the mountains are covered with a rather inferior pine and scrubby oak, while others are perfectly bare or thickly covered with chaparral. This latter constitutes the haunts of the grizzly bear, quite plentiful in this neighborhood. Several unlucky hunters have been killed by them and others badly wounded. Only last Sunday a man was found about four miles from this place, literally torn to pieces, quite dead, with his trusty rifle lying by his side. It is supposed the bear came upon him suddenly without giving him time to fire."

"This section of the country has been infested by numerous bands of Mexican guerillas, and life and property have been very insecure. Within a fortnight every morning's sun brought to light a newly murdered victim. The whole country became alarmed. Public meetings were held, and organized parties raised to ferret out and bring to justice the authors of these horrid crimes. The people grew wild on the subject and it is not to be wondered at."

"Among the persons murdered was one named Miller, of Reading, Pennsylvania. He and his partner kept a public house on the road between this and Stockton. One evening about bedtime, seven Mexicans came in and professed to be friends. After taking a drink and buying a sword, one of them made a pass with it at the man behind the counter. This was thought to be a joke and so passed off. Soon after, however, another pass was made, and this time the man was stabbed through the right breast. A scuffle then ensued between the two Americans and seven Mexicans in which one of the former was killed and the other badly wounded. During the affray an American teamster who was sleeping in a back part of the tent awoke and seizing a six-shooter, rushed out and shot one of the Mexicans through the head, killing him instantly. He then had to flee for his safety. The Mexicans plundered the tent and left the two men for dead. I saw the wounded man a few days after the occurrence. He was then very low but hopes were entertained for his recovery."

"On Wednesday morning, the tenth of July, three Indians and a Mexican were discovered burning the tent and bodies of two Americans about five miles from this place. They were immediately arrested and brought here under a strong escort of armed Americans, highly excited and enraged. They were taken before the magistrate

but before the hearing was gone through with, the excited people seized the prisoners took them to the top of an adjacent hill, selected a jury under a tree, tried and found them guilty, and sentenced them to be hung.

The sentence was about to be carried into effect, for the ropes were already around their necks and over a limb, and all that was wanting to finish their existence was the word "pull" to be given. The Mexican was even raised off the ground and was dangling in the air.

Before the rope was stretched, he fell upon his knees, kissed a cross he carried in his bosom, uttered a prayer in Spanish, and resigned himself to his fate. At this critical moment for the prisoners, the county judge with other citizens interfered and begged the people not to assume so great a responsibility but to let the law take its own course and justice would be done.

The prisoners were then brought back and placed in the jail but by this time the multitude had become so desperate that it was feared the jail would be torn down. The sheriff and his posse were very vigilant and declared that the first man who should interfere would do so at the peril of his life. No further demonstration was made and the people returned to their homes." "Yesterday one American shot another in the street and the occurrence was not noticed as much as a dog fight at home. "

Enos worked with friends he had made, panning for gold with almost no success until June 4 when he gave up and went to work for the Stockton Times newspaper where he turned out the Sonora Herald as well. He also sent an application in to the San Francisco Herald, a new paper starting up.

"Sunday, June 9 —On Tuesday morning last, I commenced type sticking in the Times office. Not having done anything of the kind for a long time, I feared that it would go rather awkwardly, but such was not the case, for I soon found my hands in and could set type as well as ever I could. I boarded myself on bread, cheese, and milk at a cost of $1.50 per day, and at night stretched out my blankets and slept on the floor of the office, where during the first night I scarcely got any sleep on account of the noise the rats made, and not only on account of the noise, but once or twice they ran over my

face. On the second night I was very sleepy and although they kept up a great clatter, it did not disturb me and since then I have not minded them."

"Saturday, July 5, 1851 —About ten days ago it was announced in all the San Francisco papers that Mr. Gunn, editor of the Sonora Herald, and myself and several other persons had been killed in a fracas with gamblers. This report, which was a falsehood from beginning to end, was published just before the sailing of the last steamer. It is probable that it will be seen in the papers at home and occasion much distress. I therefore concluded to write by the first mail, denying "KILLED IN A FRACAS WITH GAMBLERS" Clipping from the Alta California quoted in the Sonora Herald of July 5, 1851, the story altogether, and saying that no such difficulty took place."

Around the middle of October, the Sonora Herald went bust and they still owed Enos several hundred dollars. Enos went back to panning for gold, but he paid a worker $5.00 per day to work for him. Meanwhile, the Sonora Herald started back up and Enos purchased a half interest in the paper. He and a partner, *"Dr. Lewis C. Gunn from Philadelphia and a first-rate man, is now my partner. He is a finely educated gentleman and practicing physician, probably the only man in this place who does not drink, gamble or swear."*

They opened an office in an adobe building which they also lived in. On November 20th, he wrote in his journal, *"I have now been in this country almost a year and as yet have accumulated but little cash, but we have gotten our paper fairly started and it is increasing in value every day. We are not enabled to print a handsome sheet as we are in the mountains, several thousand miles from a type foundry. But we do the best we can. I think if I remain here about another year, I will be able to sell out and return home to the dearest spot on earth."*

On August 9, 1851, Enos wrote, *"I have sold out my interest in the Herald at a fair price and am now permanently engaged as printer and Deputy Recorder at a salary sufficient to save over one hundred dollars per month. My prospects are brighter than they have been at any time since my arrival in California. Sonora was a wild place to be sure. Full, of gamblers, cut throats, horse thieves, robbers and murderers.*

"Sonora is a fast place and no mistake. Such a motley collection as we have here can be found nowhere but in California. Sonora has a population hailing from every hole and corner of the globe —Kanakas, Peruvians, Negroes, Spaniards, Mexicans,

Chilians, Chinese, British convicts from New South Wales, known as "Sidney Birds," Englishmen, Frenchmen, Dutch, Paddies, and not a small sprinkling of Yankees. We have more gamblers, more drunkards, more ugly, bad women, and larger lumps of gold, and more of them, than any other place of similar dimensions within Uncle Sam's dominions. The Sabbath is regarded as a holiday, granting men and women a more extensive license to practice vice than any other day in the week."

"I feel that I am a rover, a wanderer on the face of the earth! In a land flowing, not with milk and honey, but with flapjacks and gold dust, far from home and kindred, and surrounded by the off scourings and scum of society, from all parts of the inhabitable globe. All selfish, each for himself, and his Satanic Majesty for all. I have scarcely met with half a dozen respectable women, or men with their families, since I left the Atlantic States. The women of other nations, what few there are, are nearly all lewd harlots, who are drunk half the time, or sitting behind the gambling table dealing monte. To see a woman who can read and write is a curiosity. Indeed, the majority of our females are a disgrace to woman."

"Sunday, January 25, 1852 — The weather here is not very cold and we seldom have frost or ice. Most of the trees are covered with green foliage, and the hills and valleys are carpeted with new grass. Atkins has left Sonora and gone to some new diggings, known as Cherokee Camp, about fifteen miles from this place. I accompanied him on his journey and spent the night in the camp. We were quietly stretched out on our blankets around the fire, swapping yarns with some gentlemen whose tents were close by. Suddenly we heard footsteps, as of some person stealthily approaching. As we listened, the sound grew more and more distinct and we became convinced that a number of men were stealing in upon us. As it was dark and therefore impossible to espy the intruders, each one of us quickly drew his revolver, being always on guard against marauders. But before we could fire, two colorfully dressed señoritas tripped out of the darkness into the camp. They had come out for a serenade, and proceeded to sing many merry songs, accompanying their fine voices with music picked from their guitars.

A part of the entertainment consisted of a fandango, and the dance was much enjoyed by the men participating. They had become quite boisterous in their enthusiasm. But the merry music changed, and the señoritas played softly on their guitars the sweet strains of "Home, Sweet Home," bringing to the hearts of these sturdy men the familiar words of the song, and thoughts of friends and home. Suddenly a sob was heard, followed by another, and yet another, and tears flowed freely down the cheeks of the gold diggers.

Pieces of gold were generously tossed into the tambourine held out to receive them. 'mid pleasures and palaces though we may roam, Be it ever so humble, there's no place like home! A charm from the skies seems to hallow us there, Which, seek through the world, is ne'er met with elsewhere."

On Tuesday, June 29, 1852, Enos took a stagecoach in Sonora bound for Stockton. Upon arrival there, he boarded a steamer bound for San Francisco. After arriving there, he booked passage to Panama aboard the steamship *Golden Gate,* and the following Saturday he sailed past the entrance to San Francisco Bay and on down the California coast. On July 14 they arrived in Panama harbor. The next day, Enos rented a horse for $21.00 and rode off with a group across the 25 mile Isthmus of Panama, where they rode until they arrived at the American Hotel. They spent the night. The next morning they took an hour's ride to Barbacoas, where they stopped to eat, then took a train to Aspinwall, where they boarded the steamship United States.

They sailed the next morning for New York, and it was rough going indeed. Passengers became very sick, probably with cholera and the next day several died. On July 20, they had seven or eight deaths and they were all buried at sea.

"Friday, July 23 — Wednesday night we passed two or three lighthouses and a number of sailing craft. At 4 A.M. we put another poor fellow overboard. Three hours later we passed the narrow entrance to the New York Harbor, where the fort is situated. On reaching the quarantine ground we were detained two hours in taking the sick aboard to the hospital, six in number, and also one dead man, making 15 or 16 deaths aboard. After this was finished, and just as we supposed we were going on to New York, the captain informed us that we were under quarantine for 24 hours, and if any were taken sick during that time, we would be detained longer, but that we could go ashore and remain within the hospital grounds, with a high wall surrounding them.

We were very much disappointed and some made their escape and went on to the city. I succeeded in getting ashore, where I remained until 2 o'clock when I was given permission by the hospital overseer, on giving my parole to return in the morning, to go to the city."

That night was the first time in more than three years that Enos had slept in a comfortable bed with a real pillow. In all, seventeen people had died, but the sick all recovered quickly.

In his last entry in his journal, he writes the following. *"May 9, 1853. — Wife Ellen and I were in Philadelphia yesterday to see the ship Europe which is lying at Pine Street Wharf, ready for another voyage to California. The old craft does not look much the worse of the wear, notwithstanding the manner in which she is buffeted about by the winds when she plows through the heavy seas on the passage around Cape Horn. When we came within sight of her, I almost felt as though I were being greeted by an old and tried friend. Memory carried me back to the day that I turned my face towards a land of*

Ellen Apple Christman

golden promise and I thought again of the high hopes with which I then set sail, and the melancholy reflections upon all I was leaving behind. As we were borne out of sight of home, many of us gazed at the familiar hills and vales, feeling that perhaps we might never look upon them again. What trying times were those that followed. But the thought of the dear burthen on my arm broke in upon these musings and reminded me that all was well with me. Indeed, my hopes have been gratified and I have realized a fortune."

The remarkable story of Enos and Ellen Christman doesn't stop there. This is not the end at all, but merely the end of the beginning. In only three years, Enos Christman and his betrothed Ellen Apple have already lived, in reality, or via correspondence, a lifetime of adventures, joy, turmoil, success, failure, and sorrow. There is much more ahead for them, including Civil War, various homes, several opportunities in business, and tragedy as well as great happiness. Follow along with me as we travel those roads yet untrod by Enos and Ellen as we see what lies in store for them in part two.

In November of 1852, Enos and Ellen traveled to Washington, PA, and went into a partnership in the already established Commonwealth newspaper with a man named George C. Stouch. This lasted until Stouch passed away in December 1855. Stouch was succeeded by the Honorable William S. Moore, a US congressman.

In 1858, the Commonwealth was consolidated with the Washington Reporter newspaper, at that time the oldest paper in the county. After that, the Christmans, while retaining their interest in the newspaper, returned to West Chester, PA, where Enos took over management of the Record newspaper. He performed admirably there until the outbreak of the Civil War.

Enos enlisted as a Private on June 6, 1861, and was mustered into Company K of the 33rd Pennsylvania Infantry at Harrisburg, PA, to serve for three years. The Regiment left for Baltimore in July and remained there until the end of August,

Ellen Apple Christman

when it was ordered to Tennallytown, Maryland. On April 10, 1862, Enos was promoted to Captain. There they were joined with the 2nd Brigade and were present at Mechanicsville and were heavily engaged at both Gaines Mill and Glendale, where the 33rd suffered severe losses. They were held in reserve at Malvern Hill but were active at Second Manassas, South Mountain, Antietam, and Fredericksburg.

On March 27, 1863, Enos was again promoted, this time to Major. He resigned a month later and transferred from Company K to Field & Staff.

Captain Enos Christman

Following the Union disaster at Fredericksburg, the 33rd was ordered to the defense of Washington, where it remained until January 1864. They participated in the West Virginia campaign, then were mustered out on June 17, 1864, at Philadelphia. The veterans and new recruits were transferred into the 54th Pennsylvania.

Major Christman was appointed Provost Marshal for the 7th District of Pennsylvania, comprised of Delaware and Chester Counties. He made his headquarters at West Chester and served there for the remainder of the war. He received his discharge on November 30, 1865. Major Christman had seen action during the Seven Days campaign, Second Manassas, South Mountain, and Antietam, where he fought nearly alongside his two brothers William, a Lieutenant in the 124th Pennsylvania, and Jefferson, a private with the 72nd Pennsylvania. Enos also saw combat at Fredericksburg.

Major Christman kept a journal during the war. Here, are three interesting entries.

"Monday, April 10, 1865. Westchester, PA. News received of surrender of General Lee - great rejoicing - bells ringing - salutes fired of provost guards. "

Major Christman

" Friday, April 14: 4 years today since Major Anderson surrendered Fort Sumpter. Today he again raised the flag he then hauled down over the fort. Public supper this evening at the Mansion House in honor of the surrender of General Lee and his army. Received orders to stop recruiting and drafting."

"Sat April 15: At 8 o clock received news by telegraph of the assassination of President Lincoln at the theatre in Washington last night and the attempt upon the life of Secretary Seward."

Enos endeavored to see the pomp and circumstance of the Lincoln funeral procession in Philadelphia, and to pay his respects to the fallen President. He writes further in his journal.

"Saturday, April 22, 1865. This eve Self & Willie took cars to Phila-. Witness of passage of President Lincoln's remains through Philada to Independence Hall."

And that wasn't all. He continues the next day, Sunday, April 23, 1865. *"Tried with wife to see remains of Prest Lincoln. Took station in line at Chestnut & Water Sts. 2 hours & 20 minutes reached Fifth St. Crowd too dense.*

Sarah "Sallie" Christman

And finally, his persistence paid off, as he wrote the next day. *"At 12 o'clock after two hours effort George R. and Joseph Oat & T P Apple & self succeeded in gaining Independence Hall and saw remains of President Lincoln. Came home with wife in 10:30 train."*

At the close of the war, Enos had of course returned to Ellen in West Chester, PA. They didn't remain there long as they soon moved to Somerset County, Maryland, where they went into farming and the lumber business.

They had started their family before the war with Sarah "Sallie" being first born on June 2, 1855, and William was born on January 12, 1858, both in Washington, PA. Elizabeth "Lizzie" was born in West Chester on April 2, 1859, Ella was born in West Chester on August 13, 1861, Henry "Harry" was born in West Chester on March 24, 1864, George was born in West Chester on April 9, 1866, Edwin born in Princess Ann, Maryland, on August 1, 1868, and last but not least, Charles born in West Chester on April 25, 1871. Sarah eventually married Charles Hayes of Washington, PA, and Ella was married to a Charles Wigley of Rochester, Pennsylvania.

Enos Christman

Even though Enos was still a partner in the Washington Reporter newspaper in Washington, he became associated with Edward B. Moore, and together they published the American Republican newspaper. That continued until 1872 when

Enos got word that his other partner William S. Moore got himself elected to Congress. Christman then pulled up stakes once again and returned to Washington, PA, to take over the operation of the Washington Daily Reporter.

Then it gets even more confusing because in the fall of 1876, his partner in Congress, Mr. William S. Moore, died, leaving his interest in the paper to a Mr. Alexander M. Gow. So, for those keeping score, Enos Christman now is a half-owner of the Washington Daily Reporter with Alexander Gow. Finally, sometime in 1883, Enos Christman bought out his partner Mr. Gow for $7000, and became the sole owner of the newspaper.

Elizabeth "Lizzie" Christman

As an interesting aside, the Christman home was broken into on September 13, 1888. According to the Monongahela Valley Republican newspaper the following day, *"Thieves entered the residence of Editor Christman on Thursday and ransacked the home after money.* In the Daily Reporter, Mr. Christman says *"they got none, as money is at no time kept about the house except a little change laid to one side for the missionaries."*

The Christman Publishing Company was formed in 1891 with Enos as President and his son William as Manager. William was an innovator and under his direction, purchased a Cox Duplex press, able to print 4000 copies per hour. Later, in 1897, two new Mergenthaler Linotype machines were installed, which could set type much faster than any human could.

Seeing that his company was in good and able hands, Enos retired that same year and turned the operation over to three of his children: William, Harry and Elizabeth. William managed the paper until 1903 when it was sold to the Observer Publishing Company for $55,000.

Ella Christman

Enos and Kathryn at Atlantic City Boardwalk 1903

The Pittsburgh Daily Post reported on August 5, 1893, the following notice: *The Washington Reporter deserves great credit for the magnificent paper it gave its readers on Thursday. It was in honor of the eighty-fifth anniversary of the founding of that paper, and the completion of that many years of a prosperous life. A complete illustrated history of the Reporter and the men who have made it was given, together with facsimiles of the paper at various stages of its career. The Christmans have our congratulations and good wishes. They put out a good newspaper and are deservedly successful.*

Tragedy struck the Christman family on May 6, 1899, when Enos' wife of fifty years and the undisputed light of his life, Ellen passed away after a lingering illness. A truly amazing love story that had produced ten children, and survived both time, war, and distance, was at an end. She was only seventy years old. After an extended absence of notes in his journal, Enos wrote the following. *"She was the mother of nine living children and one stillborn. The eldest died at about thirteen months of age, and the last was still-born; the others are all living at this writing."* The story doesn't end there, not by a long shot.

Major Christman mourned for but a short time, for on March 7, 1903, this announcement appeared in the papers: *"A very pretty wedding took place at the home of the bride in Middletown Thursday afternoon, March 5th at which time Major Enos Lewis Christman of Washington PA., and Mrs. Katharine E. Stofer were united in marriage by the Rev. D. S. Shoop of Mechanicsburg, in the presence of the family and a few of the friends of the bride. Major Christman was the Editor & Publisher of the Daily Reporter of Washington, PA. For many years. After the ceremony, the bride and groom drove to this city, whence they left for Florida."*

While Major Christman and his new bride, Katharyn, settled down into retirement and travel, William Christman was comfortable in his role as head of the Newspaper company. He had every right to be. When his father took a part interest in the paper in 1873, at age 15, William quit school to learn the newspaper business from his father, the Major.

He started out at the bottom and worked every position possible on the paper. From 1877 until 1883, when Enos took full control by buying out his partner Mr. Gow.

Major Christman was the sole owner until 1891 when the Christman Publishing Company was formed with Enos as President and William as Manager, although William had been the defacto Manager for some years.

On January 15, 1897, William, his sister Elizabeth and brother Harry, purchased the interests of the other stockholders in the Christman Publishing Company. William was elected President and manager, Harry was Secretary, and Elizabeth was

William Christman

the Treasurer. In May of 1902, William became the sole owner when he purchased the shares of the other two siblings.

Harry Christman

Then on January 1, 1903, William sold the Reporter to the Observer Publishing Company but remained on as General Manager until May 12, 1903, thus making exactly 30 years to the day when he started in 1873.

So, did William retire? No chance. He opened an insurance and real estate company. He was successful in that for forty years and served several terms as President of the Washington Real Estate Board. He also was a charter member of the Washington Rotary Club and a member of the Second Presbyterian Church.

We aren't finished with Major Christman yet. His story isn't complete. Information is a little sketchy on this, but Kathryn passed away at some point before 1906. Enos then married for a third time to Emma

Winebrenner. Resuming his retirement with his third wife Emma, Enos lived a quiet lifestyle at his home on West Prospect Ave., Washington, PA.

Emma and Enos Christman

His house still stands today as shown in this modern view next page. The Major and Emma lived out their lives in peace. Enos quietly passed away on January 18, 1912, of just plain old age. His death certificate states "No specific disease." He was 83 years old. The Major left his third wife, seven children, fifteen grandchildren, and seven great-grandchildren. Emma lived on alone. She returned to her family home in Harrisburg, PA where she lived until March 9, 1930.

William Christman was born on January 12, 1858, in Washington, PA. He was the eldest son and newspaper heir apparent. He did an outstanding job as described above, with both the Reporter and his insurance and real estate business. After his first wife, Fanny Morgan, passed away after bearing him three sons - Herbert S. Christman, who lived in Morgantown, West Virginia, Frank Morgan, and Herbert Spencer - he married Elizabeth Morrow with whom they had three children, Florence, Ronald S., and Robert L.

William passed away on August 3, 1946. He was 88 years old. He left his wife, four children, sixteen grandchildren, and several great-grandchildren.

The Christman Home Today

Harry Christman was a newspaperman from day one. He was born during the Civil War on March 24, 1864. He married Lena Catherine Earnestine Gerardene Henrietta Fleissner from Germany on February 3, 1887. She was only seventeen years old. They had four children: Walter, Nellie, Pauline, and Elizabeth. Harry passed away on October 14, 1947, in Allentown, Pennsylvania, at the age of 83.

When Harry was born, his father wrote in his journal the following passage. *"At 1:30 a.m., went for Dr. Hartman and Mrs. May Apple. A son was born at ten minutes of two before the Dr. arrived. In house on North New Street, West Chester. We have called him Henry. Weather moderate - clear."*

George Christman

George Christman was born in West Chester, PA on April 9, 1866. He served with Company H of the Tenth Pennsylvania Volunteer Infantry in the Spanish American War. He survived the conflict and returned home and was mustered out of the service at Pittsburgh. I do not have much else on him other than he lived in Titusville, PA. Tragedy struck when at the age of forty-nine on March 24, 1915, he was found dead in his apartment with a shotgun by his side. The reason for his suicide was unknown at the time.

Born in Westchester, PA on April 2, 1859, Elizabeth "Lizzie" Christman was unusual for a female back then. She was interested in business, the newspaper business in particular. She served many years as the Treasurer, reporter, and writer of the Washington Reporter alongside her two brothers, William and Harry.

There are big gaps in her story, as info on her is very scarce. According to her death certificate, she never married, but there is one conflicting record showing her with two daughters, Bertha and Emiline. Lizzie passed away on January 8, 1944, of pneumonia, while in Wilkinsburg, PA, near Pittsburgh. She was eighty-four years old.

Ella Christman was born early in the Civil War, on August 13, 1862, in West Chester, Pennsylvania. She married Charles Wigley in Beaver, PA, in 1903. She later married George Ward in 1912. In 1927, she was living in Washington, PA. In 1942, she moved into the Washington County Home,

Edwin Apple Christman

where she lived the final three years of her life. Ella passed away as a widow on April 21, 1945, at the age of 83.

Sarah "Sally" Christman was born in Washington, PA on June 2, 1855. Very little is known about her that I could find. She was married to Charles Morgan Hayes on June 24, 1880, in Washington. They had two children together: Harry born in 1881 and Clyde (1890-1987). Sally passed away from cancer on June 10, 1920, at the young age of sixty-five.

Edwin Apple Christman was born on August 1, 1868, in Princes Anne, Maryland. He married a southern girl named Margaret Cahill Frazier from Nashville, Tennessee. She was born in the middle of the Civil War on February 28, 1863. They

Geneveive, William J. and Edwin Roy

had five children together: Mary (1881-?), Mamie (1882 -1969), twins Edwin Roy (1887-1970), and Charles and Hazel (1889-1967). Charles only lived seven days. Ed Christman was a Pressman at the Observer Publishing Company until his death on January 29, 1944.

Edwin Roy moved to St Louis and was the manager of the Silurian Oil company. He married Genevieve Templeman. They had seven children. Their son William James (1923-2003), served as a Lieutenant JG in the US Navy in World War II.

Charles Francis Christman was born on April 25, 1871, in West Chester, PA. A year later, he moved with the family to Washington PA, where he worked as an electrician.

William J. Christman With President Ford

His marital situation is difficult to sort out. He was married four times as best as I can tell. There is conflicting information as to dates and how the marriages ended. Here was at least one divorce involved in there somewhere.

In any event, his wives, as best as I can tell, were: Lucinda Berdine who had one child, Clarence Wray Christman (1899-1962) who served in World War I as a Private

First Class. He saw action at Champagne Marne, Aisne Marne, Meuse Argonne. He received five shrapnel wounds on May 30, 1918. His son, Clarence Jr., served in the Navy in WW II. Sailing on the USS Hornet and the USS Pivot as A Motor Machinist Main engines Second Class.

Next, we have Clara F. Neff (1872-1949). She had a daughter, May Bell Christman (1893-1977), and a son Paul Randolph Christman, born in 1896. Third is Emma Christman (1860-1900). They had a son George, born in 1882.

Last we have Ocie Ora Mellon Fields. It would appear that they were married sometime in 1943 as they applied for a marriage license in June of that year. There are no known children. Charles Christman passed away on February 27, 1942.

Jefferson A. Christman (1836-1915) was the youngest of the three Christman brothers: Enos, William, and Jefferson.

Clarence Christman Jr. & Ruth

William D. Christman

He was married to Margaret J. Powers (1847-1925). They had three daughters: Leah (1865-1900), Ida (1868- 1958), Viola (1876-1938), and Eleanor (1878-1929).

On August 10, 1861, he mustered into Company H of the 72nd Pennsylvania Infantry and served until he was mustered out in August 1864. He lived in Philadelphia. He passed away of natural causes on December 30, 1915, at the age of seventy-nine.

The middle Christman brother William (1830-1911) started out in the shoe business in Chester, PA. At the outbreak of the Civil War, he was commissioned as a Second Lieutenant in Company F of the 125th Pennsylvania

Vol. Infantry. He was promoted to First Lt. In 1862 and mustered out on May 16, 1863.

He married his wife, Zilpha Ann Maxton (1831-1921) on February 1, 1854. They had three children: Ella Cora (1856-1879), George Herbert Percy (1859-1944), and Frederick Bode (1869-1953).

In 1865, he was appointed deputy provost marshall for the 7th district of Pennsylvania. After a year, President Johnson appointed him as a tax collector in the state of Mississippi.

By 1866 he was back in Pennsylvania serving as an internal revenue inspector. William pulled up

Zilpha Maxton Christman

stakes once again and moved to Washington PA, and worked on the Washington Reporter newspaper for the next fifteen years, after which he retired. He also served on the borough council of East Washington. William passed away on February 7, 1911, of "the infirmities of old age." He was eighty-one.

Major Enos Christman

And thus ends the long and winding story of Enos Christman and family. It certainly was filled with adventure and included extended family members.

He was many things: pioneer, miner, and newspaperman. It is a credit to him that his children and their children were successful for the most part. The love story of him and Ellen Apple survived such hardships, it's a wonder they made it through at all. Not only that, but they prospered in the endeavor and raised children who had the same work ethic and were successful in their own right.

I hope you enjoy the mini picture album that follows. When his country called, Enos Christman answered. We shall always remember him.

William and Florence

Rob, Ron, Florence, Elizabeth, Bill
50th Anniversary

Ronald and Robert

Ronald and Robert

Florence, Ron and Rob in Front

Florence, Unknown, Bess, Lil, Lizzie,
Sarah Morrow

Florence

Florence

Florence

Bess Lin Christman

Rob Christman

Howard, Frank, Herb,
Florence, Christmas 1998

William Christman

Rob and Wife Helen

Bill's First Wife Fanny

Chapter Six

Sheshbazzar Bently Howe

S. B. Howe was born in Bentleyville, Pennsylvania, on May 2, 1835, the son of Daniel and Charlotte Howe.

The family moved to California, PA, when Shesh was very young. Educated in the public schools, he then learned the brick molding trade and was only working at that a few years when the Civil War broke out.

He enlisted on December 11, 1862, and was commissioned as a First Lieutenant into I Company of the 1st West Virginia Cavalry. His Father Daniel and his brothers William, Samuel, and Lemuel enlisted as well.

Shesh Howe distinguished himself right from the start and was a natural cavalry leader. His commander, Colonel Henry Capehart, had much to say about his favorite subordinate. *"Captain Howe distinguished himself in*

Sheshbazzar Bently Howe

many of the hard fought battles of 1863 and 1864. In the latter year, he was selected by General Avrill to command the Company of Scouts and to report directly to the General. In this capacity, he performed some of the most daring exploits of the war, and established a reputation for gallantry in the estimation of every officer who knew him."

The Colonel continues. *"In February of 1865, he was commissioned Major and immediately in command of the 1st Regiment West Virginia Cavalry, and started on the great raid of General Phillip Sheridan up the Shenandoah Valley and to the James River." "He was particularly conspicuous at Mount Crawford on March 1, 1865, when he swam his Regiment across the river and charged the enemy in style and drove him from the burning bridge with great loss. He also bore an active part in the rout and capture of General Early's army."*

As anyone could see, Major Howe had impressed his fellow officers with his competence, bravery, and determination. His entire military career was filled with successful engagements. On January 28, he married Miss Emeline Butler from Carroll Township, Washington County. She was the daughter of Ira and Mary Butler.

It wasn't all gallantry and accolades for the Howe family. The Major's father and brother William were both killed on April 26, 1862, at Williamsville, Virginia.

Lem Howe's Headstone

Shesh's brother, Lemuel G. B. Howe, of Company I of the 2nd West Virginia Mounted Infantry, and Companies G, I, and K of the 5th West Virginia Cavalry was a boy of 18 in 1864. He stood tall (for the time) 5 foot 8 inches with a "fresh" complexion, blue eyes, and light hair. On August 27, 1863, during the engagement at Rocky Gap at Rocky Point, Virginia, Lem was wounded in the abdomen and taken prisoner. He spent some time at Richmond, then was moved to the prison at Andersonville. He died there on July 5, 1864. He rests forever at the National Cemetery there at site 2957.

The news is better for Shesh's brother Samuel. He served in the Union Army during the war, but he doesn't show up in the records, so we don't have any details. In some references, he is listed as killed, but that is incorrect. He did receive a broken leg in the service but was able to return home and he did survive the war. He married Sarah Ellen McMillan (1843-1896) on September 18, 1868, and together they had eight children.

Harper's Weekly dated November 4, 1865, ran the following story. April 8, 1865, near Appomattox Courthouse: *"A squadron of the first West Virginia cavalry under Major Howe was pressed forward to the station just before dark, and in the charge, the gallant Howe fell, shot through the body and was carried by some of his faithful men to the church, where he shortly afterward expired. The next morning he was buried, rolled up in his cloak without formality in the rear of the church. In the death of Major Howe, his Regiment lost a most valuable officer, and a man loved and respected by all who knew him."*

Subsequently, Major Howe's remains were disinterred from his grave on the battlefield and reburied in the Monongahela City Cemetery on May 12, 1865. According to the Monongahela Valley Republican, the Major's body arrived by steamer and was received by a fifteen gun salute. The flags were at half mast and an honor guard escorted the remains to the home of his father-in-law, Esquire Ira Butler, where Captain A. L. King and Adjutant Joe Hazzard *"kept the vigil through the night over the fallen hero"*.

Last but not least, there is this thoughtful and moving letter written to Shesh's mother by the Chaplain of the Third West Virginia Volunteer Veteran Cavalry, W M Slaughter.

"April 16th, 1865, Mrs. Howe, Though an entire stranger to you, personally, I have thought proper to write you a line with reference to your son Major S B Howe who fell mortally wounded on the morning of the 8th instant at Appomattox Station, Va. He was carried to Liberty Baptist Church nearby where Captain Durrette and myself was with him until he breathed his last, near ten o'clock in the evening.

Major Howe's Marker in Monongahela Cemetery

I need not say to you my dear madam, that his loss has filled our hearts with sadness. He was as brave as a lion, yet as tender hearted as a child. We have repeated prayers with him in his last moments, and his last whisper in my ear was an expression of confidence or trust in Jesus Christ for salvation.

You will miss him at the paternal hearthstone, you will miss him at the domestic circle, you will often look to that seat that is left vacant, and listen for the familiar voice that used to thrill you with delight, you will hear its rich tones no more.

Up amongst the stars may we not cherish the fond hope that your dear son has touched a nobler, sweeter strain than earth can use. I know how to sympathize with you. This war has sent the cold steel to my own heart. My first born sleeps upon the distant battlefield of Shiloh, but our children are not dead, their memory is embalmed in the great heart of the nation."

So, for Major Sheshbazzar Bentley Howe and the entire Howe family.

We shall always remember you.

Chapter Seven

Samuel Frye

Sam Frye Jr. was born in Fallowfield Township on August 25, 1827, to Samuel Fry Sr. and his wife Elizabeth Van Voorhis. He was one of fourteen siblings and half-siblings.

At the age of twenty-four, he married Miss Julia Ann Redd on August 19, 1852. The next year, his son John was born, and on February 19, 1858, they had a second son Harvey. Only a few weeks later on March 4, Julia passed away.

About a year later, he married Miss Jane Smith and they also had two sons, Calvin Keys (1862-1923), and Thomas Greer (1866-1943).

On September 24, 1862, Sam enlisted in Company F of the 18th Pennsylvania Cavalry. He was soon promoted to Corporal and served with his Regiment in all forty-four of their engagements during the war. At war's end, he returned to farming.

Corporal Samuel Frye

A year or so later, he was severely injured by a fall from an apple tree, where he lost a leg and suffered from these injuries for the remainder of his life. Corporal Frye passed away on February 4, 1904, at the age of seventy- six. He was laid to rest in the Beallsville Cemetery. His wife Jane followed him on May 30, 1911.

His son, Calvin Keyes Frye, or C.K. Frye, grew up and became a business owner, operating a general mercantile store in Bentleyville for many years.

He married Miss Martha B. (Mattie) McElhinny with whom they had a son, Oliver. When Oliver grew up, he came into the family business which became C. K. Frye & Son. Oliver eventually married Miss Lulu Phennicie and they had a son named Oliver McElhinny Frye.

In May of 1906, a new bank was organized and C. K. Frye was selected as the first President of the new Bentleyville National Bank.

C. K. Frye died on August 13, 1923, at the young age of 61. Oliver passed on November 28, 1973, at the age of 84. We shall always remember them.

An interesting note, there is a Samuel Frye Family Cemetery located on the old Frye homestead near Charleroi, PA. This is a private family cemetery with about thirty-five graves there.

Samuel and Jane Fry's marker in Beallsville Cemetery

CHAPTER EIGHT

John F. Bell

O ur story begins with John Fulton Bell being born in Jefferson, Greene County, Pennsylvania, the son of Levi H. Bell on August 23, 1841.

John attended the local schools and in 1860 enrolled in the Georges Creek Academy in Fayette County. However, the Civil War intervened and he enlisted as a Corporal in D Company of the 140th Pennsylvania Volunteer Infantry.

John F. Bell

His leadership skills soon became apparent because in June of 1863, he was promoted to Sergeant, and that November to First Sergeant. The following July 20 near City Point, Virginia, he was commissioned First Lieutenant, the rank he held until the end of the war. Near the war's end, he was the company's commanding officer for a time.

Lieutenant Bell was present during all the engagements of the 140th including Chancellorsville, Gettysburg, Mine Run, Spottsylvania, Cold Harbor, Petersburg, and Appomattox. The 140th regiment was mustered out of service on May 31, 1865.

John Bell returned to Amwell, in Washington County, where on May 6, 1868, he married Miss Lydia Ross of Greene County. Together they raised five children: Benjamin Harrod; Sarah Francis, Lyda Emma, James Franklin, and Abner Ross.

The Bells we're well known and prosperous farmers and stock raisers in Amwell Township for many years. Their youngest son, James, went on to graduate from Washington & Jefferson College in Washington, PA. He then went on to the US Military Academy at West Point, where his education was interrupted when he served in the Spanish American War. He graduated in 1902 as an Engineer and served two years in the Engineer Corps in the Philippines. He also served during World War I. He later went on to teach mathematics at West Point and further serve in Washington DC.

John F. Bell moved to Prosperity in 1903 and continued to farm and raise stock there until about 1907 when he retired to a fine brick home on West Prospect Avenue in Washington, PA.

John Bell's Home on Prospect Ave.

Time waits for no man and Lieutenant John Fulton Bell was no exception. He passed away on November 5, 1922, at the ripe old age of 79. We shall always remember him.

CHAPTER NINE
Benjamin Franklin McClure

A n interesting story is this B. F. McClure. He was a well known dealer in farm implements and hardware in Burgettstown, PA, for many years. He was born on February 12, 1846, in Washington PA, to Dr. and Mrs. (Eleanor) Robert McClure, a prominent physician in Washington County, Pennsylvania.

Ben attended the local common schools in Washington, Ginger Hill, and West Middletown, his education was secondary to earning a living. His father passed away in 1852, so B. F. was the breadwinner until February 23, 1864, when he enlisted in Company A of the 100th Pennsylvania Volunteer Infantry, the famous "Roundheads." Ben was present in every engagement with his regiment from the Wilderness to Petersburg.

During the battle of the "Crater," after a huge explosion, he found himself atop the Confederate works where he was severely wounded in the left leg. The ball had entered the leg on the outer side just below the knee and traveled downward through the leg and exited out near his Achilles tendon at the heel.

Along the way, it injured both branches of the sciatic nerve. If this wasn't enough, gangrene set in as well, eating into bone and muscle, as well as nerves and tendons, causing a large knot at the ankle. Nonetheless, he was able to survive his tortures and was honorably discharged on July 24, 1865.

His bad leg eventually gave out and the disability gradually extended to his left side, causing constant pain and suffering that was lifelong. He was able to carry on with his business affairs for quite a long time due to his sheer force of will, but the disability would eventually force him to retire, his condition progressing relentlessly.

At the close of the war, he lived in West Middletown and worked as a farmer, laborer, and teamster until the Spring of 1870. He moved to Burgettstown where he opened a hardware store.

Four years later, his brother A. C. joined him in partnership, the firm name becoming B. F. McClure & Bro. His business thrived and Ben invested in other enterprises and helped others bring additional businesses into the area. He also became a stockholder and Director in the Guardian Trust Company of Pittsburgh.

During the administration of President William Henry Harrison, Ben became Postmaster in Burgettstown and was elected to the first Town Council formed there. Needless to say, he was also a member in good standing in G. A. R. Post 120 in Washington, PA.

Following his retirement, Ben lived at 236 Center Avenue in Burgettstown. The old house is gone and an apartment building is now occupying the spot. There is currently some disagreement on the date, but B. F. McClure passed away on either June 9 or July 10, 1926, at the age of 80. We shall always remember him.

CHAPTER TEN
The Russells and the Sweetapples

Here we have a familiar story in Bill Russell. Familiar, but interesting, nonetheless. He was born in Mahoning County, Ohio, south of Youngstown near Salem, on October 7, 1839, one of five children born to Hosea and Catherine Russell.

Hosea was a bricklayer by trade and lived until 1875. Catherine passed in June of 1909, at the ripe old age of ninety-three. Bill's brothers and sisters were Lydia (1842-1909) who was married to Mr. James Armitage of Coitsville Township, Ohio; Soloman (1844-1928); Mary Elizabeth (1847- 1945) who married L. C. Cameron; and

William Russell

finally Lucy (1856-1939) who married Mr. A. L. Sweetapple. I'll have more on them a little later.

Bill attended the local schools until he started his life's work. He worked as a carpenter and in the coal mines, then called "drilling", for several years before oil was discovered in Pennsylvania. Bill became very interested in the new industry and its opportunities for employment and wealth. He relocated to near Bradford, PA, to embark on his new career in the oil business.

He eventually was able to buy an interest in an oil well and his prospects were looking very good for a young fellow starting out. They just about got the well drilled when the Civil War broke out and that brought his well to a screeching halt, at least for the time being.

Being of a patriotic mind, he enlisted for service in Company B of the Twelfth Pennsylvania Volunteer Cavalry. Composed of men from various parts of Pennsylvania, it was in Philadelphia, in the winter of 1861-62, when it was mustered in for three years. In late April of 1862, the 12th was sent to Washington and was posted at Manassas Junction to guard the Orange & Alexandria Railroad. On August 26, it was ordered to White Plains to try to locate Confederate forces. Well, they found the Confederate army, and in force. After a narrow escape at Bristoe, they withdrew to Centerville, suffering heavy losses. They continued on to Alexandria where they were ordered to guard the north shore of the Potomac from the Chain bridge to Edward's Ferry.

Bill Russell was captured at some point during all this and spent three months in captivity. He survived his imprisonment and was paroled to, ironically, Camp Parole near Annapolis, Maryland. He returned to duty and rejoined his company sometime after the battle of Antietam, while the 12th was guarding the Baltimore & Ohio Railroad near Bath. They fought several engagements during this time until they went into winter quarters for 1862-63.

They next found combat at Winchester in June of '63, where they broke through Confederate lines suffering some losses. Following Gettysburg, they captured some of the fleeing Confederate wagon trains. They then spent the rest of July in Sharpsburg, Maryland, and then went on to Martinsburg where they remained until the Spring of 1864. At this time, nearly the entire regiment reenlisted including Sergeant Russell. They were furloughed, then returned to Martinsburg in April.

That July, Confederate General Early's army was advancing toward Washington. The 12th was in his front, retiring slowly through engagements at Solomon's Gap, Pleasant Valley, Crampton's Gap, Winchester and Kernstown. The regiment was by then worn out and was ordered to Charlestown to remount and refit.

In April of 1865, they moved to Winchester and were reassigned to the Army of the Shenandoah. They received the news of General Lee's surrender while at Mount Jackson, and were assigned to receive the paroles of the soldiers of Lee's army passing through there. They returned to Winchester where they mustered out on July 20, 1865.

In 1866, Bill married Manerva Crawford (1848-1888). They had three children together: the first was a daughter named Frances (Fannie) born February 18, 1868, next came Edward Frank on June 1, 1870, and last but not least, was Lucien born in 1878.

Let's take Fannie Russell first. She was born in Sugarcreek Township, Venango County, Pennsylvania. Not much is known about her early life.

Stuart, Wilda and Fannie (Russell) Brown

She married George Stuart Brown (1870-1935) in 1898 when she was thirty years old. They had one child, Wilda Russell Brown, born in Missouri, on December 10, 1904.

In 1900, they lived on 119 Kickapoo Street, in Hiawatha, Kansas. George was employed as a printer. By 1910, they lived at 109 Maple Street, Annville, Lebanon County, PA. George was employed as a US Government meat inspector then. By 1920, they had moved to 302 Park Avenue, Lebanon City, Lebanon County, PA, where he was still employed as a government meat inspector. They ended up in Lakeland, Florida, sometime in 1934. They moved to where their daughter Wilda's second husband, Claude Lee, was a dentist.

George Brown passed away on March 26, 1935, and Fannie lived until June 27, 1948. Wilda was married twice, the first on January 31, 1925, to Grant Lincoln Miller. They were divorced in 1936. The second was to Claude L. Lee. Lee died on July 3, 1954, at the age of 45.

Edward was born in Oil City, PA on June 1, 1870. By 1880, he was living with the family at Sugar Creek, PA, in Venango County. He grew up to be a manager of an oil drilling company, no surprise there. At some point, he married Harriett Goodenough and they lived in Bowling Green, Ohio.

They had a daughter Mary Minerva, born on December 10, 1896. Harriett passed away sometime before 1900. She may have died in childbirth, but we could find no record of that. In March of 1903, Edward, who went by E. F; left the United States for Johannesburg, South Africa, and he took little Minerva with him. No doubt this was for business. They returned at the end of June 1905.

By 1910, E. F. and, I presume, Minerva too, were off once again, this time to the exotic island of Madagascar, off the eastern coast of Africa. This time, however, it didn't end so well for them. Edward passed away there from some undisclosed cause. Minerva ended up back in Ohio, where she eventually met a school teacher named Roscoe B. Thrush of Wood County, Ohio. They were married on November 28, 1917.

Last, but not least, we come to the last offspring of William F. Russell. Lucian Russell was born in Sugar Creek, Pennsylvania, in 1878. He died at the age of 7, in 1885.

Solomon Russell

So that brings us full circle in the William Russell saga. Following the war, William took a strong interest in the G.A.R., becoming Adjutant of the S. M. Adams Post 330 at McDonald, PA. He was also a member of the Union Veteran Legion No. 1 in Pittsburgh. He was a member in good standing at the First Presbyterian Church of McDonald. In 1910, he was stricken with paralysis but otherwise seemed to be in good health. On Saturday morning January 13, 1912, while seated at the breakfast table, he was taken ill with what the Doctor, W. P. Dickson, later called apoplexy. William Russell passed away within a few minutes. He was survived by his daughter, Fannie, and her family, along with his second wife, Anna.

William Russell had answered his country's call and rode to the sound of the guns. For that, we shall always remember him. But wait, there's more! The story doesn't end there.

I would be doing you all a disservice if I didn't tell the rest of the story. First, William Russell had a brother named Solomon (1844-1928).

We don't know much about him other than he was born in Boardman, Ohio, and lived most of his life in Kansas. He enlisted in Company D of the 14th Pennsylvania

Cavalry on November 23, 1862. He served through the rest of the war and was mustered out on May 28, 1865.

William Russell had a sister, Lucy K. Russell. She was born in Niles, Ohio, on March 20, 1856. At the age of nineteen, Lucy married a fellow named Albert L. Sweetapple of Kennerdell, Venango County, PA, but he was originally from Colden, New York, near Buffalo. They had seven children together. I'll tell their family story, but before we get into that, I'll tell about A. L. Sweetapple's brothers.

No one can say that the Sweetapples didn't step up when it came to serving their country. Albert L. Sweetapple was born on February 21, 1845. When he was seventeen, on August 3, 1862, he enlisted in Company D of the 116th New York

Albert L. Sweetapple

Infantry. He wasn't alone either. Two of his brothers, John and Charles, enlisted at the same time. All in the same company and regiment. All of them were paid a bounty of $80 by the town of Colden, New York. They were mustered in on September 3, 1862.

John Bailey is a little different in that he was born in England. The eldest brother was born on November 17, 1835, in Gloucestershire, England. While at Fort Monroe, Virginia, he contracted typhoid and died right before Christmas on December 20, 1862. Tragically his wife, Fidelia, had a miscarriage and died along with baby, Ida, only eight months later.

Another brother, Joseph, living in Spring, Illinois, enlisted on August 2, 1862. A month later he mustered into Company B of the 95th Illinois Infantry. During the war, he was promoted to

John Bailey Sweetapple

Corporal and then to Sergeant. He was five feet eight and a half inches tall with black hair and black eyes. He survived the war and was mustered out on August 17, 1865.

Alphred Joel Sweetapple

His brother, William, lived in Spring, Illinois, too, and he mustered in on September 18, 1861, at Chicago. He wasn't so lucky, as he died of Consumption on March 9, 1862, just five and a half months later.

In most families, there is a black sheep. It seems that Alphred was the designated black sheep in this family. Now, he wasn't all bad, but it seems he did make a mistake along the way. Alphred, was eighteen years old when he enlisted on September 20, 1861, in Company F of the 21st New York Infantry. He was five feet six, with brown hair and eyes. He was listed as "sick in hospital" in Philadelphia on April 10, 1863, and mustered out on May 18 of that same year.

He was married to Julia Calkins (1843-1916) on June 12, 1864, and they had three children: Jennie (1868-1958), Caroline (Carrie) (1879-1962) and John W. (1871-1963). Jennie married Asa Sutton when she was eighteen in 1886. Asa was twenty-seven. They lived at 468 Seneca Street, Sardinia, New York. They had a son Edward (1887-1937), and a daughter Julia Mary "May" born in 1890 and passed away at the young age of 19 in 1909 after a brief illness. Her obit read in part: *"She will be greatly missed by all who know her for her kind loving disposition. Her happy girlish life budding into womanhood has been*

Asa Sutton

transplanted into a fairer garden where it will blossom into greater beauty than is possible in this world."

The problem with Alphred was that apparently on September 21, 1879, he broke into the home of Mrs. Kingsley, a widow in Sardinia, New York, and stole what turned out to be $1,100 out of a trunk. He was soon arrested and charged. He rolled over on his accomplice, Mr. William Eastman, who was an ex-Justice of the Peace, who helped set up the heist. He was also charged. Police found the stolen money in Alphred's home, so his guilt was pretty much a foregone conclusion. He awaited trial in Buffalo, New York. Eastman's case was continued. No further word on him.

Jenny Sweetapple

Sutton

Al was convicted in short order and was sent to at the Erie County Penitentiary in Buffalo. He is listed in the 1890 census as still being a prisoner. By 1892, in a Sardinia, New York, census, he was listed as living in Sardinia with his wife Julia and two of their children, Carrie and John. He and his son, John, 20 years old, both worked as laborers.

Alphred's other daughter, Carrie who was just a baby when her father was arrested, grew up and married Lloyd Woodworth on October 26, 1898, in Sardinia, New York. On December 1, 1901, their son Aubrey was born. She looks like she might be pregnant in the picture here.

Carrie and Lloyd Woodworth
at the Pan Am Games in 1901

Alas, in a few short years, tragedy would strike this family. They had another baby on March 5, 1907. However, her husband Lloyd died on April 7, 1907. Their baby passed away, the very next day. I can find no records of what transpired there, but it must have been pneumonia or something.

Carrie remarried in April of 1920 to Mr. Harry Hawks. They had no children together. Harry had served during WW I. He was a Fireman 2nd Class on the USS Commodore. He passed away in 1971. Carrie lived a long life and after suffering an eight-month illness, she passed away at home on November 12, 1962. She was eighty-three. She was buried with her first husband, Lloyd, and their infant.

Lucy Rusell Sweetapple

Thus ends the six Civil War veteran Sweetapple brothers. There were seven more brothers and sisters in the family: Doctor, who died at one-year-old, Mary, Caroline, Louisa, Fred, Jesse, and Frank.

Now we can finally get back to the original A. L. and Lucy Russell Sweetapple. I hope you aren't confused, but this will all clear up in a minute.

Lucy Russell married A. L. Sweetapple in 1875. They had a nice large family of seven children. The first was Frederick (1876-1927), then Catherine (1879-1930), Charles (1881-1923) and Albert Lewis "Bert" Sweetapple Jr. (1890-1977). Then we have Willis (1893-1985), Doris (1895-1996), and last but not least, Mary (1900-1998).

I'm going to go down another rabbit hole with a few of these children, but not too deep. You will see why in a bit, let's take them in order.

Martha Sweetapple

Frederick Allen Sweetapple was born on January 25, 1876, in Clinton- ville, Venango County, Pennsylvania. He was an oil well driller and married Miss Lula Thomas in 1899. By 1914, they had six children: Arthur, Martha, and triplets Frederick, Albert, Francis, and Lillian.

Martha stands out because she was born on August 17, 1902. That in itself isn't earth-shattering, but she worked as a maid and passed away on March 13, 1921, at the young age of only 18 years. The death certificate says peritonitis due to premature confinement.

Francis had a tragic end. He had an alcohol problem and was found dead in a ditch in Franklin, PA. Frederick Sr. passed away on April 28, 1927. Catherine "Kittie" (1879-1930) unfortunately has a darker story.

As far as I can determine, in 1900 she was still single and living at home, but by 1910 she was listed as an "Inmate" in the State Hospital for the Insane in Conewango Township, Warren County, PA. And she was listed as a "Patient" there in 1930. She passed away on October 10, 1930. Her death certificate lists myocarditis and dementia as the cause.

The next oldest is their son Charles. He was born on February 26, 1881. Once again, it appears he had problems because he spent much of his life at the State Institution for the Feeble Minded of

Willis Sweetapple

Western Pennsylvania. He passed away from an embolism on February 17, 1923, at the age of forty-one years.

Here comes Bert Sweetapple Jr. Born April 17th, 1890 Like all the Sweetapple brothers, he was in the oil business. He married Miss Hattie Pettygrew and they had seven kids. We're unsure how that ended, but he then married Miss Sarah F. Urey and they only had two children. I guess Bert was tired by then. Anyhow, he passed away on March 7, 1977. Sarah passed in 1990.

Willis H. Sweetapple May 13th 1893-June 1985. He attended the local schools until the eighth grade when he went to work as a driller in the Pennsylvania oil fields. He probably worked

Ferman Sweetapple

for his father. He married a Miss Caroline Mary Meals with whom they had eight children. Wow, these Sweetapples liked big families.

His son Ferman was born on June 21, 1918, in Clintonville, PA. In May of 1942, he married Miss Ellen Tompsett of Bradford, PA. Together they had four children.

Ferman enlisted in the US Army on May 19, 1942, after two years of high school. He survived World War II and was discharged in September of 1945, when he returned home to his wife and little girl Carol in Bradford, PA. His wife, Ellen, died on April 1, 1981, she was only 58 years old. Ferman passed away on January 15, 1984, he was only sixty-five.

Ferman's younger brother, Willis Jr., was born on May 20, 1927. He too served during WW II. Willis served with the US Marines from January 29, 1942, until discharged on January 29, 1945. He married Miss Violet Chiarenza, and they had three children. Willis Jr. passed away on September 7, 2001, in Bradford, PA. Violet joined him on December 12, 2016, she was ninety-three.

Next is Doris and what an adorable little girl she was. Born on September 19, 1895 in Clinton, Venango County, Pennsylvania. She lived at home until the age of twenty-one when on December 29, 1915, when she was married to Mr. Issac Leroy Hoffman in Wellsburg West Virginia. And yes, he was an oil man.

By 1920, they were living in Clintonville, Pennsylvania, and had a daughter, Erma (1916-1997), and a son Harry, who tragically died of pneumonia and measles at the age of two in 1921. Another daughter came along on March 6, 1925. Her name was Evelyn.

Doris Sweetapple

She had a very interesting story, did Evelyn. She traveled all over the world with her husband, Les Donaldson, whom she married in May of 1943. Evelyn graduated high school at Clintonville, attended the Beauty Academy in Pittsburgh and worked as a beautician in the mid-'40s through the early '50s, then took a position at Wall Mfg. in Grove City, where they manufactured soldering irons and blow torches. When Wall decided to move to Kinston, NC, Evelyn moved there to set up the entire assembly line, then completed her career as a foreman with Wall in 1966.

Her husband, who after serving in WW II, worked for Cooper Cameron in Grove City from 1951 to 1966, took a field service technician position, which took him and his wife Evelyn to various parts of the world (Alaska, New Orleans, Kuwait, Peru, Pakistan, and Nigeria).

As a girl she had played basketball at Clintonville High School and began camping on the Clarion River in the late 40s, which grew into a love of river life. At every chance, Les and Evelyn would return to the good old Clarion River and their numerous river friends. When Les retired they purchased a camp and turned it into a wonderful home.

In the 1980s, Evelyn became involved with a wonderful group of friends in the area to play endless bridge and became very much involved with the Clarion Senior Center, where she became friends with a group of ladies and gentlemen and could not wait to join them daily for exercise, lunches and day trips.

She was a former member of the Union Presbyterian Church in Clintonville, a member of the Eastern Star Parker, Chapter 56, Ladies Auxiliary, Clarion American Legion Post 66, past member of the Rebecca's in Emlenton, and a member of the Clarion Red Hatters. Les passed away on June 5, 1998. Evelyn followed him home on October 15, 2015. They were married for fifty-five years. Quite a full life, I would say.

Doris and Issac lived their lives in Clintonville, PA where Issac worked as a driller and Doris either worked in or owned a beauty shop. Issac died in 1954, and Doris lived on until she passed away on September 15, 1996, at the age of 100!

Doris's sister, Mary, was born on the 14th of March, 1900, in Clintonville, PA. At the ripe old age of seventeen, she married Paul S. Pfeifer (1898-1973) of Evans City, PA, then called Evansburg Borough.

They were married in Wellsburg, West Virginia, just like Doris was. Wonder why? Paul worked for the gas company as a meter engineer, first in Evansburg (Evans City), then Franklin in West-

Mary Russell Sweetapple Pfeifer

moreland County, PA, then in Otisco, New York, and finally on to Wilkinsburg, Pennsylvania, near Pittsburgh.

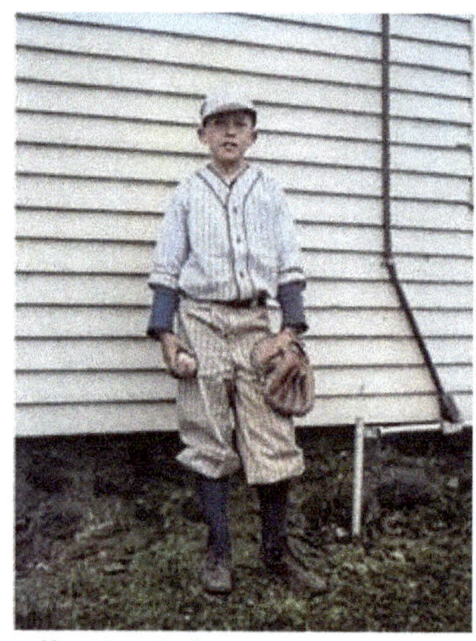

Ellis T. Pfeifer

The next Christmas, December 25, 1918, their first son was born, Amiel. Amiel grew up and served in World War II as a Petty Officer with the US Navy aboard the USS Brooklyn and the USS Cascade. He also served in Korea. He passed away on November 12, 1980.

Now we come to Ameil's brother, Ellis Theril Pfeifer, born on November 23, 1923. Ellis lived at home with the family, moving around where ever his dad's job took him. As a young lad, he loved to play baseball and was pretty good at it too.

By 1941, he was all of seventeen and just graduated from Wilkinsburg High. In August of 1942, he entered the service of his country. Enlisting in the Army, he ended up with the 8th Army Air Corp, 453rd Bomber Group, "Heavy" 734th Squadron. He eventually attained the rank of Staff Sergeant.

The Group served mostly as a strategic bombardment outfit. They bombed heavily defended aircraft factories, fuel depots, oil refineries, etc.

They also bombed anti-aircraft batteries in Normandy France in early June of 1944. On D-Day, June 6, 1944, they bombed installations between La Havre and Cherbourg and others farther inland. That July, they bombed enemy troops in support of the Allied breakthrough at Saint-Lo. During the Battle of the Bulge, they bombed enemy communications.

They went on to serve for the remainder of the war. Incidentally, American movie stars Jimmy Stewart and Walter Matthau were based at Old Buckham with the 453rd. However, we are most concerned with the air action during the July breakthrough at

Saint-Lo. On July 21, 1944, Staff Sergeant Ellis Pfeifer's B-24, flying in formation in the skies over Germany, was hit by the plane below them.

Ellis was thrown from the aircraft. The pilot later said he thought Ellis' was dead before he was thrown from the plane. A small German boy saw the crash and said that Ellis did not flail; he came straight down.

The German soldiers below were told to burn the bodies. However, the town said they would take care of them. They buried each body with their dog tags.

The pastor then labeled and kept all of their belongings. After the war, Ellis was reburied in France.

In about 1952, he was brought back to Clintonville. His casket was guarded and they were not allowed to open it. He had a beautiful funeral, complete with a horse-drawn carriage to the cemetery. Mary Pfeifer used to say "I don't know if it was Ellis we buried, but one of those boys got the funeral they deserved". Years after she died, Mary's great-granddaughter obtained Ellis's war record and it's safe to say that it was indeed Ellis that they buried. He was awarded the Air Medal and a Purple Heart. He rests now forever in Clintonville, PA.

Sgt. Ellis Pfeifer

Mary's daughter Lucy was born on October 4, 1928, in Evans City, PA.

Lucy Pfeifer Bills

She lived at home until she married Charles Bills of Ligonier in Westmoreland County, PA, on August 7, 1945.

Lucy was a traveler. In her lifetime, she visited all fifty states and every country in Europe. She liked to collect antiques as well. She and Charles lived in Murraysville, PA. They had one son and four grandchildren.

Charles passed away in 1972. Lucy went to work at Michaels Craft store in Monroeville, PA, and stayed there until her retirement in 1998. She moved to Westleyville, PA, where she passed away on March 1, 2008, at the age of 79.

Now, we can finally go back in time and return to the A.L. and Lucy Russell Sweetwater story. When we left off, it was in 1875 and they were just married. Albert and Lucy had seven children. They lived in or near Clintonville, Venango County, Pennsylvania. When Lucy's father died in 1875, her mother came to live with them, which she did for the next thirty-four years, until her death in 1909. They had a producing oil lease, part of the oil boom which began in nearby Oil City. Their descendants for the most part lived nearby and were connected to the oil industry in one way or another.

Th Sweetapple Home in Clintonville PA

Albert remained in that endeavor all his life, until February 11, 1921. At the age of seventy-six, he was out on his oil lease with one of his grand- sons, when he started up an engine but got too close to the fly- wheel and his overcoat was caught up in the machinery and threw him around several times. The little boy was able to shut down the engine, but it was too late. The damage had been done. Albert has suffered two broken arms, several broken ribs, and spinal injuries.

He passed away the next afternoon. He had spent about fifty-five years living, working, and raising a family near Clintonville, PA. He was buried in Clintonville cemetery and was a member of Mays Post No. 220, G.A.R.

He left his wife Lucy, and four of their children: Fred, Albert, Willis and Charles, all living nearby. Along with the others, Mrs. Doris Hoffman, Mrs. Mary Pfeifer. He left brothers Jesse, living nearby, Fred of Glenwood, New York, Alfred of Pough-keepsie, New York, Mrs. Louisa Vance of Collins, New York, and Mrs. Caroline Haas.

Lucy purchased a home in nearby Kennerdell, PA, just up the road from Clintonville. There, with her newfangled electrical gadget called a radio, she

The Russell House in Niles Ohio

lived the remainder of her life which ended due to cancer on the 27th of August, 1939. She was eighty-three. She was buried in Clintonville.

This brings us to the end of the Russell/Sweetapple saga.

It is a story of twists and turns that make it hard to follow at times, with so many similar names.

That will be a recurring issue because that was the norm during those times. Families would name their children in such a way that all these decades later, it's hard to keep them straight. We will do our best in that re- guard. There are stories I was forced to leave untold here as there simply isn't room for them all. There certainly was a large Civil War con-nection here, and that is only the beginning of what I want to get through to my readers. If you are

Alphred and Julia Sweetapple

anything like me, you want the whole story, you want to know what happened to everyone, especially the most interesting people involved.

So for all the Russells and Sweetapples, your names have not been forgotten by time. Your stories are within living memory still. Your pictures will live forever as proof that you were indeed once here and that you had made lives for yourselves. Those of you who answered your nation's call will hold that glory forever, and your families and descendants will rightfully bask in that reflected glory. As for the rest of us, we shall always remember you. Enjoy the mini photo album, everyone.

Pfeifer Family

Amiel and Elizabeth Pfeifer with
children Alice, Floyd and Ida

Carrie, Ida, Mary, Ray Pfeifer

I believe it's (Back Row) Lulu, Doris,
A. L. and his MIL Catherine Russell.
In front are Lulu's triplets
Fred, Albert & Frank

A. L. Sweetapple

Frank Sweetapple

The Sweetapple House near
Clintonville, PA Today

Lucy Russell Sweetapple with
Her GGranddaughter

Chapter Eleven
The Sharps and the Bebouts

Here we have the very interesting story of two families from Amity, in Washington County, PA. The family story really begins in Scotland, then moves to Pittsburgh, PA, then to Greene County, and finally to Washington County.

Cephas Sharp's father Zachariah, (1800-1874), and mother Elizabeth Yoders Sharp (1808-1881) had nine children in the early years of the nation. First came Mary Ann (1824-1912), then William Wolverton (1826-1883), Jacob Yoders (1828-1843), and Isaac (1830-1909). Then we have Cephas Dodd (1834-1863), Manaen (1837-1920), Elizabeth Jane (1840-1883), Nancy Maria (1843-1916), and finally Zachariah D (1845-1933).

We'll concentrate on Cephas, Manaen, William, and Isaac, but this will include and expand into several others who are included in this book because they served together during the war and had important contact at times of intense activity.

Sergeant Cephas Dodd Sharp

Cephas was born in the Sharp's old stone house in Amity on June 21, 1834. He was working in Amity as a clerk when the war opened. He volunteered for three months of service in Company E, 12th Pennsylvania Volunteer Infantry. Seeing no action, he was mustered out and returned home.

On August 22nd, 1862, he mustered into Company D as a Sergeant of the 140th Pennsylvania Volunteer Infantry. He saw action at Chancellorsville and was with his regiment when they arrived on the battlefield at Gettysburg.

General Sam Zook

The 140th was part of Colonel Samuel Zook's Brigade, in Brigadier General Caldwell's Division in Major General Hancock's Second Corp. Marching onto the battlefield late in the afternoon on July 2, 1863, they consisted of about 29 officers and 560 enlisted men. They were positioned on the right of the Division, across what is now Sickles Ave.

The battle had begun from the George Rose farm, up through his now famous Wheatfield, and on through what's called the Stoney Hill area. Union General Dan Sickles' line near Sherfy's Peach Orchard had all but collapsed and General Longstreet's 1st Corp was pushing back the Union defenders. The entire Wheatfield area was a whirlwind of back and forth struggle. Each side was fully engaged with the field changing ownership some six times in furious hand to hand combat.

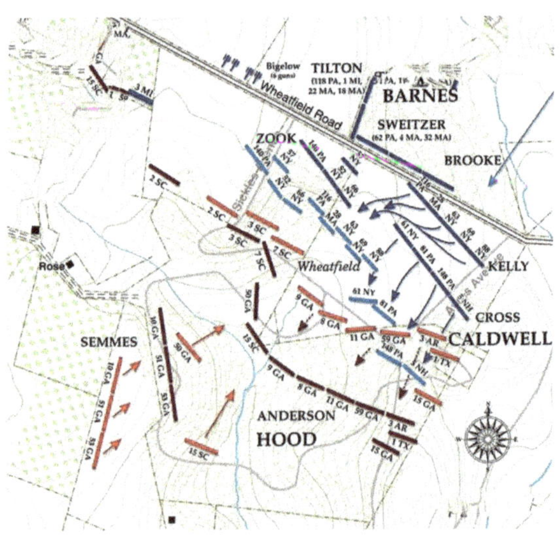

Rose's Wheatfield Then

The final Confederate assault through the Wheatfield occurred about 7:30 pm, and continued on past Houck's Ridge and into the Valley of Death. The Brigades of Kershaw, Semmes, and Anderson were exhausted, but when Wofford's fresh Brigade appeared they made one last push forward. They were met by the 3rd Division of the 5th Union Corps commanded by Brigadier General Sam Crawford, who were able to stop the worn out Confederates, and push them back to the eastern edge of the Wheatfield as dusk descended upon the battlefield.

The Wheatfield remained fairly quiet for the rest of the battle. The Confederates were six Brigades strong against thirteen Union Brigades. Of the roughly twenty-five thousand men involved, there were about 30% casualties. Today, 5% would be considered a bloodbath. Some of the wounded managed to crawl to Plum Run Creek. Unable to cross, they lay there taking what refuge they could and the creek ran red with their blood. Altogether, the 2nd day at Gettysburg is the tenth largest battle of the entire Civil War, and the Wheatfield was a big part of that.

Rose's Wheatfield Today. East Side

As for the 140th Pennsylvania, they started the day with 29 officers and 560 enlisted men. By nightfall, they listed 15 officers and 333 enlisted men in their ranks. It was a brutal day for them. Company D had a rough day indeed. They suffered with five killed, six wounded, and two captured.

The Wheatfield Today, North Side

The Wheatfield "Harvest of Death"

Cephas Sharp was wounded in both thighs and suffered a second wound in one knee. He lay on the field for several days in no man's land, surrounded by killed and wounded men. As he lay there, yet another bullet thudded into his chest, rendering him unconscious. When he awoke, he was sick and woozy. Thinking the ball had entered his heart, he felt around and discovered it had been stopped by the bible he always carried in his breast pocket.

Hearing the familiar voice of his friend and neighbor Bedan Bebout nearby, he called out and they crawled together, joined by wounded comrades Charles Cunningham and Isaac Lacock.

They lay on the field for three days plus. The next morning, July 5, they were found by Confederate soldiers who they paid to carry them to a place of safety. They went first to Mr. Cunningham's barnyard. It is believed that Bedan Bebout died there.

Elizabeth Jane Sharp

Wheatfield Today, South Side

There is some confusion as to the wounds that each of the men received. One account has Cephas Sharp, being wounded three times in the legs and once in the bible. Another account has Bedan Bebout with those leg wounds and having one leg amputated at the Second Corp Field Hospital where he died on July 11. We don't know for sure, but it most likely was a combination of those two scenarios.

It also appears that Cephas Sharp made it to the Field Hospital and possibly had a limb amputated. He survived until August 7, when he passed away. In any event, they both were wounded severely and they both passed away from those wounds.

Isaac Lacock and Charles Cunningham both survived their wounds. The same cannot be said for Corporal James Bebout, who was the brother in law, as well as friend and neighbor, of Cephas Sharp, and brother of Bedan Bebout. They all lived around Amity, PA.

Jim was a cabinet maker in Amity, as well as a maker of coffins, and became the funeral director. He married Elizabeth Jane Sharp who was Cephas' sister on May 7, 1857. They had three children: Elizabeth, Trolis, and Sarah. Trolis grew up and became an undertaker. James Bebout was killed on the field during the fighting. It was a disastrous day for the Bebout family. One bright spot was that William Bebout of Co. D 140th PVI had been discharged for disability that May.

Cephas Sharp wasn't the only Sharp represented at Gettysburg either. His brother William Woolverton Sharp was Assistant Surgeon of the 140th Pennsylvania.

Cephas Sharp's brother Isaac has an interesting story. He was born on December 16, 1830, in Amity, PA. In boyhood, he was bashful among older people, but his mother, Elizabeth, used to say that Isaac was the most troublesome of all her mischievous children.

In early life he learned the tanner's trade, working at the tannery in Amity. On March 5, 1851, he was married to Lavina Bane and they had three children: Mary Flora (1852-1920), Lindley Bane (1859-1939), and Elizabeth Ann (1854-1855), who died at the age of six months.

In August 1862, Isaac Sharp enlisted as a Corporal in Company D, One Hundred and Fortieth

Isaac and Lavina Sharp

Regiment, Pennsylvania Volunteer Infantry. He served without missing a day until the end of March 1863, when he suffered an attack of what they called erysipelas, which is a strep infection of the outer layers of the skin. This kept him in the hospital until May 1, when he joined in the march to Chancellorsville.

Isaac's Storefront on South Main

During the battle, while being overrun by Confederates, Isaac and some others from Company D volunteered to try to save the cannon of the Fifth Maine Battery. They only had manpower to move the heavy cannons. Isaac wasn't fully recovered and fell from the exertion. He quickly revived and they were able to save all the guns. He stayed with the Regiment for a few weeks. He was then forced to leave and was sent to several hospitals to try to find a cure for him. Failing that, Isaac was discharged for his disability.

Upon returning home, he found the tannery closed. Since he couldn't handle hard physical labor any longer, he started a grocery store in Washington, PA. He and his family lived at 229 South Main Street. He is quoted as saying, *"My life may not have been entirely void of some good. Be that as it may, it is of small importance to me, if at last my omissions and commissions are canceled and a clear title to the mansion of glory given me."*

Isaac passed away on New Year's Eve 1909 at the age of seventy-nine. Lavina had passed that Spring on April 16, 1909, of pneumonia at the age of seventy-four.

Lindley Bane Sharp

Their son, Lindley, apparently took over the grocery store and worked there until he retired in 1919. He died of pneumonia on March 5, 1939, at the age of seventy-nine.

William Woolverton Sharp was born on January 16, 1826. A good student, he later taught school in the winter and read medicine with Dr. Matthew Clark in the summer.

In 1847 he married Miss Margaret Jane Sharp of Washington County (no relation) and they had eight children: George W. (1848-1902), Mary Elizabeth (1850-1936), Jacob Richard (1853-1930), Isabelle (1854-1923), Henrietta (1855-?), William H. P. (1859-?), Emma Black (1863-1936)and James Black (1863-1920).

On September 12, 1862, at the age of thirty-six, he was commissioned Assistant Surgeon and mustered into the 140th Pennsylvania Volunteer Infantry. He served with them until January 13, 1864, when he was promoted to Surgeon and was mustered into the 18th Pennsylvania Cavalry.

Towards the end of 1864, his health began to wear down and he just couldn't do it anymore. So in March of 1865, with the war drawing to a close, he resigned his commission and returned home to Amity. With his health partially recovering, he resumed the practice of medicine and continued until the winter of 1882 when he contracted a bad cold that settled in his lungs.

Leaving no possible remedy untried, he fought the illness all Winter and through the Spring and Summer of 1883 until finally, according to his obituary which read in part the following. *"In the quiet of the closing hours of Sabbath, August 5, 1883, his comrades with whom he had mingled in war and in peace, in the presence of the bereaved family and friends, laid him to rest in the old churchyard, where his body shall rest until in response to his dying invitation, the loved ones shall meet him in the morning in the presence of God."*

Last but not least we have another brother of Cephas Dodd Sharp, and he did indeed serve in the Union Army during the Civil War. His name was Manean Sharp. Born in Amity, Washington County, PA, on October 22, 1837, he was by all accounts quite a character. In fact, he was remembered for this account as published in the Sharp Family records. *"in childhood was an independent, rather self-willed boy, but very careless in dress. One suspender was as good as two in his estimation, misplaced buttons were forgotten, and his boots were soon run down at the heel - in short, he was an original character. He was so fond of hunting that his older brothers gave him the nickname of "Nimrod.*

"On one occasion he caught a live rabbit, and notifying the boys to bring their dogs, prepared to have an exciting chase. Each boy held a dog, while Manean with his rabbit advanced some distance, then freeing the animal gave chase, the other boys and dogs following the pandemoniac yells and whoops, and the chase was on.

He was brought to a speedy and unexpected terminus - a large bulldog that had never seen a rabbit joined in the chase, but he was in pursuit of higher game, and catching the young leader by the leg, gave him a lasting souvenir of the rabbit chase, which the "Squire" carries to the present day. The official title of "squire" was bestowed upon him during an election when the boys held a juvenile "congress" in a tailor shop, and a journeyman tailor coming in just as the returns were made out, published the story."

And so it went until April 8, 1858, when he settled down and got married to Miss Sarah A. Bebout. They had three children: James (1859-1926), Ada (1866-1942), and Annie (1868-1915).

James grew up and married Miss Sarah Ellen Dagg. He worked at Hazel Atlas Glass Company. Ada married George McCollum in 1886 when she was just nineteen. They lived on Glenmore Avenue in Dormont, a part of Pittsburgh. She died of senility and exhaustion at age 76, we don't know what happened to George. Annie, well, we just don't know a lot about her. She married a Mr. Thomas Manown Smith,

*Annie and Thomas
Smith House Today*

(1868-1937). They had three children: Pauline (1895-1951), Hariette (1897-1937) and Homer (1906-1936). Annie died young at age 46 of a cerebral hemorrhage.

In 1861, Manean enlisted in Company B of the 85th Pennsylvania Volunteer Infantry. They were stationed around Washington, DC, at Fort Good Hope. They took part in the siege at Yorktown and the battle at Williamsburg. In September of 1862, he was discharged for Disability in Philadelphia. He returned home and became a storekeeper and owned stores in Amity, Washington, and Beallsville, all in the local area. Sarah passed away on April 29, 1898. Manaen remarried to Elizabeth Black the next year, and later passed away on May 8, 1920, of heart trouble.

To complete the link between the Civil War and those who served in subsequent wars, we need to travel down one last side trail in this chapter. As we have seen, the Bebouts were, and are, major players in the history of Washington County, Pennsylvania. We have already talked about James A. Bebout, who was killed at Gettysburg, but we haven't taken his story as far as we should have.

If you recall, Jim and Elizabeth Sharp Bebout had a son named Trolis C., who was born on August 31, 1858, in Amity. He grew up to be an undertaker and ran in the family as we know. In 1893, he went to Washington, PA, and started a partnership with M. Sharp called M. Sharp & Company. This partnership lasted seven years, then T.C. partnered with a Mr. Hallam and they operated for only about five years. Finally, T. C. broke out on his own when his son, Raymond, was old enough to join the firm and it became T. C. Bebout & Son on January 1, 1916. They were located on N. Main Street in Washington, PA. for many years, then moved to E. Beau Street.

Bebout & Barnhill Funeral Home

Sometime in the early 1870s, he married Miss Mary Gauss (1859-1888). They had three children: James M. Bebout (1876-1962), Norval Raymond (1878-1957) and

Jennie M Bebout. I don't have any dates for her, but she married a John W. Miles and had three kids.

Norval Raymond went by Raymond or N. Raymond Bebout. He had partnered with his father and in 1938, a Mr. McNary joined the firm and it became Bebout and McNary.

Well, McNary died in 1948 and a Stuart F. Barnhill (or Barnwell) joined the firm, and it changed names yet again to Bebout & Barnhill Funeral Home. Trolis had passed away on January 1, 1929, missing all the stock market crash "fun." Raymond passed on March 9, 1957. The funeral home moved from Main Street to 69 East Beau St.

The other son, James Michael Bebout, born February 22, 1876, didn't go into the funeral business. But in 1899, he married Miss Alice Bell Wilson. They had seven children: Clarence (1900-1956), Vernon (1902-1972),

James Michael Bebout

Rowena (1904-1982), Mary Elizabeth "Betty" (1915-2005), James Herbert (1923-1944), Donald (1925-1979) and Lester (1928-1993).

Clarence served in the Naval Reserve during WW II. Vernon was a miner near San Francisco, California, but he died in Florida. We don't know much about Betty. She, like many of her siblings, moved to California. She lived in San Diego.

Rowena is another story, although she did end up in Anaheim, California. She served in the US Army during WW II with the rank of Corporal. We have little info about her marriage other than his name was Frank Haught. She is buried in

Alice Wilson Bebout and Friend

Arlington National Cemetery, so she must have an interesting story to tell. No further info was available, but I would be interested in knowing more about her.

James Herbert Bebout traveled a different path than his siblings. He was only a boy of eighteen when the US got into World War II.

James H. Bebout

He just graduated from high school with his class at Hickory High class of 1941. He joined the Army Air Corps and went into flight training at Waco, Texas. His sister Betty spent six months in Waco and was present at Jim's graduation. He was commissioned a 2nd Lieutenant and went on to train as a pilot in the B-24 Liberator.

In 1944, as a member of the 8th Air Force, he was sent to England where he flew combat missions over France until June 2, 1944.

He was reported by the War Department as missing in action over France. The last his family ever heard from him was a Mother's Day card that year. As was customary, one year later, he was officially declared dead.

In August of 1949, his body was returned to the United States, and at two pm on Wednesday, August 23, 1949, Mr. and Mrs. Bebout's boy Jim was laid to rest in Arlington National Cemetery. He was only 21 years old.

Lester W. Bebout

Next, we have Lester Wayne Bebout. He was born on January 7, 1928. I don't have much info on him except that he did serve in WW II. He married a German girl from Forchheim, Bayern, named Margaret Gussregen, (1927-1982). They apparently lived in New Jersey because Les passed away there on February 3, 1993.

Don Bebout

Lester and Margaret

I found very little about Don Bebout. He was born on April 22, 1925. He served in the US Navy during WW II, and died young, at the age of 53 in Los Angeles on April 17, 1979.

And to all the Sharps and Bebouts who served our nation and who carry, even today, a legacy of service, honor, and ability, we shall always remember you.

Bebout Road in Washington County Today

Rowena and her Dad James

Don Bebout

Rowena Haugt Marker at
Arlington

James Bebout Marker at
Arlington

CHAPTER TWELVE

James F. Speer and John L. McClelland

James Speer

James Speer was born in Chartiers Township, Washington County PA, near Canonsburg, on August 12, 1843. His father, Robert (1806-1853), was a wool carder when Washington County was the epicenter of the wool industry.

His mother was Nancy Harsha Speer (1813-1903). Her father was an early settler in Chartiers Township. Nancy would recount that when she was a young girl, she could stand on their front porch and she could see the smoke from thirteen local distilleries.

Of course, that was because farmers would make whiskey from their grain as it was easier to haul it over the mountains to market and the whiskey wouldn't go bad. And that had repercussions that resulted in the famous Whiskey Rebellion.

James F. Speer had six brothers and sisters. The eldest Thomas (1839- 1861), Jennie (1841-1925), Robert L. (1845-1865), Stewart (1847-1873), Alexander (1849-1912), and Catherine (1852-?).

Jim stayed on the farm until the outbreak of the Civil War when he enlisted in 1861 as a Sergeant in Company B of the 85th Pennsylvania Volunteer Infantry.

Mr. Speer took part in the battles of Fort Wagner and Fort Gregg, Yorktown, Fair Oaks, Seven Pines, Jones Ford, Harrison Landing, Suffolk, Black Water, South West Creek, Kingston, White Hall, Goldsboro, Folly Island, Morris Island, White

Marsh Island, Charleston, Bermuda Hundred, Straw- berry Plains, Chapin's Farm, Deep Bottom, Petersburg, and Appomattox. He was wounded at Fair Oaks and on August 16, 1864, was wounded in the right shoulder at Deep Bottom Run in Virginia.

Fair Oaks

After Appomattox, he returned home and took up the bricklayer trade. On December 10, 1868, he married Miss Rebecca MacMillan. The new Mrs. Speer had one sister Mrs. H. H. Bebout. Gee, where have we heard that name before? Rebecca was the great-granddaughter of Dr. John MacMillan, founder of Jefferson College, which later became Washington & Jefferson College.

The Speers had six children including Mary Loretta (1869-1940), William L. (1871-1926), John F. (1881-?), and Dora P. (1884-?), Jim Speer was a leading citizen of Canonsburg, serving several terms on the town council, and one term as its President.

He served two terms as Commander of the Thomas Paxton Post of the G. A. R. James Speer passed away on March 18, 1924, of apoplexy. Rebecca followed him on February 11, 1929, of heart trouble.

James's brother Robert enlisted in Company G, 140th Pennsylvania Infantry. He was promoted to Corporal on September 1, 1864. He is listed as having died on February 19, 1865. No further information is available.

I also found a record on a William F. Speer of Washington County, PA. I'm not sure where he fits into the Speer family, as I found no record of him connected to them, but he must be somehow. He enlisted on October 1, 1862, as a 2nd Lieutenant in Company G of the 22nd Pennsylvania Cavalry. He was promoted to Captain on September 7, 1864, and he promptly got wounded at Opequan, Virginia, on September 19, 1864. He made Brevet Major on March 13, 1865, and Lt. Colonel that same day. After the war, he lived in Pittsburgh where he served as Post Commander of G.A. R. Post #3 General Alexander Hayes from 1889 to 1890.

So this brings the conclusion of the Speer story. There are gaps in the information that should be tracked down, but that is for someone else to embark upon. As for the Speers that served in the Civil War, that does not diminish their service one bit. We shall always remember them.

Pontoon Bridge at Deep Bottom

John Logan McClelland

John Logan McClelland was born in Florence in Hanover Township, Washington County, PA. His parents were Jackson and Mary McClelland. J L's great-grandfather, Hanson McClelland, established the family in Washington County when he came from Ireland.

Joh L. McClelland

One of his sons was named William. The McClellands and the McCooks were neighbors in Chartiers Township. William McClelland and Daniel McCook, who was the father of the "Fighting McCooks" of Civil War fame, together owned a salt well there in the township.

William married Miss Hannah Long and they had four children together: Jackson, Joseph, James, and Catherine. Jackson married and moved to Canonsburg where they raised four children: John Logan, Romulus L, Mary, and Nettie.

John Logan attended Jefferson College but accompanied the rest of his family when they moved south in 1858. They returned in 1862, but John had enlisted as a Private in Company G, of the 50th Tennessee Volunteer Infantry, in 1861. He was soon promoted to 2nd Lieutenant and then to 1st Lieutenant, serving on garrison duty at Fort Donaldson.

In 1869, John L. returned to Washington County and was a member of the civil engineering corps that built the Chartiers Valley Railroad. Following that, he worked in the Chief Engineers office of the Panhandle Railroad and worked there until 1881.

Switching gears, he was made a Deputy Sheriff in 1886. He served for three years under Sheriff W. B. Chambers. That same year, he opened a real estate and insurance office and organized a building and loan association. He later helped to organize the Canonsburg Electric Light Company, for which he served as President from 1894 until 1907.

Through all of this, he never married, and on May 21, 1920, at the age of seventy-eight, he died of pneumonia. We shall always remember him.

Chapter Thirteen

Henry Slusher

Here is a very interesting man for you. Henry Slusher was born on May 10, 1846, on the family farm in Amwell Township, Washington County, PA. His father, Michael (1809-1891), and mother, Lavinia Paul Slusher (1817-1900). were farmers. As was customary with most families and farmers in particular, they had a large family. Nine children in all, starting with Sarah (1837-1917), then Keturah "Kate" (1840-1929), Ellen (1842-1925), and just like clockwork came Hannah (1846-1915), Mary L. (1848-1918) and Christiana A. (1850-1944). Rounding out the baseball team was William C. (1853-1878), Flora (1855-1877), and last but not least, Martha (1857-1920).

Before this is over, we'll be meeting a lot of Slushers. Henry stands out for at least three reasons: one, he served in the Civil War, two, he was awarded the Congressional Medal of Honor and three, he was constantly in the middle of controversy. You can follow his life by just reading the newspaper clippings. He is our main character, but this story goes much further than him. Please bear with me as we follow the Slushers' remarkable life experiences from coast to coast. Heroes to villains, sheep barons to bootleggers, boxers, and football players, these people had it all.

Let's get underway. Who was Henry C. Slusher? Honestly, I don't even know where to start with this guy. How about we begin at the top and see what happens. Growing up on the farm was pretty hard and dull work for a young lad. When the

Civil War erupted in 1861, Henry was only fifteen years old. Now, back then, fifteen was like 18 or 20 is today. Things were different, people grew up much faster. His father was able to keep young Henry in check, because Henry didn't enlist in the Army until October 14, 1862. He mustered in at Washington, PA, as a Private in Company F of the 22nd, Pennsylvania Cavalry, the "Ringgold Battalion."

The Ringgold battalion was made up of the following companies, enlisted for three years' service, Ringgold Company, Captain John Keys, organized at Washington, PA., October 2, 1861; Keystone Company, Captain George T. Work, organized at Washington, September 6, 1862; two independent companies, Captains Harvey H. Young and M. W. Mitchener, organized at Washington, during September and October 1862; Patton Company, Captain A. J. Barr, organized at Washington, October 14, 1862. The Washington Cavalry Captain A. J. Greenfield was organized at

General William Averell

Wheeling, VA, on August 19, 1861, and the Lafayette Cavalry was organized at the same place on November 6, 1862, under Captain Alex. V. Smith. These companies had served independently in West Virginia, going to the front as fast as each was organized.

Those earliest in the field were active at Blue's Gap, Bloomery Gap, Strasburg, Columbia Furnace, Two Churches, Rude's Hill, North River Mills and Dashu's Mills. After the Battle of Gettysburg, they joined in the pursuit of Lee and were engaged at Petersburg, Lexington, and Moorefield, in the early part of 1864.

The 22nd was reorganized in February of 1864 as the 185th regiment of the line, which consisted of several six-month companies, the five companies of the Ringgold Battalion, and the Washington and Lafayette cavalries engaged in General Sheridan's campaign in the valley. It was active at Kernstown, where it displayed great steadiness and gallantry; fought at Opequan and Berryville, met with considerable loss at Charlestown; and at Halltown, Major Myers was severely wounded. A detachment of the regiment had been left behind at Cumberland in April and under the command of Major Work had been in active service all summer, sharing in the campaign against Lynchburg, the battles of New Market and Kernstown, and aiding in the decisive defeat of McCausland's forces at Moorefield, subsequent to the burning of Chambersburg.

After the union of the two detachments at Hagerstown, the regiment joined General Averell's forces and was actively engaged at Martinsburg, Bunker Hill, Stephenson's depot, Darkesville, and Bucklestown. On September 18 it charged the enemy at Martinsburg and on the evening of the following day, joined in the brilliant cavalry charge which routed the enemy at the Opequan, where the regiment captured a battery and 80 men.

It was again active at the battles of Fisher's Hill, Brown's Gap, and Weyer's Cave, where the command made a determined charge which saved the entire division train. It lost severely in this action, Major Work and Adjutant Isenberg being among those severely wounded.

*Wartime View of Morefield
West Virginia*

It was fiercely engaged at Cedar Creek, where it lost heavily, and then returned to Martinsburg, where it encamped until December 20. On that date, it moved to New Creek. During the winter it was engaged in picket and scouting duty in the counties of Hardy, Hampshire, and Pendleton, operating against roving bands of the enemy. Companies E and F were mustered out on July 19, 1865. The remaining companies were consolidated with the 18th PA Cavalry on June 24, to form the 3rd Provisional Cavalry, which was mustered out on October 31, 1865, at Cumberland, Maryland.

As I previously mentioned, Henry did indeed receive the Congressional Medal of Honor. Even during the Civil War when these were given out like candy, Private Slusher appears to have deserved his. I will let him tell his own story.

"On September 11, 1863, the rebels, three hundred strong under Captain McNeil surprised the Yankee camp of 260 men under Major Stevens on Cemetery Hill at Moorefield W. Virginia. At three AM, twenty-five men of Company E were ordered out on the Long River Road up to the South fork of the Potomac. We met the rebels two miles south of Morefield carrying off all the camp equipage and 146 prisoners.

The View Today From Cemetery Hill, Now Called Olivet Cemetery

"We took a position on the West side of the river on a bluff some thirty feet higher than the road and river, dismounted, and commenced to shoot down into the ravine, killing eight or ten men of the rebel force. At this time, I caught sight of my messmate William P. Hagner, who had been wounded early in the day, taken prisoner, and placed in an ambulance.

"When we opened fire, he threw up his hands as a signal for help." "To see him in such a predicament was too much for me. I at once crossed the river. My aim was to rescue him at all hazards, and I reached the vehicle under a heavy fire. In a hand to hand fight close by the ambulance, I was wounded and captured and had to share the fate of my comrade in Libby Prison."

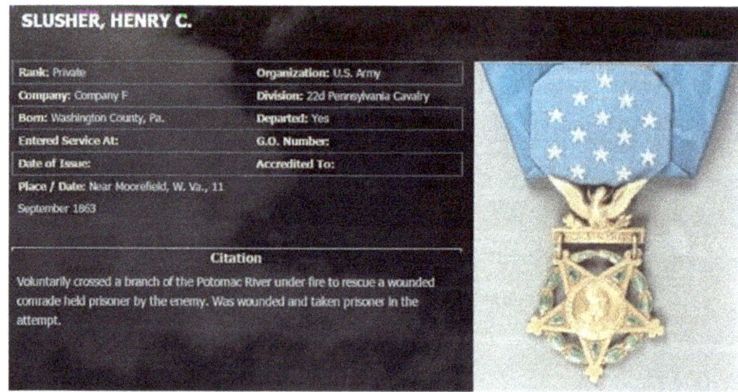

SLUSHER, HENRY C.

Rank: Private	**Organization:** U.S. Army
Company: Company F	**Division:** 22d Pennsylvania Cavalry
Born: Washington County, Pa.	**Departed:** Yes
Entered Service At:	**G.O. Number:**
Date of Issue:	**Accredited To:**
Place / Date: Near Moorefield, W. Va., 11 September 1863	

Citation

Voluntarily crossed a branch of the Potomac River under fire to rescue a wounded comrade held prisoner by the enemy. Was wounded and taken prisoner in the attempt.

Being just nineteen years old when he mustered out of the Army in 1865. I must assume he returned home to the farm where he stayed until he married Miss Margaret Jane Wilson from Cross Creek on January 18, 1868. This was to be a long and very strange arrangement as we will see a little later.

They had three children that survived, having lost an infant son in 1870. Cora (1871-1955), was the first of three daughters. Then came Della (1874- 1962) and then Oda (1876-1904). I've seen several different names for Oda. On the 1880 census, she is listed as Randa. In February of 1895, her father gave permission for her to marry a neighbor, Frank Moninger. He wrote her name as Ray Oda Romaign Slusher. Her grave marker says Oda R. Moninger, so let's call her Oda.

June 2, 1876, "H C Slusher has received a nameless boy from the Employment Office, Pittsburg, Pa whom he calls George Centennial Slusher."

The Moninger family lived on a neighboring farm. They must have been close friends because Oda's sister Della married Frank's brother John. Della and Frank had two daughters, Wilma and Margaret. John passed away in 1954, and Della at the age of eighty-eight, fell and broke her leg in 1962, she died of Sepsis that September.

November 10th 1876 "Last week, H. C. Slusher gave up the child Hannah Sutton that was bound to him by her father about six years since. Her parents separated and peddled their children over the county to have them raised. And about two years ago her father Samuel Sutton, brought a suit of abuse against said Slusher. The court discharged Slusher and he kept the child until last week when he concluded to give it up on condition that her mother would assign over a legacy of $100 left to her by her father and this money will be given to the child by said Slusher at his will."

January 17th 1877 "Commonwealth v. Michael Slusher of Amwell; selling liquor without a license, on return of constable Joseph Miller. Pleaded guilty and sentenced to pay a fine of $200 and costs."

Oda and Frank had nothing but tragedy it would seem. Oda passed away on May 6, 1904. An infant died the same day. And there is another child's name, Ray O Moninger 1904, carved on her headstone. Were there two children that died? Or was one listed twice?

November 22, 1878 "There has been a rumor current that the grave of W. C. Slusher who was buried at Lone Pine last July, had been rifled and that the skeleton was in possession of a doctor in Amwell township. We are assured by the relatives of W. C. Slusher that there is no truth whatsoever to the report. The grave has never been disturbed and the skeleton referred to was in the doctor's possession long before his death."

Circling back to Cora, she married Harrison V. Dague in June of 1892. They were divorced about three years later. In 1910, she married a real estate agent named Joseph C. Gore (1865-1941), who lived in Pittsburgh then, but was from Greene County. They lived on Hobart Street in Pittsburgh, then by 1920, they had moved to East Washington, PA, and lived on South Wade Avenue. Cora was listed as Corea on the census forms. And they also list Margaret Slusher (mother-in-law) and Marie Moninger (neice) as living in the same household. Joe died on May 6, 1941, and Cora died of pneumonia on May 16, 1955. If all this seems confusing, just wait, it gets even more unusual and interesting.

March 16, 1882 "Maj. A. G. Happer of the Washington Real Estate Agency has sold for Michael Slusher his farm of 245 acres in Amwell Township to James Foreyth, of Redstone, Fayette County, Pa for $17,000."

Let's get back to Henry Slusher who as we will soon see is quite a character.

May 29, 1891 "H. C. Slusher has leased his farm to the Carnegie Natural Gas Company for a good bonus, one half of the oil and $500 for each gas well. Operations are to begin immediately."

The best way to follow all this is to read the newspaper clippings that seem to be a constant thing with Henry. Some of them are good and some aren't. A few are simply bizarre, like this first one. Apparently, this kind of thing was a habit with Henry, because we see later that same year, this made the papers. Even Henry's father got into the act, as we see here. The Slusher family has a long history of bootlegging, as we shall see coming up a little later. Doesn't every family have a skeleton controversy? The next series of events is unclear, but bear with me.

Pittsburgh, August 20, 1902 Brother of Fighter Shot At Ball Game. "Thomas Slusher, brother of Charles Slusher, the pugilist, was seriously if not fatally shot by patrolman John W. Sage yesterday afternoon. Sage was trying to presere order at a baseball game at Twentieth and Bank streets. Slusher was disorderly and resisted arrest, firing several times at the policeman. Sage fired one shot which penetrated Slusher's bladder. Slusher is at the hospital."

July 10, 1907 "Mrs. Margaret W. Slusher has begun court proceedings against her husband. Henry C. Slusher, seeking to compel him to turn over to her, according to an alleged agreement, her interest in the joint estate. She alleges she married Slusher in 1868, and that during the last eighteen years she has lived under the same roof with him, but that they have lived as strangers, never speaking to each other except when absolutely necessary. Slusher was one of the wealthiest land owners in Amwell Township, but located in Washington three years ago after selling 300 acres of coal at a large figure. When the property was sold she alleges her husband agreed to set apart an interest in the estate for her. This, she says, he has refused to do."

Sometime before 1876, Henry acquired his Uncle David Slusher's farm. David was alive at this time, so it wasn't an inheritance. Possibly David got too old to farm and moved to town. In any event, Henry owned the farm and it turned into a huge bonanza for him. In the midst of all this, Henry's father, Michael, sold his farm, which was just around the bend from Henry's new place.

Pittsburg October 26, 1907 "A sensational case, which is soon to be disposed of in the United States district court here, is that of H. C. Slusher, a well known resident of Washington, Pa; and pension agent at that place. He is 65 years old and is charged with sending an improper letter to Mrs. J. Lewellen, a prominent woman of Washington. Slusher is now out on bail. He was indicted by the grand jury Tuesday last and Wednesday he entered a plea of nolo contendere. It is claimed by the post office authorities here that the letter on which he was indicted is one of the worst of its kind that has been received by them for some time. Slusher is a well known resident of Washington, having lived there a great many years and being active in affairs of the Grand Army of the Republic and several organizations."

Obscene Letter Costs Him $1,000 "Pittsburg, Nov 9, 1907. This was sentence day in the United States district court. H. C. Slusher, a former pension agent at Washington, Pa, was ordered to forfeit $1,000 for sending an obscene letter through the mails."

Washington, PA. July 28, 1908 "Frank L. Moninger of Amwell township has started habeus corpus proceedings against his father in law and mother in law, Mr. and Mrs. Henry C. Slusher of Washington, to secure possession of his young daughter, Maize Moninger. The mother of the child has been dead for several years and the daughter has resided with the grandparents. Mr. Moninger now wants his daughter."

November 22, 1909 "Wealthy Man Must Preserve Peace" Henry C. Slusher of Washington Pleads Guilty to Two Charges Against Him. ...The most prominent of the pleaders was Henry C. Slusher, a well known resident of Washington, who is quite wealthy and who resides at 326 East Maiden street. Slusher was charged by his wife, Margaret Slusher, with assault and battery and surety of the peace. The court let him down by ordering him to pay the costs in the case and furnish bond in the sum of $500 for one year as a guarantee that he will keep the peace."

Pendleton, Oregon June 29, 1909 Evidence of Another Mysterious Murder "Still another murder mystery may be added to Umatilla county's already long list. George McCutcheon of near Nolen has reported to Coroner Folsom that his brother, Ed McCutcheon, had discovered the bones and arm and head of a man projecting from the soil in the river bottom, three miles below Nolen on the Slusher ranch"

Perhaps this 1876 map will make things a little more clear. In 1886, Henry moved to a large eleven-room house in Amwell. Said to be the "best residence in Amwell Township." In 1899, he and two other nearby farmers sold coal and oil leases on their properties and each netted just under $100,000.00, with Henry getting an additional $500 for each well drilled. Henry still owned the farm itself, but wasn't interested in farming any longer. And with good reason. He wasn't done making moves, taking advantage of the new money making machine called oil and natural gas.

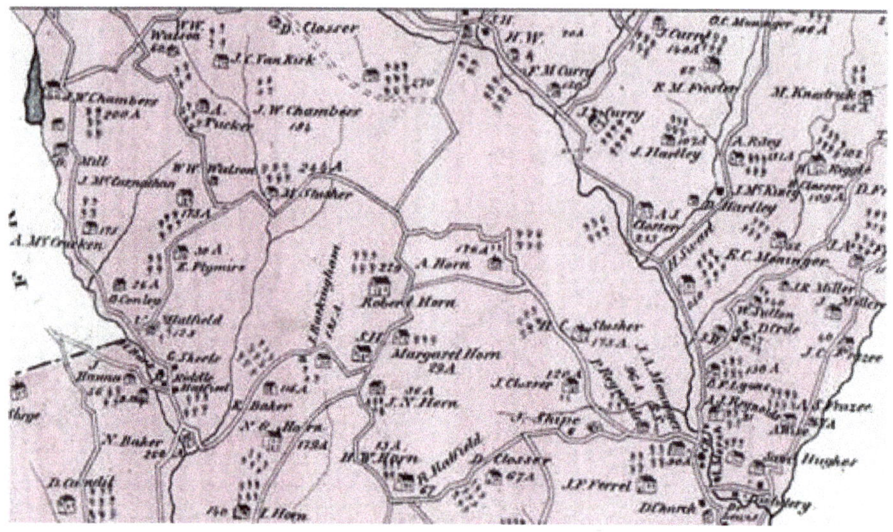

Washington, February 8th 1912 Case Against Slusher Dismissed "The court discharged the case of H. C. Slusher, accused of surety of the peace by his wife, this morning, the defendant to pay the costs of the case. The Slushers are old people and prepared separation papers some time ago. In some way the money and property of the couple ws placed in the wife's hands, with the provision that she should give her husband a home until his death. Slusher was accused of Surety of the peace specifically and with "cussedness" generally, it being alleged that he threatened to kill his wife and burn the house."

The David Slusher Farm

In 1904, he again moved. This time to the big city of Washington, PA. He and his wife, Margaret, along with granddaughter, Mazie Moninger, and a boarder named Macaulay, moved into a home on East Maiden Street. And now we see H. C. Slusher working as a Pension Agent. And then things get weird.

And the soap opera that is the lives of the Slusher family continues unabated. It would seem that Henry Slusher has a very difficult time getting along with anyone, including his own family, as we shall see. And as a sneak peek into what lies ahead, while all this was going on in Washington, PA, a branch of the Slusher family left Washington, PA, and went west to Oregon, two of whom were one step ahead of the law, were having some troubles of their own. There are Civil War veterans and others involved. Their story is even more interesting and reads like the great American success story or miniseries with wealth, power, land, family, sheep, and cattle. Only there is an undercurrent of mystery, mayhem, and yes, murder. Stay tuned.

Washington March 1, 1916 H. C. Slusher Sues His Wife For $900 "Henry C. Slusher of Washington has filed suit against his wife Margaret W. Slusher, in which he seeks to recover the sum of $900, with interest. The amount is alleged due under a certain family agreement by the terms of which Margaret Slusher, along with two daughters, were each to pay to him the sum of $100 every year during his natural life. The sum e represents eight yearly payments that it is claimed Mrs. Slusher has defaulted, and $100 comprising an alleged loan. Under the agreement, made November 14, 1907, it was agreed that Henry C. Slusher pay to Frank Moninger, his son in law, $8000, in trust for Margaret Slusher, who was to enjoy the income during her natural life. A similar sum was paid to Wildon Moninger, another son in law, in trust for Mrs. Slusher during her lifetime. Further, under this agreement, Mr. Slusher conveyed to his wife the house and lot at 326 East Maiden Street, for life. Mrs. Slusher to keep and maintain it, and to provide a home there for Mr. Slusher. He avers that he has complied with all the terms of the agreement but that the defendant has failed to comply with these terms."

The David Slusher\Henry Slusher Farmhouse As It Appears Today

Apparently, H. C. Slusher didn't learn anything from the first set of charges for surety of the peace. There was another go round with the Mrs. This time, he gets off even luckier. This is not to say that Henry was the only Slusher to run afoul of the law. No sir, there were plenty of other Slushers who just couldn't seem to stay out of trouble.

So it would seem that the entire Slusher clan is a feisty bunch, to say the least. The saga of H. C. and his Mrs. continues but for a short while longer. Let's finish it up before we move on to other members of the Slusher clan. And one final court battle to round out the lifelong squabbling that went on between the Slushers.

December 11, 1916 Slusher To Leave His Unhappy Home "Former wealthy Amwell farmer and wife agree to disagree. A new panel of jurors reported this afternoon when common please court began the third week of it's session. In the suit of Henry C. Slusher of Washington against Margaret W. Slusher a verdict of $550 was taken. The suit involved a claim on an alleged family agreement whereby Mrs. Slusher *was to pay her husband $100 a year and maintenance. The couple has not lived congenially, and by the arrangement made today Slusher is to leave home. He was formerly a wealthy farmer of Amwell township."*

Margaret Slusher passed away at the age of seventy from heart trouble on January 23, 1920. Henry Craig Slusher followed her on March 12, 1923. He was seventy-six years old. They still lived in the same house on East Maiden Street, and Maize still lived with them, despite all the litigation. They were married for fifty-two years.

They are all buried in Lone Pine Cemetery in Amwell township. Their house in Washington is gone now, it being replaced with a strip mall. I'll leave it up to you to determine if that is progress or not. Their legacy lives on in their descendants and the rest of the huge Slusher clan, many of whom served in the Civil War. Nothing can take away Henry's Medal of Honor, or the service he gave to his country. And yes, we should always remember him. A short epilogue is coming up next to complete the Slusher saga. The Oregon branch and The Kentucky Pig Feud.

Slusher Family Epilogue

The Great Kentucky Pig Feud
and
The Slusher Sheep Barons of Oregon

The Slusher soap opera would not be complete if I didn't include the following. It's two very interesting stories, but there just isn't enough solid information to fill in the blank spaces created by the newspaper clippings. The Slushers seemed to be in the papers frequently as hardly a day goes by that we don't see something concerning one of their family.

Robert and Marinda Mae Slusher

They are without a doubt one of if not the biggest families I have ever tried to research. They stretch from Virginia, through what is now West Virginia, Pennsylvania, Kentucky, Ohio, Indiana, Illinois, Arkansas, Oregon and California. And I am certain I have left out a state or two that got lost in the shuffle. Embedded in there are many Civil War veterans who deserve to be remembered. However, as far as the Oregon and Kentucky branches go, I found not one picture of any Civil War veteran in all the images I found. At most, just the basic info from the records, regiment, company etc. So in an effort to not go too far down another rabbit hole, let's catch the highlights of the most interesting stories left to tell.

What I call the Great Kentucky Pig Feud is part of a much larger ongoing feud taking place in Southeastern Kentucky. Actually, there are many such feuds, with the Hatfield and McCoy feud the most famous, but there were others that were every bit as large, long-lasting, and deadly. Let's start off with some background.

This begins with a long-standing feud between the Turner and Sowder families.

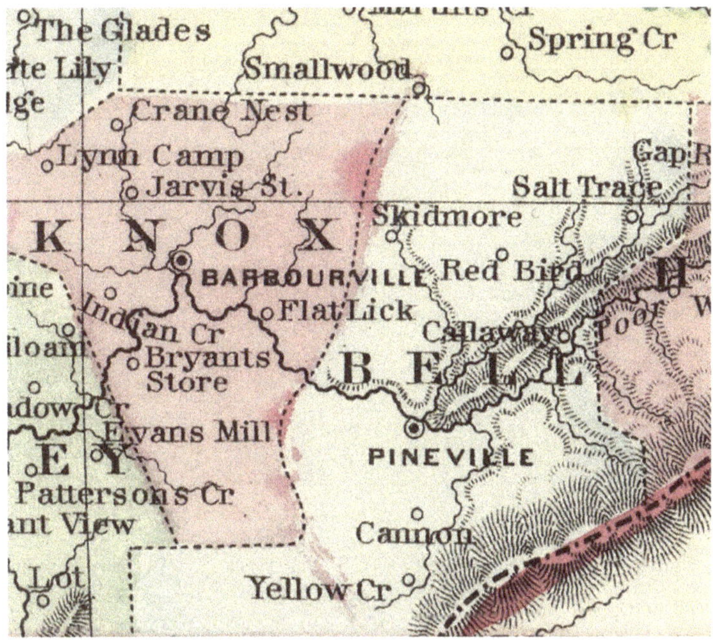

The Counties of eastern Kentucky and Tennessee are mountainous coal regions with small populations. Nearly everybody is related to everyone else, and when there's trouble, people tend to side with whoever they like the best. And it doesn't matter one bit what started the trouble in the first place, some perceived insult or a squabble over the sale price of a cow can kick off a violent altercation that can leave a dozen or more dead.

In March of 1889, there had been about a two year lull in the fighting. Part of that was because of the influx of people from the North who had no family connection with the warring tribes. These newcomers also made their way onto juries that were much more impartial and would convict outlaws who would otherwise go free.

The Sowder - Turner clash began when Marsh Turner, who was a member of a posse, went out after a relative of the Sowders for some minor offense and was pretty much shot to pieces. A man named General (his name not a rank) Sowders was accused of the murder. Now the odd part is that this Sowders was married to a Turner, but that didn't prevent him from killing her cousin Marsh, her Uncle

Lee, or her brother Tom! These people take feuds seriously! The last killing in the series was Lee Turner, who General Sowers shot down in the parlor of the hotel in Pineville. Turner quickly disappeared and went into hiding. That was just the beginning. Seven men were killed in a gunfight at the local courthouse, and in the nearby town of Yellow Creek, during a church service, five people including a woman and a small boy were killed in the church.

Yes, of course there's more. In less wholesale fashion, Tom Marcy, Jack Carroll, and Tom Turner fell victim to General Sowders, who always carried a Winchester and several Colt revolvers. After some time, Sowders was captured without a fight and jailed in the Pineville jail.

August 3rd, 1889 "A fierce quarrel has broken out between the Smiths and the Slushers near Pineville, over a hog worth two dollars. The Smith's home was attacked by the Slushers and a volley poured into the house. Smith retaliated by putting a guard armed with Winchesters on Slusher's road to Flat Lick, the nearest village. Both sides are now well armed and are watching for each other."

August 6th, 1889 "The quarrel which has been going on between the Smith and Slusher familys of Bell County, culminated in a fatal meeting last Friday. William Smith and about 40 armed men went to Flat Lick, and about 1 o'clock in the afternoon were attacked by the Slushr faction, who opened fire upon them from the mountain, about 200 yards distant...both sides kept up the firing for several hours. John Minter of the Slusher force was killed"

March 7th, 1890 Barboursville, Kentucky "E. Messner with 40 armed men of the Slusher party, arrived from Flat Creek yesterday morning and caused a general alarm. Circuit Judge Boyd placed a strong guard around the courthouse, but notwithstanding that, factions opened fire in the courthouse yard, using Colt's 45 caliber revolvers. William Day was wounded in the leg. The presence of the guards and the falling snow prevented further damage. The Messer party then threw cartridges into the stove at the depot."

Pittsburgh Dispatch December 27, 1891 A Plot To Kill A Sheriff

Middlesborough, Ky. H. W. Barker, deputy under Sheriff Slusher, was arrested here on Wednesday last, charged with embezzlement, he having appropriated nearly $2,000 collected for back taxes. His bond was fixed at $2,000, but he could not give it. On Thursday evening, while under heavy guard, Barker escaped, and is now in the mountains. It has just developed that Barker had made a plot with a notorious renegade, Gillis Johnson, to assassinate Sheriff Slusher, for which he agreed to pay Johnson $800. Fred Lynch and one Graham were arrested last night as being in the conspiracy, and Lynch has made a confession of the whole affair. The murder of Sheriff Slusher was to have been accomplished this week, during Christmas festivities. Arch-conspirator Barker having escaped, Graham was released this morning, and furnished with money to leave this section, as it was certain Johnson would kill him as soon as it was known.

Ok, so how do the Slushers fit into all this? Well, they and their friends, the Messers, sided with the Sowders. The Smith family sided with the Turners. A dispute arose over a pig, and then here we go! A fight ensued and friends of the two families ran to their aid. For several days the surrounding mountains were alive with men armed to the teeth. It wasn't long before the two sides met in a battle, where it was said that over five hundred rounds were fired, and a number of men were wounded. A Sheriff's posse was assembled to put a stop to all this, but they were driven back.

The district judge himself headed up a much larger, and more well-armed, posse, and set out. This time, the outcome was different, and they were able to gain control and arrest a handful of the combatants, including two of the Messers, and of all people Galloway Carnes who was the brother of the Deputy Sheriff.

The Judge and his posse remained in the mountains for days in sort of a running gunfight. In a pitched battle near a place called Salt Trace, four men were killed and about six wounded. Reinforcements were sent out, and the Governor of Tennessee was asked for a regiment of militia to assist. It appears that didn't happen and things quieted down for a while.

And so we come to the end of our Great Kentucky Pig Feud. There was not, as of this writing, any further reporting on the outcome that I could dig up. There were fires in 1914 and 1918 that destroyed many records. I'm certain there were further ramifications and attacks, but maybe we'll save that for another volume. In the meantime, why don't we examine the last of the Slushers?

The Slusher Sheep Barons

A little far afield? Maybe, but Civil War veterans from the Slusher family went west, all the way to Oregon. Some went to build a better life, some went for other reasons. Two went in a hurry, one step ahead of the law.

Let's begin with Thomas Winfield Scott Slusher (1848-1890). He was Henry C. Slusher's cousin, and was born in Amwell Township. He had three brothers and two sisters: James Knox Polk (1848-1894), Rachael O. (1849-1890), Simon S. S. (1851-1884), Sarah E. (1854-1909), and William M. (1856-1909). Thomas enlisted in the Union Army on October 14, 1862, as a private. That same day, at the age of fourteen, he mustered into Company F of the 22nd Pennsylvania Cavalry. He mustered out on July 19, 1865.

Sometime between the end of the war and 1878, he made his way to Oregon, where he married Miss Arabelle Hannah Durfur (1856-1939). She was originally from Wisconsin, but by 1870 was living in Oregon. Her father, Andrew Jackson Durfur, was the founder of Durfur, Oregon.

They had together eight children, with a son not surviving birth: Thomas Brinton (1879-1941), Eva Lillian (1881-1971), F. Harvy Durfur (1882- 1961), Roy Scott (1883-1974), Aleda Pearl (1884-1886), Ruby Arabel (1885-1960) and Grover Cleveland (1888-1962). We know very little about all the kids except for Eva. The rest were born, lived, and passed away in Durfur, Oregon. I could find no pictures of any except for Eva.

Eva was a very different story. On April 10, 1900, she married Mr. Charles Noble Clark (1874-1928), who was originally from Kansas.

Arrabelle Durfur Slusher

He grew up to be a Pharmacist and apparently he was a very good one. He practiced in his older brother's store in The Dalles, Oregon, where he remained for about eight years.

In 1908, he opened his own drugstore on the corner of Oak and Third Streets in Hood River, Oregon. He was known for being the leading druggist as far as the newest medicine and technology was concerned.

The Clarks had four children, with one son, Charles Edward, living but a year. The others were, Beryl Arabelle (1901-1996), Thomas Slusher (1907- 1985), and Charlotte Mary (1909-2001).

Charles Noble Clark

Beyerl grew up and attended the University of Washington and married Mr. Paul Vincenti. They moved to Los Angles and had no children.

Little Tommy grew up and married Miss Hazel White (1918-1994). They lived in California, first Los Angles, then Glendale, and finally beautiful downtown Burbank. He was a radio singer. They had two children who are still living today. Tom then married Miss. Elizabeth Pitsch (1911-1983). They have three children: Jon Christopher (1950-2005), and two who are still living.

Eve Lillian Slusher Clark

Charlotte finished high school and married Mr. Thomas Dorsey. They lived in Seattle and had a son. She died in Saratoga, California, at age ninety-two. It seems like they all migrated to California as they got older. All except for Charles Clark.

Charles wasn't just a pharmacist, he was also a horseman. Eva owned an eighty acre ranch near Durfur, where they raised fine horses, including a stallion named Scarlet Letter who was one of Oregon's most well known Hambletonian sires.

Time waits for no man and time caught with Charles Noble Clark on August 18, 1928, at the young age of only fifty-four. His wife, Eva, had a long life, ending her days in California on November 15, 1971. She was ninety years old.

And whatever happened to our Civil War veteran Thomas Winfield Scott Slusher? He was a sheep rancher, but he also was appointed to be Receiver at the Land office in The Dalles, Oregon, by President Cleveland in 1886.

Lto R, Beyrl, Tom, Charlotte

He was having serious health problems. What they were exactly we don't know. In October of 1889, he was forced to temporarily retire to his ranch for a while to recuperate and rest. He passed away at high noon in The Dalles, Oregon, on April 3, 1890, at the age of only forty-one.

Thos. W. S. Slusher Family Plot.
Pioneer Cemetery in Durfur

His wife, Arabelle, wasn't through by a long shot. She already had eight children, but I guess she liked large families because she remarried in 1896 to Mr. William Staats and she had four more kids with him! Henry, John, Val, and Oscar. That was enough for Arabelle. She went to her reward on May 7, 1939, at the age of eighty-two. William Staats died in 1943.

So what about the sheep barons you ask? Ok, let's dive into that rabbit hole and see what we find. First, how about this newspaper clip?

Washington Reporter, June 21, 1884 Sentenced to be Hanged. It was reported about town on Wednesday that J. K. P. and "Doc" Slusher, formerly of Amwell township, had been convicted of murder in Oregon and sentenced to death. They left this county some eight or ten years ago after financial trouble and a charge of forgery had been made against J. K. P. It seems that they located in Oregon established a cattle ranch and had considerable difficulty with a neighbor, who was engaged in the same business, from time to time about the mixing of their herds. A few months ago this neighbor was murdered. The Slusher boys were charged with the crime, tried, found guilty and a few days ago sentenced to be hanged. A letter was received by relatives of the accused in this county on Wednesday informing them of the above facts, of the day fixed for execution, and requesting some of their friends to visit them at once."

Permelia Jane Slusher and Flora Cox

In full disclosure, I found this newspaper clipping in several newspapers in the area. All with the very same information. I did my due diligence and researched for more information full time for several weeks. I searched all the Oregon papers, and the papers all around Washington County, PA. You would think the Oregon papers would have the entire story in all its lurid details. Well, I found nothing in any newspaper anywhere. Nothing dating from before the above clipping or for a year after. I at first thought that the sentence had been postponed or a retrial was ordered on appeal or something. But no, nothing ever turned up at the time I was researching this.

To add to that, I found no Slushers with those names that had birth and/ or death dates that corresponded with those in the newspaper clipping. There is a James Knox Polk Slusher, but he passed away in 1913, not hung in 1884. However, there are some shady goings on there. He was indeed a Civil War veteran, but he was also a bigamist, and/or maybe he was hiding from the law? He went by a false name for a while. So we'll see what happens.

There is a "Doc" Slusher, but he was living in Virginia, I believe, and had little connections with the Washington, PA, Slushers that I could find. The newspaper made it seem like these were brothers that were involved in the alleged murder. So, who knows? Did the paper make it up? Did they get it wrong? If I get time, I'll go back and dig further as I would like to know what the real story was.

Pearilla E. Slusher

So let's move on to a real mover and shaker, Thomas's brother, William M. Slusher. William's and Thomas's father was Christopher J. Slusher (1818 -1857). Their mother was Permelia Jane Reese Slusher (1824-1899). William was born on November 26, 1856, the youngest of three brothers. He lived in Amwell township until about 1870.

Between 1870 and 1880, he moved to Oregon and married Miss Pearilla Ellen Buford of Salem Oregon. We aren't sure of what exactly was going on with them, because the 1880 census listed Pearilla as E. Rilla Slusher, married, daughter, boarding in her father's home. The 1900 census shows her in Pendelton as head of household, married, living with her three children. In the 1910 census, William has turned up as the head of household with Pearilla and their daughter Edith. In any event, the Slushers had three children, William Alva 1882-?, Dale D. 1884-1937, and Edith Rachael 1891-1942.

There seems to be a huge hole in the story. There's no information about where and what William Slusher was doing for the first few years after he came to Oregon. He apparently was buying up land, because the land ownership maps show enormous acreage owned by him. However, it was not contiguous parcels, it was broken up into various sections. His occupation is listed as "stockman," but his home is in Pendelton. Later newspaper clippings show he owns a large sheep ranch near Nolin, which is a few miles west of Pendleton in Umatilla County.

East Oregonian, December 5, 1905 Mrs. William Slusher and daughter Edith will leave tomorrow for California, where they will remain for the winter at Santa Barbara, expecting to stop at Stanford

University for a short time to visit Dale Slusher, who is attending that school.

East Oregonian August 8, 1906 W. M. Slusher Now Sole Owner of the Nolan Ranch, Perry Gould, the well known sheepman and president of the Umatilla County Woolgrowers Association has deeded to his former partner, W. M. Slusher, his half interest in the Slusher-Gould ranch near Nolin...The consideration named is $1.00

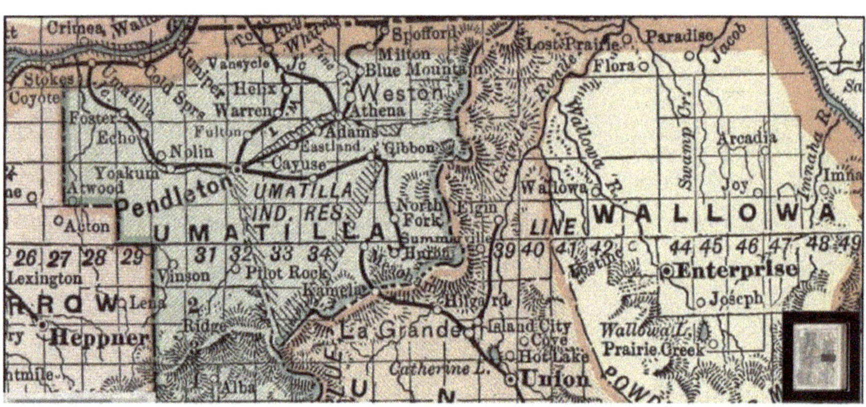

It was just after the turn of the century that things began popping for the Slushers. By 1900, the Slusher family was among the upper crust of the Eastern Oregon population. Just how they got there is a mystery, I'm afraid. William "Bill" Slusher was half owner of a large sheep ranch in Nolan, Oregon, but he had other interests as well. We know this from the following newspaper clippings.

The Hood River Glacier, May 28, 1908 Indian Land Acquires Illegally. A Federal grand jury of 23 members was selected in the United States court Monday and immediately began the consideration of evidence connected with land fraud alleged to have been perpetrated in Umatilla County. Subpoenas have been issued for 118 witnesses...The alleged fraud consists of the unlawful acquisition of about 25,000 acres of unallocated lands that originally comprised a part of the Umatilla Indian Reservation. It is reported that the evidence that will be presented will implicate several prominent citizens of Umatilla County, including William Slusher.

The Morning Astorian, June 22, 1908. Eleven of the 14 defendants included in the Umatilla Indian reservation land fraud indictments, were arraigned before Judge Wolverton in the United States district court today. The defendants who were arraigned today are J. H. Raley, John Crow, William Slusher...

So he got title to the other half of the ranch for a dollar? Seems fishy to me. As we'll see, Bill's land deals get even fishier and the law gets involved. Also, William gets elected to the State House for the 1907 term. The case, which was a big deal at the time was scheduled to go to trial on December 13, 1909. However, all the defendants except one appeared in court and took a gamble, and threw themselves at the mercy of the court. I suppose the fact that the prosecutor was a personal friend of many of the defendants didn't hurt either. They all pled guilty but claimed innocence and begged for leniency before the court. They got it. These were all wealthy men and were fined a total of $45,500. William Slusher's share of that was $5,000. Chump change to him. Were they guilty? No question about it. They swindled Indians out of some 30,000 acres of their land. They had determined that as so often happens that it was cheaper to plead guilty and pay a fine than fight the case in court. And so it goes. They probably left the court, patted themselves on the back, and were off to the club for cocktails and cigars. They would be more careful in planning their next deals.

East Oregonian, December 2, 1909 Local Men Were Fined. Judge Wolverton Assessed Defendants Total of Forty-five Thousand Dollars.

There would be much more going on for this branch of Slushers, much of it interesting but not germane to the purpose of this book. They continued on as wealthy sheep barons and high society types for many years. The clan grew and, of course, grew farther and farther past the Civil War era and its living memory. In 1916 William Slusher was elected County Commissioner, which is no surprise, as he owned much of the land in the county, well over 15,000 acres of prime land.

Dale Slusher

The eldest son, Alva, attended the University of Oregon and played some football there. He then went on to various endeavors and worked for his father as well. He married Miss Maybelle Clark in 1906, and they lived in San Francisco and had a daughter Margaret. He later married Miss Adaline Haun.

Dale attended Stanford University graduating in 1909 as a mining engineer. He worked for several years locating oil deposits for the Union Oil Company. Then he moved to Pendleton to work for his father. He worked for the Southern Pacific Railroad as an oil field engineer and spent a year and a half in Mexico serving as General manager and superintendent of an oil well in 1913-14. He married Sally Sterrett in 1914 and they had a son Dale Jr.

They moved to Portland where he worked as an engineer on the Bonneville and the new Portland Airport project. He passed away on May 30, 1937. Daughter Edith attended the University of Oregon in 1912, but the next year married Mr. Fred Gulick a dentist from Denver. They lived in Portland and had three kids, Virginia (1914-1990), William (1916-1988), and George (1922-2000).

William Slusher passed away on November 25, 1921, at the young age of sixty-four. Pearilla joined him on July 29, 1945. She was eighty-six years of age.

Edith Slusher Gulick

There are Slushers scattered all over Oregon, California, Texas, Oklahoma, Kansas, Illinois, Indiana, Ohio, Pennsylvania, Kentucky, Virginia, and just about anywhere else you care to mention. I'm certain that there are incredible stories I haven't even examined. They were and are a dynamic family, both for good and there's some not-so-good thrown in there as well. As always, I leave that call up to you to decide. I just tell the story.

We should, and we will, always remember them.

CHAPTER FOURTEEN
Philo Vance Paul

O h boy! Have I got a fun chapter for you? Big, well known Washington County family with Civil War vets who saw plenty of action and even a Spanish American war era vet.

These people were not camera shy at all, so I have plenty of great pictures for you. It's funny that they are related to the Slushers by marriage and it seems that the Slushers must not have ever heard of a camera. Nonetheless, we have a lot to cover in this chapter so let's get right to it, shall we?

Philo Paul was born in Amity, near Washington, PA, on March 26, 1824. He was one of the fourteen children of William Paul (1777-1840) and Hannah Slaught (1784-1865).

Philo grew up to be a farmer and also operated a sawmill in his hometown. He was active in the community and was a founder of the Pleasant

Philo Vance Paul

Valley Academy, which was a school sponsored by the Pleasant Valley Christian Church.

On February 25, 1843, he married a hometown girl, Miss. Sarah Hughes. They only had nine children, just enough for a baseball team. Notice their names: William Wallace (1843-1925), James Monroe (1845-1906), John Adams (1848-1937), Daniel Webster (1851-1939), Alexander Hamilton (1854- 1932),

David Clayton (1856-1936), Benjamin Franklin (1858-1939), Abraham Lincoln (1860-1951), and, finally, Laura Jewell (1862-1942).

Sarah Hughes paul

On August 22nd, 1862, Philo mustered into Company D, the "Amity Company" of the 140th Pennsylvania Volunteer Infantry. There were around sixty-seven men from Amity that enlisted from there. Not to mention another thirty or so from other parts of Washington County and neighboring Greene County as well. Perhaps you noticed the number of men from Amity or Amwell Township in this book.

Mention should be made here of the 140th Pennsylvania Volunteer Infantry. They were one of the more famous regiments in the Army of the Potomac. During and after the war. There were about eleven hundred men from Western Pennsylvania who volunteered for service in the Union army, and most of them eventually became the 140th Pennsylvania.

Survivors of the 140th PA Vols

Assembled in Reunion at the Residence of

J. B. Johnson, September 12, 1911

They were a front line regiment, seeing action throughout the war. They would see more casualties than any other Pennsylvania regiment, and only two regiments in the entire Union army suffered more. They were present at Appomattox, although only about three hundred or so men remained at that time.

From September 9 until that December, they were ordered to Parktown, Maryland, to guard the Northern Central Railroad. They were attached to the 3rd Brigade, 1st Division, 2nd Army Corps, Army of the Potomac. They were ordered to join the Army of the Potomac, then in the field near Aquia Creek, where they arrived on December 15. They wintered near Falmouth, Virginia, until April 1863. It was in the Chancellorsville campaign that Philo got his first taste of real combat. In June of 1863, near Brandy Station, Virginia, the regiment was being inspected. One of Philo's friends watched as an officer moved down the line and stopped when he came to Philo. The officer noticed how Philo stood, with a determined look upon his face, his clean rifle with polished barrel, and exclaimed *"There, is a model soldier."*

Philo Paul survived the campaigns of 1863 and he made it through the winter and then the Rapidan campaign, and the deadly, horrific carnage of the Wilderness campaign. The race to Spotsylvania now began. General Robert E. Lee's Confederate army won that race, but just barely. In the pre-dawn gloomy fog at Spotsylvania Court House, the 140th was again called on to be part of the assault upon the Confederate works at what is now known as The Bloody Angle. With their firing caps ordered removed by Brigade commander General Nelson Miles, so as not to accidentally alert the enemy, they were ordered to *"use nothing but their bayonets until they gained the enemy's works."* They moved forward, almost silently, toward the unknown until they came to the Confederate defenses.

It was there that a rebel bullet passed through the diary that Philo kept and continued on through his heart, killing him almost instantly. He was buried on the field with his best friend, Amos Swart, and a friend from church, Thomas Doty. The burial party included Thomas's brother, William, and probably James Hathaway. Those buried on the field were later removed and reinterred in the Fredericksburg National Cemetery.

Philo's diary was found and today rests in the hands of a descendant. After the war ended, the Grand Army of the Republic was formed, and in his honor, the Amity post was named the Philo Paul Post 458 G A R.

His wife Sarah wasn't done yet either. She married again to a Mr. James Smith, of which I have no information. Sarah passed away in 1914.

The Philo Paul story doesn't end there, not by a long shot. The family is big, the story is big, and I want to do full justice to the Paul family, of which there are many descendants today who have not and will not forget their Civil War ancestors. After all, is said and done, this book is all about the rest of the story. So, let's get to it.

Philo wasn't the only Paul to serve in the Civil War. Older brother William Paul (1822-1903) also served. He lived in LaSalle County, Illinois, with his wife Mary Jane Walton (1822-1896). He enlisted as a Private on August 11, 1862. Later that month, he was mustered into Company B of the 104th Illinois Volunteer Infantry. He ended up being discharged for disability on April 28, 1863.

He and Mary Jane had four children, Harrison B. (1841-1866), Lucy Samantha (1844-1919), William Paul (1852-1918), and Belle Paul (1857-1903).

Harrison registered for the draft in June of 1863, but I found no record of him having served. Belle married a man named Scott Buick and they lived in Barber County, Kansas. William married Miss Jennie Paul and they travelled around from Iowa to Kansas to Missouri and back to Iowa.

Lucy was a little different. First, she married Andrew Jackson Roberts (1826-1885). They had a son, Paul (1882-1954). Next, she married Darius Irwin (1846-1926) and they had one daughter Jessie (1874-1943). Then she married James L. Vanatta (1843-1868). They had two children, William Wallace (1864-1939), and James L. Jr. (1867-1949). You guys go ahead and talk among yourselves and work out the timeline on that one. I'm moving on to husband number four.

David McCampbell was born in Preble County, Ohio. In 1860 he was living in La Salle County, Illinois, and working as a farm laborer. He married Lucy on January 10, 1861. They had one child, Alice Eudora, who came into the world on October 19, 1861. He enlisted in the Union Army as a Private on August 11, 1862.

On August 27, he was mustered into Company B of the 104th Illinois Volunteer Infantry. He was appointed Principle Musician on August 23 of that year.

Musicians generally didn't carry arms, with a few exceptions of course, like a Musician's Sword that was carried while on parade or inspection, etc. Especially by mid war, the regulations were somewhat relaxed, due to the obvious hardships of being in the field. Musicians performed other duties as well. For example, they would help care for the wounded, fill canteens, help with resupply, etc., etc. Anything they could do to help, and that includes becoming a rifleman if necessary. This worked out well for David until the battle of Chickamauga. While attending the wounded he was captured on September 20, 1863. He was taken first to Hartville, Tennessee, then to Libbey Prison in Richmond, Virginia. On December 12, he was transferred to Danville, Virginia. Then it went from bad to worse. He was sent to Andersonville, Georgia.

David McCampbell

I must include a note here to set the record straight. Andersonville gets a lot of publicity as being some kind of torture chamber where the prisoners were treated inhumanely and brutally, the worst of the prisons in both the North and South. That's all exactly what modern day US General Norman Schwarzkopf Jr. of the first Gulf War fame called "Bovine scatology."

Andersonville prison was no worse or better than almost any other Civil War prison, Union or Confederate. The North had its share of infamous prisons that were every bit as brutal, filthy, disease-ridden, and deadly as Andersonville. Camp Douglas (no relation) near Chicago ring a bell? In Andersonville, the prisoners ate pretty much what their Confederate guards ate. By that time in the war, food was scarce for everybody in the South. The guards lacked medical care, the same as the prisoners. So let's apply the standard equally, shall we? If anything, Camp Douglas was worse for the prisoners than Andersonville was, and they had no excuse for lack of medical care, food, or shelter.

On July 10, 1864, David was taken to the infirmary with diarrhea, probably e-coli which was what most all Civil War soldiers caught at one time or another, prisoner or not. He died and was buried at Andersonville National Cemetery, Section J, Grave 3100. His family also placed a marker for him back at home in LaSalle County, Illinois.

A nephew of Philo Paul and cousin to David McCampbell is a James Pate (1840-1893), who lived at the time of the Civil War in Dearborn, Indiana. He was the son of Jeremiah Pate (1802-1860), and Levina March (1806- 1879).

He enlisted into Company A of the 3rd Indiana Cavalry on August 22, 1861, as a Farrier and Blacksmith. Company A was assigned to the Army of the Potomac and joined General Hooker's Division just South of Washington at a place called Budd's Ferry. There Company A was detached to police and break up the trade of contraband between Virginia and Baltimore, Maryland. After about four months, they reunited with the rest of the Regiment and operated in southern Maryland, then moved on to Thoroughfare Gap, Luray, and Bristoe Station, and finally to Falmouth to scout around Fredericks-

James Pate

burg. Then they went back to Washington and took part in the Maryland campaign seeing action at Antietam and South Mountain. November 11, 1862, James was discharged due to a disability from injuries received in action and returned home suffering from dysentery. He did receive a disability pension in 1862 as well.

His brother served in the 142nd Indiana Volunteer Infantry, mustering into Company K at the age of eighteen, on September 13, 1864, and mustered out on May 6, 1865.

James Pate married Miss America on November 17, 1863. Actually, he married Miss America Paul on that date. She was born in Rising Sun, Indiana, on August 8, 1841, the daughter of Andrew Sutton Paul (1812-1898), who was the brother of Philo Paul, and Ann Walton (1815-1847). They had three sons and two daughters together: Daniel (1865-1915), John (1866- 1938), Albert (1869-1933), Anna (1872-1955), and Virginia (1874-1957).

America Hart Paul Pate

Andrew Sutton Paul left home and disappeared for forty years, then returned to his second wife, Jeanette Maria Wilson, with whom he had a son, Thomas Wilson Paul.

Jeanette had divorced him to marry another man, Thomas Nighbert. He died in 1874 and she married yet another man, Benjamin Davis who also died, leaving her as a widow yet again. When Andrew Sutton Paul returned, he was cordially received, and he and Jeanette made plans to remarry, but she died before that happened.

There is a lot more to that story in Friendship, Indiana, which included at least two knife fights, two attempted murders, shootings, and much more. However, it's a very convoluted tale and hard to follow with many relatives involved over four decades of feud and double dealings and marriages and revenge, and deaths. All of this makes a great story, but it is beyond the scope of this book.

John Benson Paul

John Benson Paul was America Paul's brother. He was born on May 21, 1846, in Friendship, Indiana. On November 15, 1864, he mustered into Company K of the 142nd Indiana Infantry. He mustered right back out again on July 14, 1865, at Nashville, Tennessee. He married Miss Sarah Ann Pate on the Fourth of July, 1866.

I have no information on what was causing all the early deaths. These people all lived in the same area in Indiana, just a few miles west of Cincinnati, Ohio. But no matter where in the country John B. Paul lived, the curse followed him for the rest of his life.

John B. had apparently had enough by then and by 1880 had moved out to Battle Mountain, Nevada, where four years later he married Miss Joanna McCarthy. There are indications that he was involved with the shenanigans in Friendship, Indiana, and that is why he moved around so much. But his bad luck continued when Joanna died seven years later at the age of only thirty-four. He moved to Fresno, California in 1910, but moved again ten years later to Los Angeles. He passed away on July 12th, 1926.

James T. Paul

Better news with the son of John B. Paul. James T. Paul grew up to be a stock raiser. At least for a while. The records are sparse when it comes to his employment. After about 1920, he was listed as not working, but with another income source, so we don't know if he had medical issues or exactly what was going on with him. These old records are often incorrect, incomplete, and can be very misleading. In any event, he moved around a lot from Indiana to Battle Mountain, Nevada, to Los Angeles to Napa, California.

He married Miss Carmen Clara Luther on August 1, 1928, in Elko, Nevada. She was from Germany and twenty-two years his junior. By 1940, they were living in Napa California, where James Thomas Paul passed away on September 21, 1941, at the age of seventy-three years. John B. Paul and his son James, lie beside each other forever in the marble crypt in the Inglewood Park Cemetery in Los Angeles, California.

To wrap up the chapter on the Paul, Pate, and Slusher extended families, we need to go back and cover the sons and daughter of Philo Paul.

William Wallace Paul

Let's begin with Philo and Sarah's eldest son, William Wallace Paul. He was born in Amwell, Washington County, PA, on December 27, 1843. We don't have much of a story about him, other than he owned part of the Paul Grocery Store chain. (More on that coming up.) He married Miss Phoebe Jane Egy (1847-1926), on November 24, 1864. They had four daughters: Lillian Sarah (1868-1953), Nora Jewell (1872-1965), Minnie Paul (1879-?), and Dale Watkins Paul Gregg (1879-1970).

William Wallace Paul passed away on August 18, 1925, of influenza and senility at the age of eighty-one. Phoebe passed on October 30, 1926, from gangrene. She was seventy-eight years old.

James Monroe Paul

We move on now to James Monroe Paul, the next oldest son of Philo Paul. Oh boy! This is one huge family. Jim Paul was born on September 5, 1845, in Amity. At the age of twenty-two, he mustered into Spencer Miller's Independent Battery of Artillery on June 26, 1863, to defend the state against the invasion of General Robert E. Lee's Confederate Army.

He married a Miss Mary Magdaline Wonsettler (1849-1923), in 1867. By 1870, he was working in the Paul Sawmill along with his brother, William Wallace Paul. By 1880 he had taken to farming. He and Mary had sixteen children! Here's the lineup, starting at the eldest: David Philo (1868-1948), William M. (1870-1914), Thomas W. (1871-1950), Laura Catherine (1873-1959), Susan Annebelle (1874-1966), Mary W. (1876-1933), Sarah Alice (1879 -1958), Edna Pearl (1881-1958), Bertha Jewell (1883-1958), Elizabeth E. (1883-?), Frank Blane

(1884-1970), Lewis McKennan (1886-1952), Rosa F. (1888-1976), Nelle May (1891-1950), Allie Glenn (1893-1962), Wray Earl (1895-1983).

Mary Wonsettler Paul

David Paul

Paul's Mill was originally owned by David Frazee who later sold it to Philo Paul. When Philo was killed at Spotsylvania in the Civil War in 1862, he left it to his son William. It was located over the hill behind Flora Huston's house. The framing contractor was Isaac Keeney and Thomas Pollock was the millwright. We'll be learning more about the Pollock family a little later. John Taylor installed the boiler and got the mill up and running. In 1860, A man named Amos Khestrick added a flour mill to the sawmill.

Later, the mill was operated by H. M. Walton, then several others over the years. It was eventually made into an ice house and machine shop. During World War I, the Paul family donated the scrap iron and machinery to aid the war effort. The old mill was torn down about 1940 by a man named Harry Roberts.

Paul's Mill

William M. Paul

Frank Blane Paul

Mary M. W. Paul and 12 of her 16 children ca. 1905-1918.

Standing l to r: Susan, Wray, Mary, Lewis, Bertha, Allie.

Seated l to r: Thomas, Edna, Rosa, Mary M.W; Nellie, Sarah, Elizabeth.

Laura Catherine "Kitt" Paul w\ Husband Louis Fattman

Getting back to James Monroe Paul: he farmed all his life until some- thing went wrong. On January 6, 1906, he had a "fit of temporary dementia" and somehow strangled himself. He was only fifty-nine years old. Mary moved from the farm into a house at 510 Jefferson Avenue, in Washington, PA. She passed away on July 14, 1923, at the age of seventy-three.

But it doesn't end there. The family goes on, and on, and on. This next branch is particularly interesting, so let's take a momentary leap down another rabbit hole.

Benjamin Franklin Paul (1858-1939), and his wife Priscilla (1864-1947), only had seven kids, but they sadly lost one at birth. They were in order as follows: Daisy Estella (1884-1958), Cary (1885-1901), John Frazee (1887- 1932), Hazel Belle (1893-1971), Olive (1895-1898) and Ethel Mildred (1900- 1951).

Ben (he usually went by the name Frank) started out working in the Paul's flour mill, then by 1890 he was working in a grocery store. By 1910 he was Vice President of the Paul Grocery store chain. He managed their store in the Y.M.C.A. building

on West Chestnut Street. He also had time for public service as a school director and was active in the Washington Chamber of Commerce. He retired in 1934, and passed away on January 13, 1939, of a stroke, at the age of eighty.

Benjamin Franklin Paul

Priscilla died of old age on August 23, 1947.

Priscilla Aribel Frazee Paul

She was eighty-three years old. Interestingly, the Funeral Director listed on the death certificate (the funeral was held at the Paul home) was Ralph Piatt who bought the former home of Major A. G. Happer after the Major's wife Tilly, passed away in 1935. You will meet Major Happer later in this book.

Speaking of amazing stories, this one is right up there as well. Ben and Priscilla's daughter Daisy was quite a gal. After graduating from the Washington Seminary, she taught school in Washington, PA. She also taught Sunday School in the First Christian Church.

She was married on June 15, 1911, to the Reverend David Morris, who at one time was pastor of the Allison Avenue Baptist Church. He was born in Wales on August 9. 1882. His family came to the United States when he was about twelve years old.

He worked his way through college at Washington & Jefferson, where he graduated magna cum laude in 1919. He and Daisy had six children together, sadly only four lived: William (1911-1911), an infant (1913-1913), then Miriam (1915-1988), Ruth (1917- 1995), Esther (1921-2015), and Elizabeth (1923-2011).

Daisy Paul Morris

The Washington Seminary, where Daisy had attended, was one of hundreds of these types of schools all across the country at that time. It was a

Rev. David Morris

college prep school offering day classes and boarding as well.

Miriam, "Mim", is the eldest daughter. She grew up and married Mr. David Coelho. They lived in Ohio and had a son and two daughters. Next, we have Ruth Gwendolyn who grew up, got married to Mr. James Hall, and lived in Washington, PA, and Ohio. Next up is Esther Priscilla who was the poster child for the great American story. Actually, you could easily say that all the Morris daughters were a part of that picture. I never met the lady, but in all her pictures, she is smiling a warm smile that radiates outward and seems to capture those present.

Esther lived the American dream all the way. She married Mr. William Price just after Pearl Harbor on February 12, 1942, who was working as a clerk in a drug store, but not for long. Whatever plans they had, World War II changed them in a hurry.

Esther and Bill ended up having two sons and three daughters, and a pile of grandchildren. Like the pictures show, the American dream. America at its finest. War, victory, then peace and prosperity. The greatest generation indeed. William passed away on February 25, 1995. He was seventy-four. Esther lived on until she fol-

Miriam "Mim: Morris

lowed him on May 24, 2015, at the age of ninety-three.

The last of the Morris sisters was Elizabeth "Lib." Here we have more American dream stuff. She was married on February 6, 1943, to Paul Posa (1923-2008). Paul graduated from Washington High School in January of 1941. He served in the US Navy as a radio technician during World War II in the Pacific.

Esther Morris and Sinnie

Following the war, he graduated from Washington & Jefferson College and went on to earn his law degree from the University of Pittsburgh. He practiced law for fifty-six years. He also served as General Council for Washington Hospital, and as Solicitor for the City of Washington Municipal Authority.

He and Elizabeth had three daughters and were married for sixty-six years before Paul was taken on June 4, 2008. He was eighty-five. Libby lived on until February 2, 2011, when she then joined Paul. She was eighty-three years old. Good, solid Americans they were. That entire family were great role models we should all look up to.

Esther Morris ca 1939

David and Daisy Morris ca. 1949

In 1914, John was working in the family grocery store chain. He had married Miss Margaret Scott (1893-?) in 1909. They had a son and three daughters: Russell, Dorothy, June, and Grace. We don't know what happened to Margaret, she disappears off the radar scope and the census in 1930. More research needs to be done to find the answers.

John was sick for years with a bad stomach, being plagued with Peptic ulcers. He went into the hospital for an operation in June of 1932, but it went wrong and he passed away on June 26, 1932. He was only forty-four years old. Russell lived in Texas with his wife Aubrey. He passed in 2005. He was ninety-four. Dorothy is another mystery. She got married in 1932 to a John Brown, then poof, she disappears off the radar. June, the same thing. She was there in 1930 then she's gone. She is mentioned in her sister Grace's obituary as June Walker.

Elizabeth and Esther Morris

ca. 1938

Bill and Esther Right Before he went Overseas

Speaking of Grace, she left Washington County and moved to North Tonawanda, New York, in 1931. She married a Mr. John Perry and they had one son and six daughters, and a pile of grandchildren and great-grandchildren, and great-great, and so on. She died on April 25, 2009. At least we know what happened to her. Maybe the others moved up there as well.

Hazel Belle Paul lived in Washington PA, all her life. On December 28, 1922, she married Mr. Fred Naser (1893-1961). Fred was an elevator operator in the Union Trust Building for thirty years, retiring on New Year's Eve 1960. He had been in poor health for some time and passed away on August 30, 1961. He was only sixty-eight. Hazel followed him ten years later on January 17, 1971, she was seventy-eight.

And finally, we come to Ethel Mildred Paul. Her story was a little different from the others. She stayed at home, probably taking care of her mother. She had a job working in the offices of the power company, that she had for many years. She never married and died of heart trouble on June 18, 1951. She was only fifty years old. Interestingly, she was buried alongside her mother and father, sister Olive, a stillborn child, and brother Carey in Lone Pine. The others are buried in Washington Cemetery. There was tragedy as well, with Carey who died of pneumonia at age sixteen in 1901, and little Olive who only lived to be three. We have no info about them at all.

Bill Price

Next up is John Adams Paul (1848-1937). He was a farmer and married Miss Emma "Emily" Josephine Walton (1853-1929). Born to them were five children: May Nettie (1873-1954), Harry Hayes (1873-1976), Gleason Henry)1882-1956), Ethel Daisy (1886-1963), and Charles Hobart (1893-1972).

Bill Price WWII Germany

Seated are Priscilla and Franklin Paul

Hazel, Mildred and Daisy Standing ca 1914

Daisy, Hazel and John with Mildred in
Front

John Adams and Emily Paul

Harry. and Icy Paul

John and Emily were farmers and very prosperous ones at that. Nettie married Frank Riggle and they lived in West Bethlehem Township. We know very little else about them. She passed away on February 6, 1954, at the age of eighty. We don't know what happened to Frank.

Harry married a woman named Icy Howden. What a great name, Icy. They lived in Wilkinsburg, Pennsylvania, near Pittsburgh. They must have retired to Florida, because Harry passed away there on May 16, 1967. Icy died in 1970.

Gleason was a farmer, like so many of his ancestors before him. He married Miss Mary Frazee on September 7, 1904. They had a son and two daughters: Alvie Merel (1905-1963), Opal Romaine (1908-1994), and Wilda (1916-1957). There is no information on Alvie. Opal was a bookkeeper at the electric plant, and Wilda, again no info. Gleason passed on July 24, 1956, he was seventy-three. Mary passed away on April 1. 1974. She was eighty-nine. They all died in Florida.

Ethel Daisy married Rusell Shipe sometime before 1910. He worked as an auto mechanic. He had heart trouble and passed away in 1935. Ethel, lived in Philadelphia County in 1940. She passed away in 1963. Charles Hobart Paul served a year in the US Army during World War I. He was living in Scottsdale, Westmoreland County, PA, at the time. In 1920, he was living in Meadville for a while, then back home and worked as a store manager at a five-and-dime store. He married Agnes Fuhr, they had one child who was stillborn. Charley died reportedly in Hershey, PA, in 1972, at the age of seventy-nine. Agnes died in Harrisburg, PA. on September 2, 1957. She was only sixty-two.

Next, we have Daniel Webster Paul (1851-1939). He was a farmer married to Miss Sarah Belle Reynolds (1860-1928). They had two children: Philo Bernard (1883-1960), and Jimmy, born March 22, 1886, and sadly passed away on April 9, 1886. Unfortunately, we have no pictures of any of them.

Philo Bernard (1883-1960), married a Miss Pink Rosaca (1888-?). They had two sons and five daughters: Marion, Josephine, Harriet, Mck, Francis, Martha, and James. Marion was a school teacher and Josephine worked in a grocery store, and, I'm sure, one of the Paul's Grocery stores.

Icy and Harry Paul

Alexander H. Paul (1854-1932) married Miss Mary Horn in 1880 and they had seven kiddies: Clyde (1879-1963), Grant born 1880, Edith Irene (1881-1891), James B. (1884-1952), and Walter Scott (1886-1924).

Gleason and Mary with Alvie and Opal Paul

Walter served for six years in the US Infantry and made Corporal. He was a glass worker in Washington, PA, and a railroad fireman. The poor man died at the Torrance State Hospital of "paralysis of insanity." The other two children were

Clarence Horn (1890-1969) and Roy H (1892-1969). Roy served overseas in World War I.

Alexander Hamilton Paul was a farmer like several of his brothers. He lived and farmed all his life and passed away of old age at seventy-nine years.

David Clayton Paul (1856-1936). Sadly, little information on him. The man lived eighty years and nobody knows anything about him or his life, other than he was retired, he had a wife named Hannah, a daughter named Estella and when he was 80, he fell down and four days later he died. There should be much more of a record of a man's life than that.

Gleason & Mary Frazee Paul
1904

Franklin & Mary Paul Riggle

Abraham Lincoln Paul started out as a farmer, then opened a butcher shop for a while, then a candy store.

He was married to Miss Ida May Baker (1860-1892) and Belle Day (1857-1904). Between the three of them, they had eight kids: Shelton (1883-1883), Ivy Florence (1884-1892), Albert Wallace (1886-1948), Benjamin Harrison (1888-1890), Sarah Minerva (1890-1891), Howard Lincoln (1896-1918), Laura E. (1899-1972) and Daniel James (1891-1974).

Howard Paul enlisted in the US Navy during World War I and served from April 9, 1917, until he was washed overboard while a Gunners Mate 2nd class on the U.S.S. Columbia while steaming from Hampton Roads, Virginia, to New York.

Albert worked in his dad's butcher shop. Laura married John Martin Pence, who was an interior decorator. They had two sons: Wilbert and John Jr.

Danny Paul On HIs Cool Harley with I Assume, Sarah

Danny Paul also served in World War I. He was already married at the time he was inducted, to Sara White, and had two sons, Daniel, 14, and George, 12.

Paul Residence at Lone Pine

Dan was a musician and was with the Headquarters Company of the 330th Infantry. He served from September 20, 1917, until February 13, 1919. He was sent overseas with the American Expeditionary Forces in France and was there from June 12, 1918, until January 30, 1919. He was discharged that February at Camp Sherman, Ohio. He was a serviceman for Carothers Dairy Company and owned his very own ice cream factory. Their son George was a Motor Machinist's Mate during World War II and was wounded in action.

PA State Trooper Brady Paul

And we come now to Laura Jewell Paul (1862-1942). She grew up and married a farmer by the name of Elijah Dawson Day. Together they had three children: James Philo (1890-1950), Elmer Paul (1882-1983), and Sarah Estella (1896-1987).

Laura lived and kept house until she was eighty when she fell at home and fractured her femur. She passed away twenty days later on April 15, 1942. Elijah farmed until he retired. In March of 1943, he suffered gangrene in his foot and passed away at the age of eighty years.

Corporal Brady C. Paul, son of William and Vinta Paul, of Hickory, Washington County, PA, was slain on Route 422 about three miles east of New Castle, at Rose Point, Lawrence County, PA. A three-year veteran of the force, Corporal Paul was setting up a road-block, accompanied by Patrolman Earnest Moore, on the night of December 27, 1929. The two officers stopped a vehicle with Ohio registration, when a woman, one of three people in the car, fired a pistol at the officers.

Brady Paul Memorial on Old Rt. 422 Between Butler & New Castle PA.

The Corporal was killed by Irene Schroeder who fired the fatal shots. Patrolman Moore was wounded during the altercation. Brady Paul was only twenty-nine years old. So many tragedies seem to happen around Christmastime.

Jennie Vincent "Vinta" Paul

Ok, that wraps up the Paul and Pate saga for this book. There is even more to this family that I may go into in another volume. I know it's a long one, but their stories deserve to be told before they fade completely away. We shall always remember the Paul family of proud Americans. There are some amazing images I think you might enjoy seeing that may just bring some additional clarity. It's one thing to read about someone, but the story changes when you can see a picture of the subject. Enjoy the photo album.

Huston Paul House built 1838
South Strabane Twp.

Daisy Paul's Graduation Picture from Washington Seminary. She's bottom right.

Daisy is Second From Left

One of the many Paul reunions This one, probably September 1905 in Washington County

The Morris Family with Sunday School Class ca. 1924

Gleason, Charles and John Adams Paul with wives Mary, Agnes and Emma

William Paul, father of Philo Paul

Ethel Daisy Paul

Paul Family ca. 1914 at Lone Pine, PA.

Addie Sowers Paul

Dr. John & Lida Pate ca. 1910

Bill Price Breaking Ground for
First House 1950

Emma Walton Paul

Charles H. Paul
Son of John Adams Paul

William M. Paul with wife Jennie
McGugin Paul and baby Vincent
Niagara Falls ca. 1895

William M. Paul
Son of James Paul

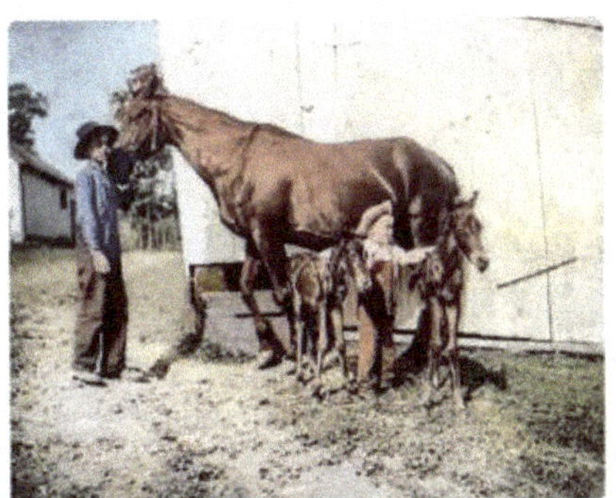

Vincent and Mack Paul, sons of
William Paul

Walter and Bertha Paul Nightengale with
Mable and Helen. Walter served with
Troop I, 12th Regiment US Cavalry

M. M. Paul House Jefferson Ave. Washington
ca. 1915
Elizabeth & Bertha with Mary M.W. Paul

Amiel and Elizabeth Pfeifer with
children Alice, Floyd and Ida

Sarah Hughes Paul Smith with her children.
Probably taken in 1914 on Sarah's 90th Birthday

2nd Row Phoebe Edgy, Mary Magdalene, Laura Jewell
Paul, Emma Watson
1st Row Sidney Frazee, Sarah Reynolds, Sarah Hughes,
Mary Horn, Hannah Birch

The Morris Sisters With Daisy 1940's

The Morris Sisters ca. 1970's
Mim, Ruth, Esther and Libby

Esther Morris
ca. 1924

Paul Posa
US Navy WW II

Sarah Alice Paul
ca. 1887

John and Margaret Paul ca. 1910

Mildred Paul

Paul's No. 6 Highland Av. ca. 1929

Paul's No. 1 Jefferson Av.

Chapter Fifteen
William C. Ramsey

William Ramsey was a son of Reuben and Margaret Horn Ramsey of Amwell Township, Washington County, PA. He had four brothers - Robert Hamilton (1845-1880), George Washington (1848-1874), Nicholas Murray (1854-1923), and John Nelson 1857-1873.

Reuben was a farmer and worked as a cooper as well. Margaret was a daughter of Michael and Elizabeth Closser Horn.

William C. Ramsey

When the Civil War erupted, Reuben enlisted in Company F of the famous 11th Pennsylvania Volunteer Infantry "The Bloody Eleventh" on April 23, 1861, and served for a three-month enlistment, mustering out on July 31, 1861.

William attended the common schools and what was then called the normal school. He was preparing to go to work teaching school when the Civil War broke out. On August 8, 1862, he enlisted in Company D of the 140th Pennsylvania Volunteer Infantry, where he served as a color corporal. He saw action at Chancellorsville and Gettysburg, where he was wounded in the lower leg. He spent ten months in the hospital, but survived and was transferred to the Eleventh Veteran Relief Corps where he was a quartermaster sergeant. He was finally discharged at Albany, New York, on June 25th, 1865.

Modern View of The Wheatfield at Gettysburg

During 1863, most likely before he was wounded, he married Miss Eliz- abeth Jane Sower of West Bethlehem Township. When he returned home, he worked the farm in the summer and taught school in the winter. He was also politically inclined and in 1870, he ran for and won the office of Washington County Sheriff. He served a three-year term, and then went back to farming, buying a two hundred and twenty-five acre farm.

He and Elizabeth had five children: Ulysses Bernard (1865-1944), Levi Har- lan (1868-1944), Kate Florence (1870-1930), Wilmetta Maud (1873-?) and Lillie Blanche (1876-1955). Bill served as an Elder in the East Buffalo Presbyterian Church and was a Director in the Farmers and Mechanics Bank of Washington, PA.

Bill Ramsey passed away on December 2, 1902, at the age of only fifty- nine years. His wife Elizabeth bought a home on Duncan Avenue in Washington, where she lived with her daughter Kate. She lived on for another twenty years until October 23, 1922, when she quietly passed away. She was eighty-four years old.

Once again we see the people of the small Township of Amwell, ride to the sound of the guns and serve without hesitation both their country and their community. William C. Ram- sey was one of them, as was his father.

We shall always remember them.

CHAPTER SIXTEEN
The Swarts

It's getting to seem as though the entire book is about Company D of the 140th PVI.

That is just the way it's worked out so far. So many interesting veterans and others happened to be from Amwell Township, and most of the military-age men there enlisted and then came home and made something of their lives, for better or worse.

The Swarts are no different, they were a prominent family in Washington County and also neighboring Greene County as well, where they had a station/village named after them - Swarts, PA. The ancestors settled in Washington County in about 1740.

There were four brothers who served in the Union Army during the late War of the Rebellion:

Andrew Jackson Swart

Andrew, John, Henry, and Amos, along with John's son James Monroe, and a brother-in-law James Andrew Jackson.

The parents of this band of brothers were Phillip (1797-1876) and Asenah Walton (1798-1870). By 1800, Philip and Asenah lived in Amwell Township, Washington County, and began building their family. First, there was David (1818-1890), then John Walton (1819-1890), Jacob (1820- 1898), Jonathan W. (1823-1903), Henry Clay (1825-1895), Amos J. (1828-1864), Sarah Ann (1830-1920)

Keziah (Cassie) (1833-1915), Andrew Jackson (1836-1899), and, finally, Mary Jane (1838-1921).

I would take the veterans one at a time, however their stories are so closely intertwined that I'll just tell the story, then fit in individual stories as appropriate.

It may sound like a broken record, but that cannot be helped this time. The Swart family mostly enlisted in the "Amity Company," which became Company D of the 140 Pennsylvania Volunteer Infantry. So many in this book served in that very Company that it may seem as though all of Washington County, PA, consisted of that one small community. But that is far from the truth, as there were thousands more Civil War veterans spread all over the county. There were twenty-eight Regiments from Pennsylvania and West Virginia (Union) that had men from Washington County in their ranks, some in more than one Company.

The 140th Pennsylvania consisted of ten Companies of soldiers. On paper, there should be one hundred men in a Company, but that was far from reality. By mid-war, a Company was from around thirty to sixty men. Of the ten Companies in the 140th PA, five were from Washington County.

So let us return to the war and tell of the Swart's bravery and fearlessness. John W. Swart, the eldest of the Swart brothers, enlisted in Company H of the 53rd Pennsylvania on February 27, 1864, at the age of 46. His son, James, had enlisted into Company A of the 140th on September 4, 1862. He was only eighteen years old.

Henry Clay Swart enlisted in Company D on August 22, 1862, as a Sergeant. He was thirty-six years old at the time. Amos Swart enlisted in Company D the same day as his older brother, August 22, 1862, He was thirty-four. Andrew Jackson Swart enlisted at first in E Company of the 12th Pennsylvania Volunteer Infantry on April 25, 1861. He served his three-month enlistment and was mustered out on August 5, 1861. He wasn't done quite yet because he reenlisted in Company D of the 140th with his two brothers on August 22, 1862. He was twenty-four when he enlisted the first time. And, last but not least, their sister Mary Jane's husband, James A. Jackson, enlisted with his brothers-in-law in Company D on the same day.

The 140th was organized in early September of 1862 and spent their time training and guarding railroads until that December. They were then moved to the 3rd Brigade, 1st Division, 2nd Army Corps. Richard P. Roberts of Beaver County was their Colonel, John Fraser of Washington County was their Lt. Colonel and Thomas B. Rodgers of Mercer County was the Major. They missed the battle of Fredericksburg but were heavily engaged at Chancellorsville at various positions around the Chancellor house. They were moved to another position and remained there under artillery fire until they crossed the river and returned to their previous camp at Falmouth, Virginia.

Ruins of the Chancellor Mansion 1865

They started with the Corps in the pursuit of Confederate General Robert E. Lee as he moved northward. They had a brief skirmish at Thoroughfare Gap and then crossed the Potomac on the 24th of June 1863. From there it was on to Pennsylvania and destiny at Gettysburg they marched. Arriving on July 2, they took a position along Cemetery Ridge toward the Round Tops.

In a previous chapter, I described the carnage at the Wheatfield battle, and the Swart family was not able to escape the carnage completely. Andrew J. Swart was wounded in the Wheatfield and was taken to the field hospital where he remained for about two weeks. He was then removed to Camp Parole near Annapolis, Maryland, where he stayed until that October.

He was just well enough to be given a furlough and was sent home. When his furlough ran out, he reported for duty near Philadelphia and was admitted to a hospital there. He still wasn't well enough to return to duty. In March of 1864, he was transferred to a Pittsburgh hospital where he remained until September of 1864 when he finally received his discharge and went home for good this time.

He had been married on Halloween Day in 1861, to Miss Mary J. Greenlee of Greene County, PA. They produced seven children: Florella (1862- 1913), Viola (1867-1937), Minnie (1870-1956), Annie M. (1874-1920), Harold Glen (1898-1965) and an infant son and daughter that didn't survive. Their daughter, Florella, was only two weeks old when he re-enlisted into the 140th PVI. He left home strong and healthy and returned home an invalid due to wounds suffered while attempting to help a wounded comrade to safety in the Wheatfield in Gettysburg. Being unable to do manual labor on the farm, he had to hire someone to have it done. He suffered greatly for thirty-five years, without complaint. His shattered legs were all but useless.

On Sunday, July 23, 1899, Andrew J. Swart passed away at home. He was only sixty-two years, seven months, and seven days old. He had belonged to the Philo Paul G. A. R. Post and they took part in the funeral, along with members of other G. A. R. posts. He was buried in the Amity Methodist Cemetery. Mary Jane joined him on February 21, 1913.

John Swart

The eldest brother, John Swart, is a mystery. There are many conflicting sources of information on him. I cannot figure out which one, or which parts of which ones are accurate. There isn't even agreement on a birth date or wife or wives or children. I found at least three dates of death. I have no idea which one is correct or if any are correct.

This is one of the problems you run into when researching large families. Multiple people with the same names in which descendants trying to do genealogy got confused at some point in the past, so it all gets mixed up and there is just no figuring it out. In this case, apparently John Walton Swart may have had a brother named Jonathan Walton Swart.

Why on earth would people give two brothers essentially the same name!? And that is the root of the problem here. Add to all this, there were also two Uncle Jonathans, an Uncle John, and a Grandfather Jonathan! So, instead of giving you all this conflicting information, I'll tell you the parts I'm pretty sure about.

He was born in Amwell Township, Washington County PA, around 1819. By 1850, he had bought about two hundred acres in neighboring Greene County. In 1838, he married Sarah (Sallie) Huffman (1819-1889) from Greene County.

Sallie Huffman

James Monroe Swart and Sarah Allum and Family. L to R
James H. A. standing, John, Dessie, Elita, Relica, Unknown.

My best estimate is they had fourteen children, seven boys, and seven girls: Asena Jane (1840-1920), Sarah Ann (1842-1888), James Monroe (1844-1915), Philip Warren (1846-?), Sidney (1846-?), J. W. Scott (1848-?), Mary Louisa (1849-?),

Henry Clay (1853-1926), Octavia (1854- ?), Sidney (1856-?), William Montgomery (1858-1941), Clara B. (1860-1884), Walton Ellsworth (1862-1941) and John L. G. (1864-1886).

In 1864, at the age of forty-five, he enlisted in Company D of the 140th Pennsylvania Vol. Infantry. He served with his Company clear through until the end of the war. In the Wilderness, he got a bullet lodged in his rifle muzzle, he sat down and dug it out with his knife while under fire, and then continued with the fight. Also at the Wilderness, John's tenant on the farm named John W. Pedan, of Company A in the 140th PA, was severely wounded in the leg at Todd's Tavern. His leg was amputated, but he did not survive. At Cold Harbor, John's rifle butt was shattered by a Rebel bullet, but he found another rifle and continued on once again.

Isaac Allum

Spotsylvania Court House turned into a bloodbath for the Swart family. While assaulting the Confederate works, John happened to be right beside his brother Amos. He turned and saw his brother go down, never to move again. Another brother, Henry Clay Swart, suffered a serious leg wound and lived, but was a cripple for the rest of his life. John's son, James, was in Company A of the 140th PA and somehow survived the battle unscathed. James fought at Chancellorsville, at the Bloody Angle, then went on to the battles at Cold Harbor, Petersburg, and Appomattox. One of John's sons-in-law, John Jones, was serving in Company A as well and made the assault on the Bloody Angle, but was lucky and survived unharmed.

By the way, another son-in-law, Isaac Allum, served in Company K of the 5th Pennsylvania Heavy Artillery. He served in the forts north of Washington City and in the Shenandoah Valley supporting General Sheridan.

Getting back to John, he was wounded at Spotsylvania and later transferred to Company H of the 53rd Pennsylvania Volunteer Infantry. He served until June 17, 1865. He was mustered out on June 30, 1865, at Washington City. He was listed as absent/sick at muster out. He returned to his farm in Greene County, PA, until

1884 when his branch of the family picked up, packed up, and moved to Leroy, Audubon County, Iowa. The next year, he joined the Allison Post of the G. A. R.

John Swart passed away after a short illness which was described as "a congestion of the lungs". He was seventy years, eleven months, and eight days old. He was buried under the rituals of the G. A. R. and the Stuart Camp of the Sons of Veterans. *"His toils are past, his work is done, and he is fully blest; He fought the fight, the victory won, and enters into rest."* His remains are interred in Maple Grove Cemetery in Audubon County, Iowa. His wife, Sally, joined him on March 4, 1889, and is buried beside her husband.

John's son, James Monroe Swart, survived the war and had married Sarah Jane Allum in 1864. They had eight children: Sarah Rebecca Arbelle (1866-1955), Bertha Viola (1870-1898), James Henry Allum (1872-1961), Laura Dessie Ardella (1875-1957), Asenath Etta Ann (1878-1966), Clara Leona Venetta (1880-1887), John Thomas Garfield (1882-1951), and William Lester Blaine (1883-1896).

They stayed in Washington County, PA, and later Greene County, PA, where they led a farm life. James passed away from cancer on February 6, 1913. He was only sixty-nine years old. Sarah Jane died on February 8, 1915, her too at the age of only sixty-nine.

Charles Monroe Swart

Their son, James Henry Allum Swart, is the boy standing at the left in their family picture. He worked the family farm in Greene County all his life. He married Nancy Virginia Scott on August 18, 1892, in Washington, PA. They were blessed with four boys: Charles Monroe (1893-1988), George Harley (1895-1985), James Hobart (1896-1918), William Ross (1988-1920); and two girls.

Let's check on the boys, shall we? First Charles. He worked the family farm until January 28, 1918, when he enlisted as a private 1st Cl. (Cadet) in the Air Service.

He served until that November when he was honorably discharged. He never made it overseas, making him lucky.

He married Miss Bessie Smith of Wheeling West Virginia, on August 11, 1945. They had two children: Charles Monroe Jr. (1922-1983) and Martha V. (1924-2014).

Charles worked as an IRS agent in the 1920s and later worked at the Block Brothers Tobacco Company in Wheeling, West Virginia. He passed away on August 23, 1988, at the age of ninety-five years! He's buried in Greene County, PA. Bessie passed some time in 1984 at the age of ninety- three. She rests beside her husband. By the way, their son, Charles Jr. (1922-1983), served in the US Navy during World War II.

George Harley Swart

George Harley Swart (1895-1985) married Miss Mary Jenkins (1895- 1967), on April 10, 1918. He was working the family farm in 1910, so he probably left home with his brothers to enlist when World War I broke out. Harley served in France in Company K of the 110th Infantry in the 28th Division. After the war, he graduated from Penn State College and was a vocational-agriculture teacher at Waynesburg High School for thirty-three years, retiring in 1955. He was active in the Future Farmers of America and 4-H clubs. He maintained the family farm all through this, and also ran a milk route in Waynesburg, PA.

Harley helped organize the Greene County Farm Bureau Coop Association and served as a Director of the Association. He was a member of the American Legion and the East Franklin Grange. Two of his sons grew up to be medical doctors. Harley passed in his home on February 15, 1985. He was ninety years old. He and his wife are buried in Enon Cemetery in Greene County, PA.

And now, it gets tougher. James Hobart Swart (1896-1918). That 1918 date should tip you off to what is coming. And you are right. We have scant information on Hoby Swart. He lived and worked on the family farm until World War I started. He enlisted probably with his brother in Company K, 110th Pennsylvania

Regiment on April 14, 1917. He was sent overseas with the American Expeditionary Forces on May 2, 1918, and served in France, seeing action at Ourcq River, Vesle sector, and the Argonne Forest. He carried the rank of Corporal when he was killed in action on September 27, 1918, in the Argonne Forest. He was only twenty-one years old. He is buried in Enon Cemetery in Greene County, PA.

One more son to go and his name was William Ross Swart. His story is tragically short. He lived on the family farm in Greene County, for twenty years and was a pretty good carpenter until he contracted Tuberculosis in March of 1920, and passed away that September on the twenty-first. He was only twenty-one years old. He was buried in Enon Cemetery.

James Hobart Swart

As I mentioned before, John W. Swart's sister, Mary, (1838-1921), had married a man named James Andrew Jackson (1832-1910), who had enlisted with the Swart brothers into Co. D of the 140th Pennsylvania. Jim was a good soldier, but was not able to handle the rigors of soldier life it appears. He was sent to the Lincoln General Hospital in Washington City in hopes that he would recover and be able to return to his regiment. The following is an excerpt from a letter he wrote to his brother-in-law, David. I will leave the spelling and punctuation as he wrote it, with corrections in parentheses for clarity.

William Ross Swart

"...I was glad to hear from you, and that you are all enjoying good health or wer (were) at that time, and to hear of your patriotic declarations, for our beloved country and government, may god sustain you and all of our relations in there indevers (endeavors) to restore our govern and thrush out this hell born rebellion. I have indevered (endeavored) to do my duty to my country, but

my health has faled (failed) me. But I hope to be restored, in health, if not sofisient (sufficient) to go back to the front, to return to my family agane (again). I would rather be with my regiment and dear friends and fellow soldiers that (than) be in this hospital."

James Andrew Jackson 1903

Mary Jane Swart Jackson

Lincoln Hospital was opened in December 1862. It was the largest of the hospitals around Washington and was built by the US Army, located right on Capitol Hill just a few blocks east of the Capitol building. It was quite a facility, especially for that time. There were twenty pavilions, arranged in two lines forming a large V, with 25 additional tent wards which gave them a capacity of about 2,575 patients.

The kitchens and dining rooms were connected to the pavilions by means of a covered walkway. There was a headquarters, officer's quarters and quarters for the nuns who served as nurses. There were barracks, a guard house, and separate quarters for contrabands. Also, there was a laundry, barber shop, carpenter shop, stables, and a "Dead House." (mortuary) along with a large water tank. The hospital was demolished right after the war ended and is a residential area today.

James's wish was granted somehow because he returned to the 140th PVI and was present at the Battle of Gettysburg, where he lost an arm. He was discharged by a surgeon's certificate of disability on the 31st of December, 1863, from "Convalescent Camp Virginia." By the way, James was 5 feet 9 inches tall with a fair complexion, dark eyes, and brown hair. We try to be complete around here.

James was a shoemaker before the war and he returned to that profession after he came home from the war. By 1880, he was listed as a farmer in Amwell Township.

He and Mary had nine children along the way: Permelia Isadora (1855-1952), Addell (1857-1857), Asenah Ann (1858-1864), Viola (1860-1864), Lilla Frances (1862-1866), John Amos (1865-1926), Anna Mary (1867-1936), Philip Swart (1870-1898) and Kittie Belle (1872-1951).

James Andrew Jackson passed away on September 5, 1910, at the age of seventy-eight years. Mary Jane died on December 16, 1921. She was eighty - three. They are buried in Amity, PA.

Henry Clay Swart, as I mentioned earlier, was seriously wounded at Spotsylvania. He was born on November 18, 1825, on the family farm near Amity. Early on, he dealt in stock, mostly horses and hogs, which he drove on foot to Cumberland, Maryland.

J. A. Jackson's Gettysburg 50th Anniversary Badge

In August of 1852, he married Miss Abigail Day and they lived on the Swart farm until 1857 when he purchased a farm of their own one mile south of Amity. They had two children, John and Laura. John stayed on the farm while Laura grew up and in 1862 married a man named Horn and moved to Denver where he practiced law.

After Henry was wounded, he was taken to first a field hospital, then was taken by wagon on the fifteen mile agonizing trip to Fredericksburg where he remained for two weeks. Finally, he was taken aboard a transport boat and sailed to Washington City and placed in Lincoln Hospital. He stayed there for ten days before receiving a leave of absence and was taken home on a stretcher to recuperate. After several months of suffering and agony, Henry was finally able to report to a hospital in

Pittsburgh, where he applied for an honorable discharge. After a month of waiting, he was granted his discharge and returned to his home and family.

Jackson Home in Amity Mary Jane Jackson Out Front

He remained an invalid for the rest of his life, his hip wound never healing completely, but successfully managed his farm until 1872 when he retired to Washington, Pennsylvania.

John Amos Jackson Family

He was active in his Methodist/Protestant church for many years and joined the temperance cause he had supported from early on. He eventually lost sight in one eye and had limited vision in the other. He was a member in good standing in the Templeton Post 120 of the G. A. R. as well.

Henry passed away on June 13, 1895. He was only sixty-nine years old. Abigail joined him on March 31, 1901. They are buried in Washington Cemetery.

So there you have it. The remarkable story of an entire family that sacrificed and served their country with a patriotic fervor that was unmatched. They continued this service in the generations to come and lost more of themselves to protect the freedoms we all enjoy today. We shall always remember them and the debt we all owe to them and others like them.

Chapter Seventeen

Joseph Bradford Johnson

Joseph Bradford Johnson was born September 26, 1842, on the family farm in North Strabane Township, Washington County, Pennsylvania. He was the son of John and Rebecca Johnson.

His grandfather Richard was an early settler in the area. Joseph had two brothers, Richard and John.

Joe had just completed his sophomore year at Jefferson College when he decided to enlist in the Union Army in 1862. Another 140th Pennsylvania Volunteer Infantry recruit, but Joe was in Company G.

He saw action at Chancellorsville and Gettysburg, before transferring out to the Signal Corps on April 1, 1864. That October, he was captured and spent a little over three months at Libby Prison in Richmond, Virginia. He was paroled on

Joseph B. Johnson

January 22, 1865, but was unable to leave due to the icy river. He remained in prison until February 5, when he was finally transported to Annapolis, Maryland's Camp Parole. Given a thirty-day furlough, he then returned to service, but by then General Lee had surrendered and the war was nearly over. Joe was discharged at Washington City.

Returning home he resumed what he knew best, farming. He was able to purchase his Grandfather's old farm located about a half mile north of Houston,

Washington County, PA. He married Miss Hannah Jane "Jennie" Crothers in 1867 and they had three children, Ella, John, and Charles.

Ella ended up marrying Reverend Charles Williams and they moved all the way to Denver, Colorado. They in turn had two boys Bradford and Jay. John stayed on the farm all his life, and Charles became President of the Citizens Trust Company of Canonsburg, PA. He married Miss Grace Henderson.

Charles Bradford

Jennie Johnson passed away in October of 1897 at the early age of fifty- seven. After a respectable period, Joe married Miss Anna Harper on April 4, 1900. He became a Director of the Citizens Trust Company and was an Elder in the Central Presbyterian Church.

Joe Bradford retired from farming and moved to town. He and Anna lived on Pike Street in Canonsburg, PA.

Right before Thanksgiving 1912, Joe and Anna traveled to Denver to spend the holidays with Joe's daughter and her family. He was stricken with a severe case of pneumonia and passed away on December 11, 1912. He was seventy. His son Charles passed away on August 10, 1922. John died on November 30, 1954, and Ella passed on December 29, 1926. Her son, Bradford R. Williams (1894-1970), served as a Sergeant in the US Army during WW I. Her other son, Jay (1897-1977), also served and was a 2nd Lt. in the US Army in WW I.

The Bradford Hone in Canonsburg Today

Again we have a family tradition of service to the nation. Although there is scant information about this family, they deserve to be remembered, and we shall always remember them.

CHAPTER EIGHTEEN
Absalom Baird

The Baird family is one of the most famous of all the old families in the county. Theirs is a story of achievement and accomplishment. We will focus on one particular Baird named Absalom. He is only one of several with that unusual first name. It is an old family name, so he comes by it honestly.

In order to get the full picture of just who our Absalom Baird was, let's take a very short trip down a rabbit hole for some interesting background, shall we? Don't worry, we won't go far and we'll be right back to our main focus of this chapter.

Major General Absalom Baird

The original Absalom Baird (1758-1805) became a physician in Chester County, Pennsylvania. He served in the Revolution as Surgeon of Baldwin's Regiment of Artillery Artificers from March 20, 1780, to March 29, 1781. Three years later, he moved to Washington County, PA, and opened a medical practice there. He was elected to the state Senate in 1794, and to the state House of Representatives in 1798. The following year, he was elected Sheriff of Washington County.

He married Miss Susanna Brown (1763-1802) on July 14, 1783, and they had six children: John (1784-1836) was a doctor in Ohio and Washington County, PA, George (1785-1860) was a storekeeper, Thomas (1787-1866) was a lawyer and

President Judge of the 14th Judicial District of Pennsylvania, William (1789-1834) practiced law, Sarah (1793-1833) married William Hodge of Kentucky and Susan (1796-1824) married Dr. Hugh Campbell of Uniontown, PA.

The Home of Dr. Absalom Baird

His father, John Baird, came from Scotland and entered the military service of the Colony of Pennsylvania. He took part in the 1758 expedition of British General Forbes against the French at Fort Duquesne. While waiting for troops and supplies, Major Grant was given orders to reconnoiter Ft. Duquesne. Grant had about 800 men and marched from Ligonier toward the fort located at what is now Pittsburgh. He reached what is now called "Grant's Hill", which is about a mile from the fort. Instead of merely checking out the fort, he decided to try to take the fort on his own. The French were reinforced by Indians and troops that arrived from Illinois, thus vastly outnumbering the Brits.

They quickly had Grant surrounded and they actually captured him while the rout was on. Many of Grant's men drowned in the Allegheny River that chilly September night. Grant was taken to Montreal by the French and eventually released. He later fought for the British in the American Revolution. So he was still an incompetent loser.

To finish out this story, that November, General Forbes, and 2500 troops marched on the fort once again, this time the French troop's fort had been depleted and they were abandoning the place. On a cold and rainy, miserable night on November 18, 1758, none other than George Washington along with

Grant St. Today in Downtown Pittsburgh

General Forbes watched the British flag being raised over the fort that was now named, Fort Pitt.

Grant's Hill became a park for a while but was troublesome for increased wagon traffic, so they decided to "cut the hump" in 1836 and cut it down even more in 1847. In 1913-14, they lowered it even more, a total of about sixty feet have been shaved off the hill. Today, it's the main artery in downtown Pittsburgh. It's lined with vintage buildings from the 1800s and modern skyscrapers. It's been widened as well, along with other improvements.

John's grandson, William Baird, married Miss Nancy Agnes Mitchell (1799-1881) in 1823. They had eight children along the way: Susan (1823-1851), Absalom (1824-1905), Gabriel (1826-1827), William M. (1827-1923), Jane (1828-1903), Catherine (1830-1868), Maria (1832-1834), and John Mitch- ell (1833-1834).

William studied to become a lawyer with his uncle Thomas H. Baird. He prac-ticed law from 1812 to 1816, then served as District Attorney from 1816 -1824.

He resumed his law practice until he passed away on October 6, 1834. He was only forty-five years old.

Now we can get back to our Absalom Baird. There is much more to tell about the Baird family. They were a huge family and they all have interesting stories because they all were movers and shakers and achieved success in the various enterprises they undertook. But they are beyond the scope of this work, so we move on to the subject at hand.

Absalom Baird was born in Washing-ton, Pennsylvania, and attended the Normal schools and then on to Washington Academy, now combined with Jefferson Academy and called Washington & Jefferson College. Following graduation, he enrolled in the United States Military Academy at West Point, where he graduated ninth in a class of 43 in 1849. Baird served as Second Lieutenant during the Seminole War in Florida in 1850-1851. He served as an assistant mathematics instructor at West Point from 1852 to 1859, being promoted to First Lieutenant in 1853. He served the next two years on frontier and garrison duty in Virginia and Texas fighting Indians.

General William T. Sherman

In March of 1861, he took command of the light battery for the Department of Washington, and on May 11th was brevetted Captain. In July of that same year, he served as Adjutant General for the defense of Washington. On November 12, 1861, Baird was promoted to Major in the Regular Army while serving as an Assistant Inspector General. He then served under Brig. General Daniel Tyler during the battle of First Manassas. He became Chief of Staff to Major General Erasmus Keyes at the start of the Siege of Yorktown and was engaged in the battle of Williamsburg, and that service earned him another promotion to Brigadier General of Volunteers.

Gen. Absalom Baird

Absalom Baird commanded the 27th Brigade in the 7th Division of the Army of the Ohio from May to September of 1862 under Major General Don Carlos Buell. He helped capture the Cumberland Gap as well. That October, he took command of the Third Division of the Army of the Kentucky and after the battles of Thompson's Station and Harpeth River, they were absorbed into the Army of the Cumberland. Baird's Division became the 1st Division of Major General John Henry Thomas's Fourteenth Corps.

Baird earned great fame for his heroics in the Battle of Chickamauga and in the Chattanooga Campaign. He won a brevet promotion to Lieutenant Colonel in the Regular Army for "Gallant Action" at Chickamauga where his tenacious defense of Horseshoe Ridge helped save the Union's bacon that day. But for Absalom Baird, the best was yet to come.

Union General William Sherman was parked west of Atlanta, Georgia, in August of 1864. He had the city virtually surrounded, but the Confederates were still getting supply trains in via the Macon & Western Railroad which ran through Jonesboro, then spelled Jonesborough. So, on Friday, August 19, about 4,000 Union cavalrymen under General Judson Kilpatrick made an assault on Jonesboro. After brushing aside the scant Confederate force there, the cavalry went to pulling up rails of the vital supply line and burned the depot. Heavy rain prevented them from heating the rails and twisting them into

General William Hardee

"Sherman's Neckties." They then departed and returned to duties elsewhere.

Confederates quickly repaired the tracks and the supply line was reopened. Sherman determined that infantry was needed to shut off that rail line at Jonesboro permanently. He had three armies available to work with, and he used them all. Tuesday, August 30, Major General O. O. Howard and his Army of The Tennessee crossed the Flint River and dug in just west of Jonesboro.

By this time, Confederate General John Bell Hood woke up and realized that the railroad was Sherman's objective. His intelligence was not very good and he thought that there were only two Federal corps near Jonesboro. He planned an attack there and sent two Confederate corps, one led by Lt. General William J. Hardee and the other commanded by Major General Stephen D. Lee. Major General Cleburne would command Hardee's corps, while Hardee commanded the entire attack.

Cleburne's troops planned a wheeling maneuver to assault the Federal 16th Corps. Lee's corps was on the right up against the Union 15th Corps. According to the Confederate battle plan, Cleburne would launch the attack, and when Lee heard the sound of Cleburne's guns, he would strike the Union left. However, Lee, hearing the skirmish line firing, mistook that sound for Cleburne's assault and pre-maturely ordered his troops forward. S. D. Lee's force was decimated in the ensuing attack.

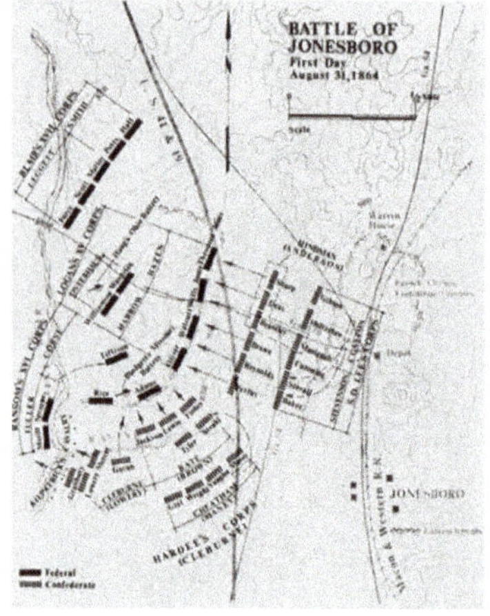

Cleburne made a gallant effort, driving the Federals back and capturing two cannon. Still, the fight began to come unglued as Lee's weakened force could not support Cleburne as planned and hold the ground they had gained. The Confederates were forced to pull back and form a defensive position and await further events.

During this lull in the action, General Hood, fearing an attack from another direction on Atlanta ordered Lee to return to the city. When the battle resumed on September 1, General Hardee's army, being vastly outnumbered, had no chance to stop the Federal onslaught. A private in Cleburne's Division wrote later that the boys in blue *ran over us like a drove of Texas beeves.* Hardee was forced to abandon his position and retreat to Lovejoy Station. The Confederates suffered around 2,000 casualties, while Sherman's army lost about 1,200 killed, wounded, and missing.

Gen. Absalom Baird

Later that night, General Hood, seeing that Sherman's army had cut the last rail supply line to Atlanta and were threatening to block off the southern escape route for his army, ordered the evacuation of Atlanta. General Hardee in his report, later placed the blame on General Hood for misreading Sherman's plans.

During the battle on September 1, in a moment of extreme emergency, General Baird voluntarily led an assault by a detached Brigade upon the Confederate works. For this gallantry, he was awarded on April 22, 1896, the Congressional Medal of Honor.

General Baird participated in and led his Division in the "March to the Sea," and the march through the Carolinas, he was heavily engaged at Bentonville and Raleigh and was present at the surrender of General Joseph Johnston's army at Durham Station.

On January 23, 1865, President Abraham Lincoln nominated Baird for appointment to the brevet grade of Major General of Volunteers, to rank from September 1, 1864, and the U.S. Congress confirmed the award on February 14, 1865. On April 10, 1866, President Andrew Johnson nominated Baird for appointment as brevet Brigadier General in the Regular Army, to rank from March 13, 1865, and the U.S. Senate confirmed the appointment on May 4, 1866. On July 17, 1866, President Andrew Johnson nominated Baird for appointment as brevet Major General in the regular U.S. Army, to rank from March 13, 1865, and the U.S. Senate confirmed the appointment on July 23, 1866. Baird was mustered out of the Volunteer service on September 1, 1866.

General Baird then served as Commander of the Department of Louisiana. Then he served as Inspector General of the Department of the Great Lakes from 1866 to 1868, and Inspector General of the Department of the Dakotas from 1868 to 1870, and of the Division of the South until 1872. Later, he was Inspector General of the Division of the Missouri. General Baird was then named Inspector General of the Army on March 11, 1885. In 1887, Baird traveled to France to observe military maneuvers and was named a Commander of the Legion d'Honneur. Absalom Baird retired from the Army on August 20, 1888, having

General Absalom Baird

reached the mandatory retirement age of 64. He was a Veteran Companion of the Military Order of the Loyal Legion of the United States and a member of the General Society of Colonial Wars.

Other than that, he didn't do anything. Oh, and one more thing. I personally award him a brevet promotion to Lt. General for the best mustache in the Union army during the Civil War.

As we know, General Baird was born in Washington PA, on June 20, 1824. He graduated from West Point in 1849, and the next year he married Miss Cornelia Wynte Smith (1828-1883) on October 17th, 1850. They had only one child, William (1851-1930). William was born in Philadelphia, Pennsylvania, on August 22, 1851. Like father, like son, he graduated from the US Military Academy at West Point on June 16, 1875. He was ranked twenty-eighth out of forty-three in his class.

William Baird

He was appointed a Second Lieutenant and assigned to the 6th US Cavalry Regiment for frontier duty. He served there on the frontier throughout the Indian Wars, rising in rank slowly to 1st Lt. in 1882. From November 27, 1884, until November 1, 1886, he served as Regimental Adjutant.

Finally, on his way, he married Miss Minnie Dawley (1865-1935) in San Francisco on June 18, 1885. He was promoted to Captain on February 24, 1891 and served again on frontier duty until he retired with a disability on December 3, 1897.

But wait, Captain Baird wasn't through just yet. He returned to active duty in 1900 and 1901. He continued on active duty in September and Oc- tober 1917 before finally retiring as a Lieutenant Colonel in 1918.

William Baird passed away on January 3, 1930, in Washington, DC, at the age of seventy-eight. Minnie followed him on July 15, 1935. She was only seventy years of age. Bill and Minnie had only one child as well. John Absalom was born on June 23, 1890, in Fort Myer, Alexandria, Virginia. He went a different route than his father and grandfather. He went to the US Naval Academy at Annapolis, Maryland, and was a Cadet there from 1907 until 1911. He graduated a Midshipman and became an Ensign on March 7, 1912. He was promoted to Second Lt. in April of 1912 and to 1st Lt. on July 1, 1916.

At some point around this time, he switched to the US Army. Why? I have no idea. He rose through the ranks from 1917, when he was made Captain, until he retired as a Colonel on January 31, 1947. He served with the Coast Guard Artillery Corps from 1912 until 1923, then went with the

Chemical Warfare Service from 1923 until 1947. He's credited with the Chemical Warfare School in 1923. And was a student at the Army Industrial College from 1927 to 1928 and a student at Command and General Staff College in 1932. At some point, he was awarded the Legion of Merit. He passed away on September 30, 1951, in Virginia. He was only sixty-one years old. Helen followed him on July 6, 1972. She was eighty-two.

General Absalom Baird's wife Cornelia passed away on May 6, 1883, in Washington DC. She was only fifty-four years old. Absalom Baird passed away on June 14, 1905, in Relay, Maryland. He was eighty years old.

We have one last member of this family to make mention of. And that is General Baird's sister, Jane Baird Jacob. General Baird's younger sister Jane (1828-1903) grew up and married Mr. John Jeremiah Jacob (1829-1893), of Fairfax Virginia. Hampshire County is now part of West Virginia of course and John Jacob was a big part of that new state.

He graduated from Carlisle College in Dickinson, Pennsylvania, then returned home to teach school and practice law.

In 1853, he moved to Missouri to teach at the university there and again, practice law. At the end of the Civil War, he once again returned to the new state of West Virginia.

While practicing law there, he caught the attention of local politicians who liked his skill as an orator in the courtroom. They persuaded him to run for public office, and he did just that. The first time out, he won a seat in the House of Delegates, and a year later was his party's choice as their nominee for Governor. He won the Governor's race in 1870 and became the first Democratic Governor in the young state's history.

Governor John Jacobs

He had an aggressive style and rubbed his political adversaries the wrong way as he established the structure that began the state's university system. He also implemented a plan to rid the state of its debt. He also helped to establish a new state constitution that helped unite the state divided by the Union sympathizing counties and the Confederate sympathizing counties in the southern part of the state.

This caused a rift between him and his Democratic party friends and he lost their nomination for Governor in his try for a second term. Nevertheless, he ran as an Independent with help from Republicans and won a second term. Following his second term, he returned to the House of Delegates and also served as a Judicial Court Judge. In 1888, he retired from politics, and passed away on November 24, 1893, at the age of only sixty-three, while practicing law in Wheeling. His wife, Jane, died of pneumonia on February 22, 1903. She was seventy-four.

General Absalom Baird, his wife Cornelia, their son William and his wife Minnie, and their son John and his wife Helen, are all buried in the Arlington National Cemetery together. I would think that fitting for the enormous service that that great family has given freely to the United States of America. We shall always remember them.

Chapter Nineteen

John C. French

John C. French enlisted in the Union Army as a Private on June 6, 1861, at the age of 27. He mustered into E Company of the 2nd West Virginia Infantry. He served with them until January 26, 1864, when he apparently got tired of walking and transferred into Company E (I) of the 5th West Vir- ginia cavalry. He rose in rank to 1st Lieutenant and mustered out of the army on June 16, 1864.

He was born in Washington County, Pennsylvania, on October 10, 1836, to George and Mary (Porter) French. His mother passed away when John was only three years old, and a lot of his early life was spent with relatives in Fayette County, PA. John's Great Grandfather served as a member of General George Washington's body-guard during the Revolution. His maternal Grandfather, Charles Porter, was Speaker of the House of Representatives of Pennsylvania in 1906.

John C. French

At the age of twelve, John returned home with his father where he lived for about four years. Then, he lived with the family of William Lindley, Esquire, where he worked all summer and went to school in the winter. At nineteen, John went to work in the mercantile house of Robert Porter in Ritchie Court House, Virginia. After a year, he went into business with three others starting up a barrel supply business on the

B. & O. Railroad. Their company was the first manufacturer of oil barrels in that area after the development of the Kanawha oil field.

George French, Father of Captain French

When the war broke out, their business went bust and John found himself without a job and few prospects for employment. He decided to enlist in the Union Army. In that area, most were siding with the South, so he was able to make an agreement with six others to meet at an agreed-upon place on the night of June 14, 1861. They made their way to St. Mary's, some sixteen miles away, to catch the boat going to Wheeling. They arrived there the next morning and proceeded to Camp Carlisle where they enlisted in what became what is listed as Company E of the Second Virginia Mounted Infantry, Union. I believe it was Company I, as they were from Washington County, PA and Co. E was from Ohio. Later they were changed by order of the War Department into the 5th Virginia Cavalry.

For fifteen months, John French served as a Private, Duty Sergeant, and Orderly Sergeant. At Second Manassas, the Company commander was killed and the Lieutenant was severely wounded, so John was left in command of the Company. He served in that capacity until September 9th when he was commissioned a Second Lieutenant and assigned to Company H. That same year on December 3rd, he was commissioned 1st Lieutenant and transferred back to Company E. While in command of his Company, they made a charge upon the enemy works at Rocky Gap on August 26, 1863. There, John suffered a serious wound near his left knee. The thigh bone was broken and the knee was dislocated. This ended up crippling him for life.

Rescued by his comrades and removed from the field, he was taken by ambulance some one hundred miles or so to Beverly, Virginia, where he was sheltered and nursed by Mrs. Jonathan Arnold, a sister of Confederate General Stonewall Jackson.

He was able to recover enough to return home to Pennsylvania, and eventually to his regiment. He served as Adjutant until they were mustered out and discharged.

John returned to Washington County, and on September 7, 1864, married Miss Sevilla Jane Vaille (1840-1931). They were blessed with four children: Edward John (1836-1926), Leah Mary (1868-1958), Charles Clinton (1873-1874), and John Calvin (1874-1963).

Edward French

By the way, John had two brothers who also served in the Civil War. Andrew was mustered into Company K of the 37th Pennsylvania Volunteer Infantry. He was killed at Fredericksburg on December 13, 1862. And Enoch mustered into Company D of the 140th Pennsylvania Volunteer Infantry. He survived and was discharged on September 14, 1863.

John worked in retail for some years, then in 1873, he was elected County Treasurer. When his term was up, they moved to Prosperity in Morris Township, where he did his best to work at farming. They joined the Presbyterian Church of Upper Ten Mile, where John served as Superintendent of their Sabbath school, and was chosen to be a church Elder. He was also a member in good standing of the Grand Army of the Republic, being a charter member of Luther Post 395, and served as its Commander for some time. In 1894, John was elected to the Pennsylvania General Assembly, and again in 1896. He also served in other important political positions in the County.

On April 21, 1926, John caught a case of pneumonia and went to his reward while living with his family at the home of his son-in-law Dr. A. N. Booth in Bentleyville, Washington County. He was eighty-nine years old. The love of his life, Sevilla, followed him on March 19, 1931, of pneumonia. She lived to be ninety-one years old.

Their son, Edward, attended Washington & Jefferson College, then studied medicine under Dr. E. H. Carey. He then went on to Jefferson Medical College in Philadelphia and graduated from there in 1887. In 1889, he went into partnership with his brother-in-law, Dr. A. N. Booth, and they established an extensive practice in Bentleyville. In 1903, the town of Ellsworth, PA, hired Dr. French to open a practice there, which he did. Dr. French married Miss Sarah "Sadie" Young of Pittsburgh, whose father was a Civil War veteran. Not having any children of their own, they adopted a niece, Miss Ada Young who grew up to be a successful teacher.

A. N. Booth M. D.

Dr. French was a member of the Odd Fellows and was a Mason and also held membership in the Knights Templar and the Elks. He was a member of the Washington County Medical Society, the Pennsylvania State Medical Society, and the AMA. He was the Health Officer for the Townships of Somerset and West Bethlehem and secretary of the Ellsworth Board of Health. Gee, when did this guy have time to practice medicine? He died at the age of fifty in Belleview, PA, on February 11, 1916, of once again, pneumonia. Sadie passed on March 14, 1943, at the age of seventy-two years.

The Captain's daughter, Leah Mary French, grew up and married Dr. Alexander Nelson Booth (1864-1934). They had two children: Sevella Gaile (1892-1978) and John Calvin "Doc" (1896-1956). "Doc" graduated from Washington & Jefferson College and served in the Army Air Service during World War I.

John Calvin "Doc" Booth

The Captain's other son, John C. French (1874-1963), followed his calling and became a Reverend. He married twice, first Miss Priscilla Day McVay with whom they had a daughter, Leanna May (1902-1990). Priscilla passed away in 1911 and he married Miss Donetta Crumrine (1885-1969). They had a daughter as well, Donetta F. (1921-2015).

We give a sincere and heartfelt thank you to the French family for your service to our nation. We shall always remember you.

CHAPTER TWENTY

Alexander Hawkins

Alexander Hawkins wasn't born a Colonel, but maybe he should have been. He was a fourth-generation soldier going back to the Revolutionary War.

Born on September 6. 1843, Alex spent his early days on the family farm on the border between Washington and Greene Counties in Pennsylvania.

He came by his military roots honestly because his earliest ancestor in America was Robert Hawkins, who arrived here in about 1715. He was smart and industrious, becoming wealthy in the bargain. Robert was well known as a strong supporter of the colony's fight for freedom from Great Britain. He put his money where his mouth was, donating over 2,000 pounds sterling to the cause.

Alexander Hawkins

But it wasn't only money he gambled with, he also risked three of his sons who fought in the Revolution, and lost one of them in that horrible winter at Valley Forge.

On the other hand, James Crawford Hawkins (1808-1891), the father of Alexander was a farmer and along with that, he was a carder of wool. Washington County, Pennsylvania, was at one time the center of the wool industry, with some of the finest sheep and wool in the world. James was a man of character and believed in hard work and impressed upon his family the value of frugality. Residing on the Hawkins homestead in East Bethlehem Township, he was an excellent steward of the land that had originally come to him via his father Thomas who patented the land in 1772 by the Commonwealth of Pennsylvania.

Alexander was the fourth of the Hawkins children his mother, Margaret Wise Hawkins (1818-1892), gave birth to. There were six more. First, there was Emeline W. (1837-1864), then Absalom W. H. (1839-1876), Cynthia A. (1841-1900), Elizabeth W. (1847-1877), James R. (1852-1916), and William Newton (1855-1922).

Alex made his way through the public schools and went on to prepare for college at George's Creek Academy, and then on to Waynesburg College. Working toward his future success was all he had on his mind until it was all blown up, literally by the attack on Fort Sumpter. The Civil War what the future had in store for a young man not even finished with his schooling. How would all this turn out? How long could this possibly last? How would it affect me personally? Me, Alexander Hawkins. What should I do?

Alexander L. Hawkins enlisted in the US Army and was mustered into Company K of the 15th Pennsylvania Volunteer Cavalry on August 30, 1862. One of a company of farm boys from Washington and Greene Counties, many of which Alex was well acquainted with.

Part of Co. K 15th PA. Volunteer Cavalry 1907 Reunion

The history of the 15th Pennsylvania Cavalry is unusual and confusing. There isn't time or space to get into that mess, so I'll give you some of the highlights to give you an idea. The men were hand picked by officers of an independent troop named Anderson Cavalry. The men had to submit letters of recommendation by prominent local citizens to be considered.

They originally were supposed to be part of the Anderson Cavalry and be part of the 1st US Cavalry. Anderson Cavalry decided to remain independent, however. So only companies B through G mustered into the 1st US Cavalry. The rest had no commissioned officers and were equipped with only sabers, about half of those then in camp were sent to help out the Army of the Potomac during the Confederate invasion of Maryland. Those four hundred men were issued horses and carbines and were used as pickets near Hagerstown. Those men returned to Carlisle for more drilling and to await their next assignment. They ended up serving in Tennessee and Kentucky and all over with the Department of the Cumberland.

They had a mutiny while at Nashville over still not having enough commissioned officers and non-commissioned officers. About 415 of them were jailed for a short time for insubordination. Eventually, it got worked out and they provided great service throughout the war. They captured Confederate General Braxton Bragg, and were on the hunt for President Jefferson Davis.

Private Hawkins worked his way up through the ranks, first as Corporal, then quickly rising through the other non-commissioned ranks until he was named acting Lieutenant while in Nashville. Later at the battle of Nashville, he was serving under General Thomas with the rank of Captain.

He remained in the service after the war ended as a staff member of Major General Clinton Fisk. He finally mustered out on January 21,1866. Following the war, he opened a drug store in Pittsburgh, but that didn't last and after two years he sold his store and returned to the family farm in East Bethlehem Township. On February 4, 1869, he married Miss Cynthia H. Greenfield of Beallsville, PA. They had three children born to them as follows: Clyde E. (1869-1950), Jessie B. (1871-1946), and Frank B. (1874- 1929).

Alexander was taken with politics and served at various times as the Chairman of the County Republican Committee. In 1875, he was elected Treasurer of Washington County, and also began service with the 10th Pennsylvania National Guard.

Back in 1872, Company H, the local company of the 10th, was disorganized and demoralized to a point at which it was close to being retired. However, Major Wilson spoke up and recommended that Alex Hawkins be named commander. Alex knew about organization, as he agreed and received his commission on January 1, 1877.

Hawkins quickly whipped them into shape and they were used to put down the Pittsburgh riot. He was elected Colonel in February of 1879 and was re-elected in 1884, 1888, and 1894. During his twenty years of service as commander of the regiment, Alex never missed an encampment or was absent at any function the regiment was a part of. He commanded during three inauguration ceremonies in Washington, DC, Garfield, Cleveland, and Harrison.

Colonel Alexander Hawkins

When President McKinley issued his call for volunteers for the Spanish- American War, Colonel Hawkins once again rode to the sound of the guns with his regiment. They were the only regiment from Pennsylvania that was selected to go to the Philippines. While aboard ship, he was elected to the Pennsylvania State Senate.

While in the Philippines, Colonel Hawkins was taken ill. He was urged to return home to recover but refused to leave his boys. While on board the transport ship "Senator" Alexander Hawkins died on July 18, 1900. He was only fifty-six years old.

His eldest son, Clyde, was educated in Washington PA, and was in his junior year at Washington and Jefferson College when he received his appointment to the U S Military Academy at West Point. He graduated from there with the class of 1895 and was stationed at Fort Riley, Kansas. He served in the United States armed forces starting in 1891. Then the Spanish American War of 1898, the Philippine Insurrection of 1899-1900, the Cuban Occupation of 1901-1902, the Moro Campaigns 1911, and was Colonel of the 352nd Infantry, 88th Division during World War I from 1917 and served overseas from August 8, 1918, until July 31, 1919. He retired from the US Army on March 15, 1928.

Colonel Clyde Hawkins

Being single, he retired to live with his sister, Jessie, and her husband, Robert, in Beaver, Pennsylvania. By 1940, he was living with his sister, his niece, and a servant in Terrell Hills, Texas. Clyde passed away on September 8, 1950. He was eighty years old.

Clyde's brother, Frank, has much the same story to tell. He was born in Beallsville on June 14, 1874.

He graduated from Washington and Jefferson College with the class of 1896. He enlisted in Company H of the Tenth Pennsylvania National Guard while still a student and he rose to the rank of First Lieutenant, which he held as the regiment entered the US service in the Spanish-American War. He rose to Captain of Company D and still served during the Philippine Campaign and the Insurrection that came after. When that ended, he remained in the regular army as a Second Lt. in the Third infantry, and later 1st Lt. in the 27th infantry. He continued in the army all his life, and in 1905 he married Miss Rebecca Streator of Washington County, PA. They had one child, a daughter named Emma.

He served in France during World War I from June 4, 1918, to July 20, 1919, first as a Captain then promoted to Major, then to Lt. Colonel, and then full Colonel. He saw action at St. Mihiel, Meuse-Argonne and the Toul Sector. Col. Hawkins was awarded five medals for Distinguished Service in the Philippines and World War I. He also was awarded the Distinguished Service Cross for his actions in the World War. Ten years later, he served for two years in Panama. In early November 1929, he be- came ill and was admitted to Walter Reed Hospital. His condition worsened and he passed away on December 7, 1929, he was only fifty-five years old. Rebecca went to live in Detroit. She is listed as a lodger in

Colonel Frank Hawkins

a family's home there. She passed on July 15, 1974, at the age of ninety-four in San Antonio, Texas. No mention is made anywhere of their daughter Emma.

Former Hawkins Home on S. Wade Ave. Washington PA.

Last but not least is Alex and Cynthia's daughter, Jessie. She grew up and on November 14, 1901, married Mr. Robert Weyeth Darragh 1870-1957, of Beaver, PA. He was a descendant of a signer of the Declaration of Independence. He had a long career as an attorney and judge in Beaver. He also was a delegate several times to the Republican State Conventions. He has many business interests in Beaver County, especially in banking and real estate. He also served on the Beaver School Board for eleven years. They had two children, Alexander Leroy Hawkins 1902-1994, and Elizabeth G. who was born in 1907. Jessie and her daughter Elizabeth were living with Jessie's brother Clyde near San Antonio Texas when she passed away on June 19th, 1946. Robert died in Washington PA in 1957.

So once more we see an entire family whose personal ambitions were tempered with the patriotism that won out the struggle between the two. They chose service before personal gain. And even today, we are all better off for it. The name of Hawkins is a name we shall always remember.

CHAPTER TWENTY ONE

John McConnell Berry

John M. Berry was born on January 14, 1839, in Cecil Township, Wash- ington County, PA. He was the son of John Berry (1805-1881) and Jane Eagleton Berry (1812-1844). John was one of three brothers and two sisters along with one half brother.

This family has one of the best stories of the Washington County, PA. veterans. A long history beginning even before there was such a thing as America. Let's begin at the beginning, shall we?

John's Great-Great Grandfather John Berry, was a native of Ireland and came to America before it was America, near the be- ginning of the Revolutionary War. He arrived in Lancaster, PA, and before even settling in, he enlisted in the Continental Army for five years as a Private with Colonel Daniel Broad- head's 8th Pennsylvania Regiment.

John McConnell Berry

While at Valley Forge during the win- ter of 1777-1778, he married Miss Elizabeth Gilmore. She and her sister had immigrated on the same ship as John Berry had and all three of them were present at Valley Forge that winter. The sisters were serving as nurses, but there is a record of Elizabeth also carrying a rifle at times as well.

John Berry and Elizabeth were married in 1780 and both served in the same Company for the remainder of the war. There are records of her in the Pennsylvania archives that show her being paid as a "Ranger on the Frontier." The Rangers were created by the Pennsylvania Constitution as a militia and were provided arms and uniforms by the state. They would patrol the western parts of the state and protect settlers from Indian attacks. Elizabeth is on record as participating in several battles and remained with the Rangers for four years after the war ended.

She and her husband John settled in Washington County in 1794 and after two years purchased land owned by George Washington. They had eight children: William, John, Elizabeth, Nancy, Isabelle, Mary, and Ann. John Berry passed away on June 7, 1809, and Elizabeth joined him on August 21, 1824.

William G. Berry (1781-1866), married Jane McConnell and nine kids came from that marriage. John (1805-1881), James (1828-?), Matthew (1823- 1914), Prudence (1821-1885), William (1819-1898), Jane (1817-1888), Elizabeth (1815-1898), Mary (1810-1893).

The eldest son John was married three times and had five sons and two daughters. In 1829 he married Jane Eagleton with whom they had Jane (1833-?), Rachael (1835-1909), William (1837-1906), "our" John Berry (1839- 1912), David (1841-1864) and Carson (1843-1922).

His second wife was Mary A. Barr (1824-1864). They had only one child, Joseph (1858-1881). His third wife was Miss Sarah Logan (1820-1880). They had no children.

Private John Berry

Now we come to the Honorable John McConnell Berry, the main subject of this chapter. John grew up on the family farm in North Strabane Township, now grown to 187 acres. In August of 1862, he enlisted in Company G of the 140th Pennsylvania Volunteer Infantry and served with his regiment until he was severely wounded in the left shoulder at Spotsylvania. He was present at the "Bloody Angle" and was supposedly one of those to breach the Confederate works.

Thure de Thulstrup. "Battle of Spotsylvania and the Bloody Angle."

The battle at Spotsylvania Court House was one of the most brutal and horrific engagements of the entire Civil War.

The action at the "Mule Shoe" and "Bloody Angle" on May 12, 1864, occurred in a steady rain which affected the powder in the soldier's rifles and they wouldn't fire reliably.

The fighting was hand to hand with many being clubbed to death and the most bayonet wounds of the entire war. The bodies on both sides piled up three and four deep on each side of the parapet with wounded in among the corpses trying to wriggle free of their ghastly tangle.

The Union soldiers were desperate to dislodge the Rebs, and the Rebs were determined to hold on at all costs. Men were being fed into the giant meat grinder at an alarming rate and the casualties were astounding.

General Ambrose Burnside

Private David Holt of Mississippi wrote this vivid account of his experiences: *"We were in the V-shaped salient that had traverses thrown up to prevent an enfilading fire. The line was mended, and we [had to] keep it mended. Soon the Yanks made a determined charge with fixed bayonets, but the mud fought for us. "The breastwork was in a bog, and to make a charge in such a place against a line of fierce men close up, who have no idea of giving way, was more than those gallant Yanks could do. Many of them were shot dead and sank down on the breastworks without pulling their feet out of the mud. Many others plunged forward when they were shot and fell headlong into the trench among us. Between charges we cleared the trench of dead and wounded and loaded all the guns we could get hold of for the next charge. I was shooting seven guns myself. We stacked them up against the breastwork with the butts on the trench, and when the Yanks came, we picked them up one by one and fired and sent them down again. Many times we could not put the gun to our shoulder by reason of the closeness of the enemy, so we shot from the hip. All the time a drizzling rain was falling. The blood shed by the dead and wounded in the trench mixed with the mud and water. It became more than shoe deep, and soon it was smeared all over our clothes. We could hardly tell one another apart."*

A Union staff officer wrote later: *"The appalling sight presented was harrowing in the extreme. Our own killed were scattered over a large space near the angle, while in front of the captured breastworks the enemy's dead, vastly more numerous than our own, were piled upon each other in some places four layers deep, exhibiting every ghastly phase of mutilation. Below the mass of fast-decaying corpses, the convulsive twitching of limbs and the writhing of bodies showed that there were wounded men still alive and struggling to extricate themselves from the horrid entombment. Every relief possible was afforded, but in too many cases it came too late. The place was well named the Bloody Angle."*

Spotsylvania Earthworks Near the "Bloody Angle."

John spent six months in the hospital, then went to Washington City and served in the Veteran Reserve Corps. He served until he was mustered out on June 28, 1865.

After returning home, he went to work on the farm as a farmer and prominent stock raiser, mainly interested in sheep.

He served as President of the Pennsylvania Wool Grower's Association, and for ten years he was President of the Black Top Spanish Merino Breeders Publishing Association.

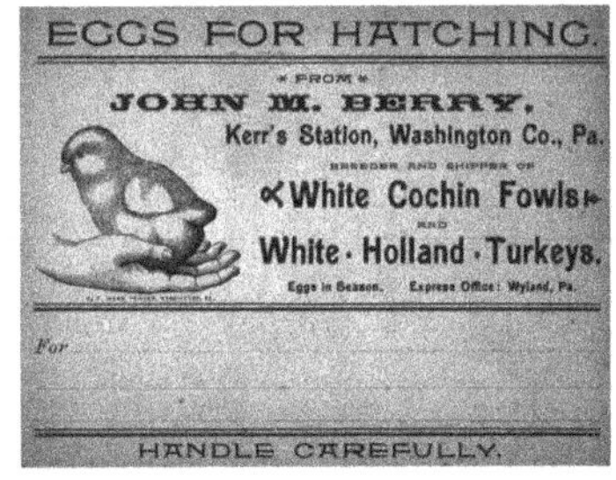

If that wasn't enough, he was also a member of the Washington County Agricultural Association and the Canonsburg Association. He served as the crop reporter for the US Department of Agriculture in Washington, DC, as well.

If that wasn't enough, he also sold and shipped White Cochin Fowls and White Holland Turkeys, plus eggs for hatching.

Mary Weir

John married Miss Mary Weir of Somerset Township. They had a son, Samuel, who died at the age of one year. They sadly also had three others that died in infancy. They did have Minnie Jane born in 1875 and John in 1878 and William (1881-1970).

John Berry was also interested in politics and served on the township Board of Assessors and as a member of the Republican County Committee for nine years. He spent eighteen years as Justice of the Peace beginning in 1885, before he was elected to the state legislature in 1902.

Interestingly, in 1890, he built one of the most modern homes in Washington County at that time. It was said to be "finished in natural woods and equipped with all the latest improvements in plumbing with hard and soft, hot and cold water in both the first and second stories.

John M. Berry Home and Family

ca. 1890

Squire John was a Sunday School teacher at the United Presbyterian Church at Pigeon Creek, as well as an Elder in that church. John had been ill for about a week in March of 1912. He recovered but unexpectedly passed away from heart and liver failure at home on March 16. He was seventy-three years old.

His older brother William, born February 23, 1837, was interested in sheep raising as well. He lived on the family farm in North Strabane Township. In May of 1862, he married Miss Jane Barr. Sadly, she passed away on August 26, 1865. Three years later, William married Martha Patti- son (1840-1910), and they settled on a farm near Clokeyville where he continued raising and breeding sheep. They had five kids: Margaret (1868- 1950), David (1869-1964), Robert (1872-1966), Mary Etta (1876-1933), and Martha "Pearl," (1879-1933).

He was able to put all his children through college. William had health issues and he passed away on April 5, 1906, at the early age of sixty-nine years.

David Berry, born in April of 1841, never married but he too lived on the family farm and attended the local schools. He entered Jefferson College in Canonsburg and studied through his sophomore year when, along with his brother John, he enlisted in Company G of the 140th Pennsylvania Volunteer Infantry. He was present at every engagement up to Cold Harbor, where on June 2, 1864, he was mortally wounded. He was treated in a hospital in Alexandria, Virginia, where he passed away on July 4, 1864.

William Berry

David Berry

The battle of Cold Harbor was yet another in the Summer of slaughter that comprised the Overland Campaign. General Grant had about 120,000 troops with an unending supply in the pipeline.

General Lee had about half as many with no more available anytime soon. Grant sent wave after wave of men against dug in veteran Confederate troops. The union men got mowed down time after time, "like hay before the scythe." It was a disaster for Grant, losing ten percent of his army about 12,000 men or more. Afterward, he lay in his bunk and wept.

General U. S. Grant

Now, we have Carson Berry, born on December 22, 1843, who resided on the family farm in his youth. On November 22, 1871, he married Miss Abigail Thome Boyd. They settled on their farm in South Strabane Township. They had three children: Alvin (1908-1909) and the twins Bankhead (1878-1938) and Elizabeth (1878-?). Carson was a prominent Republican like his brothers and was very active in their church, Emmanuel United Presbyterian Church. Abigail passed away in 1910 at the young age of seventy. Carson followed her, passing on April 25, 1922, of the "infirmities of old age."

Carson Berry

Again we see a family of strength, courage, and the desire to help their fellow man. They served their nation with courage and honor and spilled their life's blood in the hope that the Union might live on.

We shall always remember them.

David W. Berry

John M. Berry

Carson Berry

Abigail Boyd Berry

Martha Stewart Pattison Berry

William Berry

Church Elders. Back Row, Wilson Meyers, Adam Weir, Will Martin
Front Row. James Pollock, Rev. Comin, John M. Berry

CHAPTER TWENTY-TWO
Major A. G. Happer

Of all the prominent families in Washington County, Pennsylvania, the Happer family from the time of the very first settlers in the county, through the first half of the twentieth century had no match in virtually any civic endeavor, or efforts to advance the welfare of the community.

I can say here and now with one hundred percent confidence that Major A. G. Happer accomplished far more than any other person in the history of Washington County when it came to achieving remarkable results that had an incredible and permanent effect upon the entire City of Washington and the County at large. Applying his extraordinary vision and other abilities to the betterment of the entire County, and the entire State of Pennsylvania, Happer improved the lives of every one of his fellow citizens. But, I'm getting ahead of myself. Our story should begin with the beginning. To understand who Major Happer was, you must know the history of what came before him and who and what his ancestors were.

Major Andrew G. Happer

If I left that out, I would be doing you, and the people involved, a great disservice. So let's begin shall we? John H. Happer was born in Ballygawley, County Sligo, Ireland in 1745 to Robert and Isabel Happer. He took up the weaving trade and in 1778 at the age of thirty-three, he married Miss Margaret Paton, 25 of Lonmay in Aberdeen Scotland. They set up housekeeping and he plied his chosen trade. The following year, their first child came along, a son they named Andrew Patton. For nine more years, they lived and worked as more children came, Agnes in 1781, Baptist in 1783, and John in 1786. Weaving was a good trade, but things were tough in Ireland for the Happers. John and Maggie decided that a better life was possible in America. Who wouldn't?

Leaving his family in Ireland, John set sail for the land of opportunity in 1787. Planning ahead, he had applied for and was granted a Pennsylvania Land Grant for three hundred and sixteen acres in what is now Union Township, Washington County, Pennsylvania. Union Township was a bustling and prosperous farming community near a big bend in the Monongahela River in the southwestern corner of Pennsylvania.

John cleared enough of his land to build a cabin and sent for his family to come to America. They arrived safely the following year, and they all worked together to clear the land and start building a farm they named, Happerwell. In 1789, they were blessed with another child they named Jennet. Their first tragedy struck when little Jennet died before her third birthday. In 1793, Jane came along, and in 1812, Samuel arrived.

The family had what they needed to survive, making most of that themselves. Whatever they couldn't make had to be packed over the mountains on horseback. They probably had very little furniture, the fireplace and a punched tin lantern with a tallow candle provided what light they had after dark. For food, they had what game they could take in addition to what they could raise on the farm. They ate a lot of cornmeal mush and beans as well. When there was salt, they could cure pork, and they made a kind of Rye coffee from what was then the predominant grain in the area. Corn, cabbage, taters, and some wheat were grown as well. Later on, Barley became popular as well. Travel was by horseback or on foot.

By the 1840s, sheep were imported into the county, the Saxony breed mostly. A little later, Spanish sheep from Vermont arrived with their heavy, greasy black-tipped wool. In 1891, the Dorset-Horn breed was imported from England, and Washington County began furnishing breeding sheep to all the wool producing states in the country. Large flocks were driven to Iowa and Illinois after the Civil War, and Texas and Kansas received shipments as well. Washington County sheep were known worldwide for their fineness, density, weight, and overall quality. At one time there were over 600,000 sheep in the county, and John Happer was proud to have a good sized flock of his own.

In the 1790 census, the population of Washington County was about 24,000, including 263 slaves. Most of the population was of English, Welsh, Scottish, German, and Irish descent, with a few Dutch and French as well.

Mingo Creek Presbyterian Church

John and Maggie along with their children of course were very involved not only with farming but with the creation and welfare of the local church. They helped organize the *Mingo Creek Meetinghouse,* known today as the *Mingo Creek Presbyterian Church,* in 1786. It was a log building that stood not far from where the present day *Mingo Creek Presbyterian Church* is. It stood fifty feet wide by fifty-five feet long. John Happer as well as his grandson John Arrell, the father of A. G. Happer, were Elders in the Mingo Creek Meeting House. The Mingo Militia met in the Meeting House on July 15, 1794, and left to incite open defiance against the Federal Government, thus setting into motion the events that tested our young republic for the very first time. Many notable Revolutionary War and Whiskey Rebellion figures are buried in the Mingo Cemetery. In the fall of 1794, John and many of his friends and neighbors had to swear an oath of allegiance following the Whiskey Rebellion. They swore that oath before none other than General Henry "Light Horse Harry" Lee, the father of Confederate General Robert E. Lee.

John and Margaret Happer worked their farm and produced a very successful and prosperous enterprise to hand down to their children. John passed on August 25th, 1818 at the age of seventy three. Margaret passed away on May 12, 1838, she was eighty five. They are both buried in Mingo Cemetery near Finleyville, Washington County.

The Happer Farm in Union Township, Washington County, Pennsylvania

One thing about the Happers. Most of them had large families, and they all named children after relatives, so there are always multiple people with the same names. Along with that, various branches and generations would name children after the same ancestors, sometimes with variations in spelling. This makes telling their stories somewhat confusing. So, if you see names spelled differently, it probably isn't a typo, it's the correct spelling. I'll try to keep this as simple as I can. We'll pare this down to the most relevant people, even though others may well have interesting stories of their own. It would be great to tell every bit of the incredible history of all the Happers, but that will have to happen in a future book.

I'll focus in on John H. Happer's son Baptist, born July 15th, 1783. Baptist grew up working with his father on the farm. He married Miss. Nancy Ann Arrell on September 21, 1801. They produced six offspring, all of which led very interesting lives. There was Sarah 1809-1849, John Patton 1811-1812, John Arrell 1816-1890, the father of A. G. Happer, Andrew Patton 1818-1894, we'll delve into his story in a minute. It's too good to overlook. James Edward 1821-1876, and Margaret Jane 1823-1903.

Sarah married Mr. Thomas Gault on October 6th, 1834. They moved west to Sangamon County Illinois and had seven kids. Sarah passed away on January 25th, 1849 at the young age of only thirty nine years.

Margaret Jane ended up marrying a distant relative, Mr. David Breading Arrell in 1846. They had seven children. They too moved west to Illinois, eventually settling in Moline in 1887. David died there in 1899. Margaret passed away on October 28th, 1903. She was eighty.

James Edward Happer married Miss. Mary Ann Gardner 1823-1883. They too journeyed west to Illinois where they began their family which totaled six children. John Gardner 1848-1917, Sarah Adeline 1849-1937, Mary Caroline 1849-1919, Lura A. 1853-1927, Andrew Francis 1854-1903, and Margaret Helen "Maggie" 1860-1935.

James took the boat to St. Louis and from there to Illinois where he bought a hundred and sixty acres of land which included a cabin already on it. In 1837, he returned to Washington County for his bride Mary Ann.

James Edward Happer

John Gardner Happer

They became very prosperous and were well thought of by all who knew them. Jim was an Elder in the Farmingdale Church, and Superintendent of the Sunday School for many years. He served as School Trustee for four years. They had acquired two hundred and forty acres of the best farmland in the county, when James died at the early age of fifty five on May 20, 1876. Mary Ann remained at home until she passed on June 20th, 1883. She was only fifty nine years old. No info is available on why they both died so young.

Sarah Adeline Happer was born in Farmington, Illinois. She married Mr. John Parsons 1848-1914, in March of 1873 and they had eight children. Harriet 1874-1964, Edward 1876-1880, Mary 1878-1969, Isaac 1882-1948, Carrie 1883-1961, John 1885-1957, Leila 1889-1974, Margaret 1892-1892.

Mary Caroline Happer was born in Manhattan New York on July 29, 1849. In 1870 she married Mr. John Storrs Lyman 1841-1907 in Sangamon, Illinois in 1875.

Sarah Happer Parsons

John Lyman served in the 101st. Illinois Vol. Infantry. They had four kids, Edward H. 1872-1961, Nellie C. 1875-1878, Frank L. 1879-1950, and Mabel A. 1883-1936.

Lura A. Happer was born on Christmas Day 1853 in Gardner Illinois. She married Mr. William Simms 1854-1929, of Kentucky. Four children were the result. There was Florence May 1879-1945, Adele 1881-1970, Nellie 1883-1967, and Jack Happer Finley 1887-1952.

Next is Andrew F. Happer, who was born in Gardner Illinois as well. He was a farmer and married Miss. Ida V. Harrison 1856-1949, of Richland Illinois. They produced two children, James H. Happer 1886-1970, and Mary M. 1891-1973.

And last but not least we have Miss. Margaret Helen "Maggie" Happer, from Farmingdale, Illinois. She has a strong resemblance to her sister Lura. She grew up and married a Medical Doctor, Dr. Elijah Aaron Morgan 1854-1918, of Niantic Illinois. They had two daughters, Marie H. 1887-1957, and Helen G. 1889-1956.

Rev. Andrew P. Happer

Andrew Patton Happer 1818-1894 was a different story altogether. His parents, John H. and Margaret being devout Presbyterians, especially his mother, heavily influenced his life. His mother pushed him toward the ministry at an early age, and by the time he was eleven, she sent him to the ministry prep school at Jefferson College.

He graduated from there in 1835 and went on to teach school for five years. From 1840 to 1843, he studied theology at Western Theological Seminary, was licensed to preach, and then ordained to the Presbyterian ministry in 1844. Then he went on to earn his medical degree at the University of

Pennsylvania. The opening of China to the West, due to its defeat in the Opium War, presented an opportunity for Reverend Happer. He decided that China was the place to begin his missionary work.

After a four month voyage, he arrived in Macao. There were only two other Presbyterian missionaries in southern China at the time, and the Reverend Happer made three. Happer ended up taking over the Morrison Education Society in Hong Kong. After about a year, he moved back to Macao, where he established a boys' boarding school. He had two Chi- nese teachers working for him teaching the classics to 27 students. In early 1847, Happer moved his school to the outskirts of Canton. Canton itself was closed to foreigners. While it proved difficult to convert the Chinese to Christianity, they were open to education and medical care. With the assistance of a Chinese doctor, he opened a dispensary, and within five years he had become one of the pioneer medical missionaries in China.

In November of 1847, Happer married Elizabeth Ball of the American Board of Commissioners for Foreign Missions. They had six children together: Andrew, Lucy, Lillie, Mary, Alverada, and John, all born in China. In 1854, the Happers opened a second dispensary and were now treating over 10,000 patients. This pleased the Reverend of course. "A widely spread missionary influence is exerted in this way. The sufferings of many persons are relieved, and the Christian in- structions addressed to them by their benefactors have been in many cases received with grateful attention." That year, Happer turned the dispensaries over to a young missionary, Dr. John Kerr, who eventually built a major medical center out of the foundation laid by Reverend Happer.

Happer built day schools as a way of attracting Chinese from the higher classes. He offered them both Chinese and Western education. The Happers' health had been suffering for some time. The Reverend decided that a brief return home would be in order. They returned to the United States in 1855. Their good health returned, but war had broken out in China again before they could return there. The war lasted until 1860, but the Happers returned to China in the fall of 1859.

The results of the war finally gave Happer access to Canton where he founded the First Presbyterian Church in 1862. In the next two years, he established both boarding and day schools in the city along with a training school for teachers and preachers.

For the rest of his career in China, the training school produced his dream of Christian higher education in China. Happer had a desire to provide Western education to the future leaders of China as well. For two years, he headed the Chinese government's Interpreter's College in Canton. He taught Math and English to special students preparing to enter government service. The Chinese were being more receptive to Happer's work and his efforts showed steady growth. Just as things were looking up, disaster struck. In 1864, Elizabeth became ill. It was decided that she would return to America for treatment. On the voyage home, she passed away, leaving her husband of seventeen years and their five children back in China. Reverend Happer had his hands full taking care of the children and continuing his work, so he had to send the children home to Washington County. He followed them home a year later in 1867. Happer did not think he would ever make it back to China to continue his work. However, he met and married Miss A. L. Elliott. The Happers returned to China in 1870 where he continued as pastor of the First Presbyterian Church. The schools Happer started had reached about a thousand students by 1884, and the hospital had performed some 1200 operations.

Things were going well professionally for the Reverend, but his personal life was a shambles. In October 1873, his second wife passed away. He continued with his work and in March 1875 he married his third wife, Hannah Shaw. She was a Presbyterian missionary in Canton.

By this time, Happer had a national reputation in China. He began to write about current events and issues with theology, and Chinese culture. He translated Presbyterian statements of faith and parts of the Bible, and Confucian classics. His growing prominence landed him a job as editor of the Chinese Recorder and Missionary Journal, the most important Western language periodical in China.

He also was elected President of the Chinese Religious Tract Society in 1880. His writing expanded into books and pamphlets published by the Presbyterian Press in Shanghai. After 1870, Happer commented a great deal on Chinese relations with the West, often taking the Chinese side when a conflict would arise. He did not approve of the way the Western businessmen acted in China, nor the way Chinese were treated in America. Over the years Happer had come to admire much about the Chinese. He believed that China would eventu-ally come to "a position of power and wealth in the future which she had never attained in the past."

Happer now had a new vision. He wanted to start a Christian college in South China. He received resistance from Presbyterian ranks, so he decided to found a non-denominational college. In November 1884, Reverend Happer and his wife, both very ill, returned to the United States. After several months, their health improved and he started a fundraising campaign for the college he had in mind. The advertised purpose was "to train a class of man that will renovate and Christianize China."

By June of 1886, he had raised over $110,000.00, and he became its first President. The Happers returned once again to China in 1888. He had given thought to locating the college in a larger city such as Shanghai, but a large outpouring from Cantonese officials convinced him to stay in Canton. He once again in 1890 gave thought to relocating the school, but his declining health prevented him from moving it. Reverend Happer left China for the last time in late 1891. The college eventually became Lingnan University and remained in Canton. Andrew Patton Happer D.D; M.D. died in Ohio on October 27, 1894.

Reverend Happer was a gruff and somewhat distant man, but he took pride in his children, two sons Andrew Patton Jr. and John Stewart, and four daughters Lucy, Lillie, Mary, and Alverada. His elder son Andrew Jr. tried missionary work for a time, but it wasn't for him and he went to what was then Peking and became Imperial Commissioner of Customs. He traveled extensively and passed away sometime before 1904.

John Stewart Happer became a businessman who worked for Standard Oil. He went to Japan in 1891 and fell in love with the country and in particular the woodblock prints of artist Ando Hiroshige. These prints were unknown in the West and Andrew became a world renown authority of Hiroshige's art. In fact, his friends called him Hiroshige-Happer. He was transferred to London in 1904, but by that time he had collected several thousand of the prints. He used the prints for exhibitions and to illustrate lectures on Japanese art. John returned to Japan in 1909 where he met and married Mabel Bacon of San Francisco. The couple was never blessed with children and made Japan their home until John passed away in 1936. Interestingly, Happer was cremated and had his ashes placed at Togaku-Ji, a Zen Buddhist temple in Tokyo, right beside the grave site of his favorite artist. On his marker reads the inscription that John Stewart Happer himself picked," Here lies one who loved Hiroshige."

Reverend Happer's daughter Lucy married George Glover but suffered from poor health and died in childbirth. Mary Rebecca married Frank W. Damon of Honolulu, Hawaii whose father Samuel was a missionary who landed in Hawaii in 1841. They settled there, raising two sons and two daughters: Mary Violet Happer, Daphne Mills, Cyril Francis, and Bernard. They all traveled quite a bit, but they all made their homes in Hawaii.

Mary Violet married Dr. Franklin L. Putman, a well known Honolulu doctor. They had a daughter, Geraldine. Her brother Cyril was a well known financier and business leader. Daphne lived in Hawaii, as did Bernard who married Charlotte Baldwin. There are Damons and Happers in Hawaii still today.

John Arrell Happer

The last of Baptist Happer's sons, John Arrell Happer was born on the farm on October 1, 1816. He inherited his father's love of the land and was particularly interested in the breeding and raising of livestock. He was the first to bring Berkshire hogs into the area, and among the first to introduce Durham cattle (now called Shorthorn) in Union Township in addition to his herd of sheep. He attended the local schools and then on to attend Jefferson College. He became very active in the local schools and served on the school board for many years. He was also an elder in the Mingo Creek Presbyterian Church. In 1838, he married Miss Violet Gardner of Allegheny County, Pennsylvania. They had eight children: Andrew Gardner; Margaret, Mary Belle, Oliver Paulinis, Frank Arrell, Elizabeth, John Wilmer, and Ella Blanche. He served in the state legislature in 1861 and 1862, then came home to continue his life's work as a gentleman farmer and stock raiser. He remained active in community affairs and was held in high esteem by all who knew him. He passed away on November 11, 1890. Violet joined him five years later.

Margaret, born on October 14, 1841, married the Reverend John J. Beacom in 1868 and moved to Allegheny County, Pennsylvania, and later to Ohio. They had two children, Frank Happer Beacom born in 1870, and Mary Beacom born in 1875. Frank became a clerk in the Revenue office and Mary married Reverend George Rowland. Reverend Beacom passed away in 1902 and the family moved back to Coraopolis, Pennsylvania where Margaret died in 1927. Mary and George had two sons George Jr. born in 1910, and John born in 1914. Mary passed away in 1968, and George Jr. in 1996. John died in 1979. Frank married Elizabeth Speer and they had a daughter Margaret born in 1905. Frank died in 1934, and his daughter Margaret in 1976.

Mary Belle was born on October 12, 1843. She married Dr. George Cheesman (1829-1910) and they lived in Allegheny County, Pennsylvania. They had two sons and two daughters: Mary Bertha (1874-1940), Leroy Happer (1875-1945), Harry Cameron (1879-1942), and Helen Violet (1884- 1921). Mary passed away in 1920. Leroy served with the 10th Pennsylvania Volunteers in the Spanish American War. After the war, he attended the Western Pennsylvania University, now the University of Pittsburgh. He graduated in 1903 as a Doctor of Medicine. He became a prominent surgeon at Passavant Hospital in Pittsburgh. In 1909 he married Laura Drake Boehm and had a daughter, Dorothy, who died in infancy. In 1919 he was commissioned as a Captain in the U.S. Medical Corps, but the Great War ended before his services were required.

Helen married a farmer named Louis R. Smith (1881-1966) in 1909. They lived in Union Township, Washington County. Lewis became a carpenter in a coal mine. They had one son, Robert Leroy, born in 1910. He married a woman named Mary and they lived next to his parents. He was a machinist in a coal mine. Robert passed away in 1978.

Oliver Paulinis was born in 1846. Not much is known about him. He attended Princeton University in 1870 and died in June 1877.

Francis Arrell Happer was born on January 12, 1848. In 1874 he married Miss Emily Foster. They lived in Westmoreland County, Pennsylvania, for several years where they had four children, John, Henry F, Mary, and Florence (1883-1939). Sometime around 1890 they moved to Mobile, Alabama where he was the Chief Clerk in US Engineers Office. Francis passed away in 1923, and Emily in 1914.

John, born in 1875, married Miss Zuelma Ball, (1870-1968). They lived in El Paso, Texas where John was a real estate agent. He tried his hand for a few months working on the railroad in North Dakota, but that wasn't for him. He returned to his family in El Paso and sold real estate. He went to Washington D.C. for the Chamber of Commerce in 1920. He apparently liked the D.C. area and he settled down there to sell real estate once again. They had a son and two daughters: John Millard (1899-1974), Lydia Gardner (1901-1997), and Mary (1904-1965). John Millard "Jack" Happer went to Yale. He left school in 1918 to join the US Navy, where he served only a year before returning to El Paso and becoming a banker.

Lydia Gardner Happer was an interesting one. She married a military man, a Captain named Maxwell Davenport Taylor. Theirs is a story that is interesting and historic.

Francis's son, Henry F. Happer, never married and became a car salesman in Pittsburgh. Francis's daughter, Mary Happer lived in Pittsburgh and became a stenographer, then moved to Illinois where she married an attorney named John Macauley. Francis's other daughter, Florence Happer, however, had a very interesting life. She married an Englishman named Alfred P. Rose. Apparently, it didn't work out and they were divorced in about 1915. She moved to Evanston, Illinois where she became a copywriter. During WWI, she was a secretary for the International Committee for the YMCA and was sent over to England and France to work for the canteen there. In 1920, she married a man named William James Morden (1886-1958) of Chicago. His family was in the railroad equipment manufacturing business. William started out working with his family, but not for long. He was an explorer at heart.

They moved to Bronxville, New York, where he became a director of the Explorer's Club and was an honorary fellow at the American Museum of Natural History. He led an expedition to the Yukon Territory in 1921 in search of White Sheep. He didn't stop there, he led six major expeditions. In 1926 he went to Asia. Then, on to the ancient city of Angkor in Cambodia, Africa, Pakistan, Tibet, Burma, Sri Lanka, and India. These expeditions were filmed and are available at the AMNH. Florence died in 1939. William remarried and went right on exploring until he died.

John Arrell Happer's son, John Wilmer Happer, was born on January 23, 1858. At the age of 45, he married a woman named Sylvia and they lived in Lancaster,

Pennsylvania where John worked as a lumber salesman. They moved to Harrisburg, Pa. around 1920. John died in August of 1933 when they were living in Waynesboro, Pa.

Andrew Gardner Happer

John Arrell Happer's eldest son, Andrew Gardner Happer was born on August 15th, 1839, on the farm in Union Township. Little is known about his early childhood except he possessed the same love of the land as his parents and grandparents did. As a boy, he roamed the farm with his father, taking it all in and learning about all things agriculture. He did the typical farm chores all boys had to do, splitting wood for the stove, milking the cows, helping to plant in the spring and harvest at the end of summer into the cool crisp days of autumn when the leaves turned all the colors of the artist's pallet. This instilled in him a lifelong desire to be close to the land.

He was an excellent student in the local school and was an active participant in the affairs of his church, yet another interest that would last all his days. In 1859, he enrolled in what was then Washington College in Washington, Pa. Even though it was his first time away from home, it wasn't all that far away, and he was able to visit with family often. He breezed through his classes, learning about all the things that interested him.

There was more to this, however. Even though the Happers were spread out all over the country and overseas as well, they all knew each other and kept in touch. A. G. Happer was well aware of the success that his grandfather and father and many of his relatives and ancestors had achieved. He knew that much was expected of him, that he was to carry on what had become a tradition of accomplishment and service.

Many of us are aware of the saying, "May you live in interesting times." Usually referred to as an ancient Chinese curse, there is some disagreement, but it probably is an American invention going back only a hundred years or so. Be that as it may, it relates to the times that A. G. Happer found himself. The year 1860 was a time of great debate and turmoil, a real powder keg that was rapidly coming to a head.

The election of Abraham Lincoln that fall lit the fuse and sealed the deal, and the country was blown in half, North and South along the Mason-Dixon Line which runs only a few miles south of Washington County.

The following spring, Fort Sumpter was fired upon and the shooting war began. A twenty-two year old young man just starting out in life was trying to make heads or tails of the whole thing. What was he to do? Stay in school and pursue his dreams or heed Lincoln's call for troops and join the army. What happened at a small town southeast of where he was, called Manassas, Virginia probably made his mind up for him. For young A. G. Happer, "interesting" would not begin to cover the rest of his remarkable life.

A. G. Happer was enrolled in school at Washington & Jefferson College when the Civil War broke out. As a student, he of course followed all the newspaper accounts of the political and military events of the day as did everyone else. His primary interests however still lie in agriculture and business.

Andrew had other things on his mind this day. The secession of the southern states had troubled him greatly. What troubled him, even more, was the rout of the Union army at Bull Run. Like a lot of people, he had figured the war to be a short affair. Now, he wasn't so sure. He wanted to continue his education, he had big plans. His father, uncle, grandfather, and the rest of the family being so successful, was putting pressure on him to measure up. He wanted a career in business and agriculture. However, it seemed his country needed him. Everyone said it would be a short war, go ahead and sign up, it's only three months. Yes, he was anxious to start his life's work, but his patriotism won out, and he went ahead and enlisted in Company K 1st Pennsylvania Volunteer Cavalry. He didn't know it then, but this would not be a brief detour on the road to his dreams. It would be a life changing decision. Andrew was never to return to school or earn his degree.

Under the command of Colonel George D. Bayard, late of the 4th US Cavalry, the men trained with saber and revolver throughout September. Carbines were issued only ten per company at first. Gradually, all the men were equipped with carbines. Most of the horses were chosen by the company commanders, with the remainder chosen by Colonel Bayard from the U. S. stables in Washington.

The regiment was stationed at Tennallytown until October 10 when it moved to Camp Pierpont Va; attached to McCall's division. On November 27th, Colonel

Bayard was ordered to scour the area around the village of Dranesville. The area was reported to be a hotbed of guerrilla activity. After surrounding several houses and conducting a search, several suspicious persons were arrested. On the march for camp, the column was ambushed by guerrillas hiding in the roadside thickets seeking to release the prisoners. Men from D company were dismounted and sent into the woods after them. In a short time, they killed or captured all the guerrillas. Private Joseph Hughling of Company D and Assistant Surgeon Samuel Alexander were killed, and two men were badly wounded. Col. Bayard was slightly wounded in the action.

On December 20, 1861, Federal Brigadier General George McCall dispatched a Brigade under Brigadier General E. O. C. Ord, reinforced with two cavalry squadrons and a battery of artillery, to forage in the vicinity of Dranesville. At the same time, Confederate Brigadier General J. E. B. Stuart patrolled north from Centreville with four regiments of infantry, a detachment of cavalry, and one battery of artillery. The two forces met at Dranesville. Of the 1st Pennsylvania Cavalry, only companies C, D, E, H, and I were involved. Companies A, B, F, G, L M, and Company K with A. G. Happer were left behind in camp. Stuart's Confederates were eventually driven off by the Federal artillery, and General Ord's Federals held the field.

The 1st Cavalry mostly spent the remainder of the winter in camp, waiting for the spring campaign to begin. However, when it began, they would be without A. G. Happer. In April 1861, following Lincoln's call for troops, ten companies from six counties altogether nearly a thousand men arrived in Harrisburg, Pennsylvania, and were formed into the 11th Pennsylvania Volunteer Infantry. The men quickly elected their field officers, selecting Fhaen Jarrett as their Colonel and Richard Coulter as their Lieutenant Colonel. The regiment's Chaplain, Reverend William H. Locke, kept a dairy and wrote a partial history of the regiment after the war.

"Companies A through G rendezvoused at Camp Curtin, where they were mustered into the State service during the months of July and August 1861, and then moved to Camp Jones, near Washington DC. Three companies H, I and K, rendezvoused at Camp Wilkins, near

Pittsburgh, where they were mustered into the State service during the month of August, and soon after joined the other companies at Washington DC." "The Eleventh Regiment of Pennsylvania Volunteers was thenceforth a corporeal reality. From the 23d of April, 1861, to the surrender of General Lee at Appomattox Court House, the history of the "Old Eleventh" so designated to distinguish it from the Eleventh Regiment of the Pennsylvania Reserve Corps is the history, in part, of all the grand movements of the Army of the Potomac."

The 11th belonged to the Department of Pennsylvania under the command of Major General Robert Patterson. Three days after organization, they were assigned to duty on the Baltimore and Wilmington rail road. When the Confederate army soon after captured Harper's Ferry, a general alarm took hold of both Pennsylvania and Washington city. The 11th was relieved of guard duty and marched through Baltimore and Washington to Hagerstown, and assigned to Abercrombie's Brigade of Keim's Division.

General Patterson's army was given the task of retaking Harper's Ferry. On the morning of June 1st, General Patterson's men stepped off with a spring in their step toward the Potomac. The rebels however had other plans. The Confederates had pickets along the Potomac up as far as Shepherdstown. As soon as the 11th moved out, Confederate General Joseph E. Johnston evacuated Harper's Ferry, falling back to Martinsburg. Patterson began to pursue Johnston's troops, crossing some seven or eight thousand troops over the Potomac. Patterson was halted however by a message that Washington was threatened and he must detach his Artillery and Cavalry to General Scott. Once the troops across the river had been recalled, General Patterson had to sit and wait it out.

The Confederates moved right back up to the Potomac near Shepherdstown under the command of Colonel Jonathan T. Jackson. General Johnston was headquartered at Bunker Hill with the reserve. About the third week of June, Patterson had received a battery of six guns and a small detachment of cavalry. He was finally ready to resume his forward movement. On July 2, 1861, the entire force crossed the river at Williamsport with little opposition. Advancing with skirmishers out in front, rebels could be seen in the distance falling back. The column reached Falling Waters, Virginia that afternoon. Turning a sharp bend in the Martinsburg Pike on the Porterfield farm, the pickets confronted both pickets and the main body of Colonel T. J. Jackson's Brigade consisting of the Second, Fourth, Fifth, and Twenty-Seventh Virginia regiments. Also, J.E.B. Stuart's cavalry regiment and Captain Pendleton's battery of four guns. The 11th Pennsylvania and the 1st Wisconsin led the way on either side of the pike, with Hudson's battery in the middle of the road. At the sound of the guns, with shouts and cheers the federal line went forward toward the rebel line drawn behind the Porterfield house.

Stuart's cavalry tried to flank the 11th but with no success after several tries. The fight became general with all federal troops moving forward, extending their lines toward Jackson's flanks. After a sharp fight of about an hour, Jackson had to retire.

It was after this battle that the 11th Pennsylvania regiment won the distinction for meritorious service and earned the nickname "The Bloody Eleventh."

The 11th was present at every engagement of the Army of the Potomac. They saw heavy action at Antietam, Fredericksburg, Chancellorsville, and Gettysburg. They were in the thick of the fighting at all these battles and served with distinction. A. G. Happer was present in every instance. He was wounded in the famous "Bloody Cornfield" at Antietam, but refused to leave his men.

Mr. Miller's "Bloody Cornfield" Today

In the after Gettysburg lull, when General Grant took over the Army of the Potomac, a restructuring took place but the 11th Pennsylvania remained together.

On the 20th of March 1864, the 11th Pennsylvania reassembled at Harrisburg, Pennsylvania, and men, an aggregate of five hundred and eighteen men. On the 3rd of April, the regiment rejoined the brigade at Culpeper, and also at this time, our Lieutenant A. G. Happer was promoted to Captain A. G. Happer of Company I, of the 11th Pennsylvania Volunteer Infantry.

The Battle of the Wilderness is the defining moment of the character of the two army commanders. Generals Grant and Lee finally coming head to head, eyeball to eyeball, locked in a struggle of immense importance. We now come to one of the most historic moments in the entire Civil War. The fact that Captain Happer was present illustrates the unusual number of times he seemed to find himself in the midst of those moments that withstand the test of time and are remembered still today.

The 11th PA was loaned temporarily to General Hancock, who had Confederate General A.P. Hill's Corps on the defensive. General Heath's division was nothing more than a thin skirmish line hunkered down along a low ridge in the huge smoky briar patch. Hancock launched an all-out assault on Hill's line in the all but impassable jungle of the Wilderness. Hancock's men charged again & this time the Rebs couldn't hold and fled back toward their artillery in their rear.

Baxter's Brigade with the 11th Pennsylvania in front had reached the Orange Plank road and was charging toward the meadow to their

General Winfield Scott Hancock

front, where Lee could see them coming. General Baxter fell, severely wounded in the chest, and carried from the field. Brigade command fell to Colonel Coulter, and command of the 11th went to Major Keenen. Law's Alabamians whooping across the field with the rebel yell struck Baxter's Brigade and sent them streaming back. Some of Wadsworth's men ran all the way to Grant's headquarters at Lacy Meadow, where Grant remained on his stump, whittling as he had been doing all day yesterday and so far today. Wadsworth himself was shot in the head near the meadow. His men left him on the field where Confederate troops carried him to an aid station where he died two days later.

General Henry Baxter

It is most likely, all things considered, that it was in this part of the battle that Captain A. G. Happer of Co. I, was wounded and fell. Captain Happer was very seriously wounded this time. He was hit low in the abdomen and suffered a broken pelvis. He could not even sit up, let alone stand, and walking was out of the question. The battle lines wavered back and forth in the middle of this dark and smoky tangle. In all this confusion, it's no wonder he was left behind what became enemy lines when Law's men drove the Union right back. Baxter's Brigade fell back some distance, where they were ordered to support the left.

That night, when darkness fell, the night wind came up again to fan the embers into flames. Worse than the night before, the underbrush ignited and the fire spread quickly. The moans of the wounded were punctuated with screams of terror as men too injured to escape the flames were caught and burned to death. The cartridges in their cartridge boxes ignited and cooked off, sounding like skirmishing fire. Volunteers and stretcher bearers did all they could to pull the wounded that were reachable from the flames. Just one more bit of horror the exhausted men of both sides had to deal with as they lay on their arms in that briery inferno. Over two hundred men both blue and gray were incinerated that long and dreadful night. Later, skeletons were found with rifles turned around pointing at their skulls. Unable to escape, and pulling the trigger with their feet, they shot themselves rather than burn to death.

Somehow, miraculously, Captain Happer survived that hellish night. As the blue and gray armies moved off on their race to Spotsylvania, Captain Andrew Happer still lay on the field severely wounded. Somehow, he had escaped the fires of the previous night. He had given up calling for help that never came.

Skirmish In The Wilderness by Winslow Homer 1864

His throat was parched anyway. He was resigned to whatever fate had in store for him. If his life was to come to an end here, at least it would be for in his mind the greatest cause of all, freedom.

But this is not where his story ends. By some miracle, a slave stumbled upon the Captain by accident! He had a canteen and gave Happer a drink. Looking over his wounds, he washed them & cleaned them as best as he could. Captain Happer passed out and when he awoke, it was dark and the man was gone. Oh no, he thought. He's left me for dead. All night, Captain Happer lay there, hearing off in the distance now the moans of the other wounded, waiting to die.

Dawn broke and the old slave was back. This time he had a piece of hardtack along with water. While Happer did manage to eat the food, the man poured water over the wound, cleaning it out, then Andrew drank again. He once again tried to move Happer to no avail. He at least was able to make him a little more comfortable. He placed his coat over his wound to keep the dirt out and then left saying he'd be back tomorrow to check on him.

True to his word, the man returned the next afternoon with more hardtack and water. Captain Happer asked him if he could bring someone to help. The man cleaned the wound yet again and left. The following morning, he returned. This time he was in a hurry. He gave Happer some hardtack and hurried off. The Captain would never see him again or even know his name. Just then Andrew could hear some noise and voices nearby. A Confederate ambulance and men were picking up the wounded from both armies, it wasn't long before they stumbled upon Captain Happer. They rolled him onto a stretcher and carried him to the ambulance with some other wounded.

Happer was taken to a Confederate field hospital where he lay on the ground with the others until a surgeon could see him. They put him on a makeshift table made of an old shed door. They had some chloroform and dripped it onto some cotton over Happer's face. The surgeon examined the wound and probed for the ball. He decided that the ball was lodged in the pelvic bone, which was broken, and could not be removed, and the wound would in all likelihood be mortal. Happer was set outside in the shade to await his fate.

Andrew G. Happer survived yet again. The wound had not become infected. The surgeon told him *"Whoever cleaned your wound has saved your life, for now."* He remained at the field hospital for some time. Improving bit by bit. He could not move much without great pain, but he was able to be propped part way up for short periods to receive what nourishment the Confederates could provide. At some point, he was loaded on a wagon with others and moved to the hospital at Libby Prison in Richmond.

Libby Prison

The hospital at Libby prison wasn't much of a hospital at all. The inmates got to lie on a straw mat on the floor instead of lying on the bare floor. Some of the hospital rooms held as many as 125 patients, lying shoulder to shoulder. All were kept in deplorable conditions by today's standards. Even though the conditions were bad, they were no worse than the conditions found in the Federal prisons up north. Southern prisoners suffered just as badly up there, as the Union prisoners did down in Richmond. A fact very much glossed over today.

Happer's condition improved little while in prison. In fact, he started getting worse as his confinement went on. The bone fragments in his shattered pelvis had started to knit back together some, and his bullet wound was healing sufficiently to allow him to sit up enough to sip some weak broth. That and the lack of serious infection is what saved his life so far. He had a long way to go before he would be out of danger. The longer he had to stay at Libby, the greater the chance that disease and infection would send him to the boneyard like so many others. It seems that Happer's luck held for him because, after only six months, he was paroled with other sick and wounded prisoners. Prisoners were to be shipped up north on one of the steamers used for that purpose. Still unable to walk, of course, Happer was transported to the dock in a cart where he was unceremoniously dumped onto the deck of the ship to fend for himself.

The Captain passed out from the pain and remained unconscious for the entire voyage up the Chesapeake and into Annapolis Maryland. Camp Parole it was called. Confederate prisoners when paroled were allowed to simply go home to wait to be exchanged, then they could

Camp Parole

return to their regiments. On the Union side, however, when this was done, it soon became apparent that many soldiers would disappear into the civilian population never to return to their regiments. It was decided to keep the men under military control until they were exchanged. So in June of 1862, they built a camp of eight wooden barracks for paroled prisoners from New England and the "middle states." At first, the camp was established on the campus of St. John's College. The men were brought in by steamer and the first thing they did was to remove their clothes. These they simply threw into College Creek, where for decades afterward, fishermen would be reeling in the discarded boots of the men.

The camp soon proved to be entirely too small and quickly became woefully overcrowded. A new camp was built on a 250-acre parcel of land on the outskirts of Annapolis near the Elkridge- Annapolis railroad. The new camp included a 168-bed hospital. The camp eventually became a sort of way station for exchanged prisoners and paroled men before being moved to other facilities. In 1864, General Grant ended all paroles once and for all, so by June of 1865, there was no more use for the camp. The hospital remained until the patients either died or were well enough to be sent home. Nothing remains of the camp. The Annapolis Towne Center shopping mall occupies the site today.

Captain Happer arrived in October 1864 and was sent straight to the hospital. He finally received the care he needed and slowly recovered from his wounds for the most part. The Confederate mini ball was never to be removed, and he carried it for the rest of his life.

Captain Happer's Eleventh Pennsylvania Volunteers were heavily engaged in all the battles of the Army of the Potomac as they slowly fought their way toward Petersburg. When that city finally fell, they marched through Richmond and participated in the battles leading to Appomattox where they were present at the surrender of the Army of Northern Virginia. At least what was left of them. They went on to march May 23rd in the Grand Review in Washington and were mustered out finally on July 1, 1865.

The Court Martial Board

Captain Happer wasn't with them of course, and he wasn't mustered out either. The army wasn't finished with Captain Happer it seems. In March 1865, he was given permission to stay with the army during his recuperation and was detailed to report to Harrisburg to serve as the Post Adjutant in the office of the Chief Mustering and Disbanding Officer for the Western Division of Pennsylvania. While there, he impressed his superiors with his abilities, diligence, and work ethic. He also served on the Court Martial Board.

The summer of 1864 was one of turmoil in Pennsylvania. In the central part of the state, there was widespread resistance to the military draft of 1863. Some 618 citizens were drafted, but very few reported for service as ordered. There were also a significant number of army deserters in the area. An initial search for these men was conducted in Columbia County by a Lieutenant Robinson and several civilians. They could not find the men they were looking for but the alarm had gone out about the search & a group of citizens opposed the searchers. One thing led to another and there was an exchange of gunfire. Lieutenant Robinson was wounded and later died.

When this news reached Harrisburg, a detachment of 48 soldiers was sent to the mouth of Fishing Creek near Bloomsburg to round up the deserters. Two days later, 250 more soldiers arrived along with Major General Darius Couch arrived. By August 21, 1864, there were about a thousand soldiers in the party. Scouring the county, the soldiers ransacked farms looking for the so-called disloyal men and their supposed fort.

Major General George Cadwalader arrived to take charge of events. Some 45 people were arrested and charged and sent to Fort Mifflin. As late as November, people were still being rounded up as deserters. On Election Day 1864, soldiers guarded polling places in Columbia County.

Military commissions were formed to try the accused prisoners. Over time, there were three courts set up for the trials. On January 10, 1865, the third court was seated to try a man named Valentine Fell. The court consisted of Lt. Colonel George Zinn, Lt. Colonel John Murray, and (then) Captain A. G. Happer. This entire series of events was a major story

PA Governor Andrew Curtin

statewide, with newspapers fanning the flames on both sides of the issue for years. Even decades later, the discord was still evident. It also had a major effect on the 1864 local and state elections. Large numbers of citizens who supported the draft resisters were denied their right to vote in many polling places by the soldiers posted there.

These events are little known today but were a major issue in the state at the time. This was included in the Histories of Columbia and Montour Counties published in 1887, The History of Columbia County From The Earliest Times, 1888, Civil War Dissent in Columbia County, 1991.

Pennsylvania Governor Andrew Gregg Curtin was a staunch supporter of the Lincoln administration. The commonwealth supplied more than 360,000 white soldiers and 9,000 black soldiers during the conflict. However, there was sustained opposition to the war throughout the state, much of it fanned by the pens of Democratic newspaper editors. Though most opposition was disorganized and spontaneous, other aspects of the antiwar sentiment in the state occasionally erupted as major incidents.

Presient Abraham Lincoln

In Columbia County, Pennsylvania in 1864, egged on by the anti-Lincoln newspaper editors, a number of men avoided the draft and formed ad hoc groups to protect themselves from arrest. The shooting of a Union lieutenant confronting draft evaders in July 1864 resulted in military intervention in the northern townships of the county. The troops arrested more than one hundred men, sending about half of them to a prison fort near Philadelphia. Some of these men were subjected to military trials in Harrisburg, the state capital, that fall and winter. The arrests led to bitter feelings that were slow to die. The military intervention eventually impacted a Pennsylvania gubernatorial election and led to a murder trial.

The President of the United States was assassinated at Ford's Theater on the evening of April 14, 1865. Captain A. G. Happer was not yet recovered from his wounds suffered in the service of his country. Nevertheless, he had finished his duty serving as a judge in the draft resistor trials and was serving in Harrisburg Pennsylvania in the Mustering Out department as Post Adjutant and on the Court Martial Board.

Plans had been made for the departure of the President to be taken home to Springfield on a special train called the "Lincoln Special," or "The Lincoln Funeral Train." The train would travel from Washington City to Baltimore then to

Harrisburg Pennsylvania, Philadelphia, and on to New York and various other cities westward, taking the slain President back home.

The Lincoln Funeral Train

As the train entered each new state, that state's Governor would embark with his own staff and invited guests if any. On April 21, 1865, Pennsylvania Governor Andrew Curtin would have the train make an unscheduled stop on the PA border at about 5:30 p.m., where he would board with his staff of the following men.

Adjutant General A. L. Russell, Inspector General Lemuel Todd, Surgeon General Joseph G Phillips, Major General Cadwalader commanding the Department of Pennsylvania, Colonel R. B. Roberts, Colonel S. B. Thomas, Colonel Frank Jordan, and Colonel John A. Wright. Not noticed or paid attention to by reporters, being a mere Captain lost in a virtual sea of politicians and Army brass, was A. G. Happer.

Captain Happer was personally invited by Governor Curtin to accompany him on the Lincoln Funeral Train as recognition of his arduous and

Brevet Brig. Gen. J. B. Kiddoo

outstanding service. His painful and extraordinary ordeal of being severely wounded and left on the battlefield for dead and then unable to move, thrust into the hands of the enemy for six long months of confinement in Libby Prison with little or no medical treatment. Governor Curtin did not invite any other soldiers in this way. There was only one. Captain A. G. Happer. On September 1, 1865, the following letter was sent.

Headquarters Military Post of Harrisburg, PA. Sept. 1, 1865 Brig. General E.L. Townsend Asst. Adj. General USA. *General, I have the honor to recommend Capt. A. G. Happer of the late 11th PV for the appointment to the rank of Major by Brevet. I know of no officer in the volunteer service of his rank who has a better record or is more justly entitled to promotion. He entered the service as a private soldier at the commencement of the war, passed honorably through every grade to his present rank non- commissioned included and participated with gallantry in the battles First Bull Run, Dranesville, Thoroughfare Gap, Second Bull Run, Chantilly, South Mountain, Antietam at which battle he was wounded, but refused to leave the field on account of being left in charge of his regiment as senior officer with the rank of 1st Lt. Fredericksburg, Burnside's Advance, Chancellorsville, Gettysburg, Mine Run, and the first and second days battles of the Wilderness in the latter day of which he was severely wounded and left on the battlefield for dead, fell into the hands of the enemy and suffered all the barbarities of Rebel imprisonment for several months. While still suffering from wounds, he was ordered to this post for duty and acted in the capacity of post adjutant for some time. I take great pleasure and consider it my duty to report him as a most competent, faithful and gallant officer, and respectfully insist that he receive in justice to him and the government he has so faithfully served, the promotion above recommended.* I have the honor to be very respectfully Your obt servant, Brvt. Brigadier General, J B Kiddoo

There were several other letters of recommendation from senior officers sent along with the above letter, and several other endorsements written along with the letters. The Assistant Adjutant General forwarded all this to Army headquarters. It's quite apparent that the soldiers that Happer served with all thought very highly of him, both on the battlefield and later. The recommendations were quickly approved by order of Lieutenant General U. S. Grant on September 21, 1865. Captain Happer was now Major Happer. Not long after this, on October 20, 1865, Major Happer was finally mustered out of the service. The war was over.

Part Two

This was perhaps the most spectacular time of the year for Major Happer to arrive home. Southwestern Pennsylvania in late October is a splendid array of the most brilliant colors imaginable. The hills are painted with the deep reds and browns of the oak leaves, the dazzling yellows and golds and scarlet reds of the sugar maples, the wine red of the dogwoods that dot the hillsides, the pale yellow of the chestnuts that dominated the woods at that time, before the blight took them all away. Splashed here and there with the deep greens of the pine and hemlock stands, the countryside was a sight to behold. The hog butchering was done, and fresh hams, pork shoulders, and slabs of bacon were hanging in the smokehouses. Kettles of soap were being rendered over the fire in the farmyards, along with iron kettles full of bubbling apple butter that the ladies would put up. In the spring house, crocks of freshly churned butter would be lined up in the cold spring water beside perhaps a can of buttermilk or two. The "punkin" patches and apple orchards were a splash of color in the tans and browns and grays of the landscape in the valleys. Fields of feed corn dotted the landscape, some harvested, some not yet cut, providing food and cover for the deer, raccoon, and the occasional black bear that roamed the area. The farmers didn't mind the deer so much because although they did eat quite a bit of corn which was supposed to feed the farmer's cattle and other livestock over the winter, the farmer hunted the deer for the meat and they were an important source of food and leather, so in a way the deer were yet another farm animal. The air was cool and crisp, with the scent of all the ingredients of the season in every breath. It was a very pleasant time when the backbreaking labor of the long hot summer was mostly done, and folks were making ready for the long, cold winter to come.

The Major stopped and stood in the yard. Home, finally home. After four long years of war, the contrast of where he now was, and where he had been and experienced these last four years was not lost on him. It was like stepping into a different world. What he had seen of Virginia last year was very different from what he saw around him here and now. Virginia, once a commonwealth of great abundance, was now stripped bare by the war. Barren and spent in the great effort, it was now rendered a mere shadow of what it once was. The Major knew it would take years before it recovered if it ever would.

The Major would take some time to rest and to think. There was still some recovery to be made from his battle wounds. It was a miracle he was even alive and able to stand and walk. He knew that the old man in the Wilderness was responsible for saving his life. He had tried but was never able to find out his name or who the man was.

He had to give his mind some time to process all that had happened and to figure out just what exactly he wanted to do with his life. His previous plans were all now a distant memory. In the last four years, he had done so much, and seen suffering never before seen in America. It seemed he had lived an entire lifetime. But he was only 26 years old and had a long way to go.

He went from being a student in a small school in Pennsylvania, to a Major in the U.S. Army, and accompanying the slain President in only four years, that was a lot to try to comprehend. He had been a real-life witness to history. Not only was he present in most of the major battles fought during the Civil War, he was in some of the hottest spots in those battles. He had seen the horror of what war was really like, very different from the fiery rhetoric spewed by the politicians and the newspapers in every town and city. He had seen his friends, boys he had grown up with, blown to bits. He had heard the rattle of musketry and felt the ground shaking thunder of cannon. He had smelled the gunpowder and peered through the smoke. He had heard the zip of Confederate minis whizzing past his head. Oh yes, he had indeed "seen the elephant." He'd known the shock and pain of being wounded and still didn't know just how in the world he ever made it out alive from Miller's cornfield at Antietam. Jumping over the wall on Oak Ridge and charging the Confederates at Gettysburg just seemed like the right thing to do at the time, orders or not. Being left for dead in the Wilderness was the lowest point for the Major, naturally. But somehow, the man upstairs must have had something important for him to do. There must have been a reason he was able to survive his devastating wound, and be found by a kindly stranger and then endure months in prison, to be returned to relative health and to be recognized by his fellow soldiers, and to be finally able to go home. There must be something more, some purpose for him to go through all that and come out alive. That was what the Major had to discover. What was he to do now? He had some serious thinking to do, and this farm was the place to do it.

The Major, everybody around these parts called him Andrew or Andy, and he went by A. G. but that would soon change. The Major was not able as of yet to perform the heavy labor required to work the farm. He did what he could to help out his father, who retired from the state legislature to become a gentleman farmer along with one of his other sons, Wilmer.

The Happer farm was the largest and most prosperous farm in the area, but all the neighboring farmers were friends and helped each other out. The McVays and the Kennedys, the Nicholsons and Klinefelters, the Pattersons and the others all worked their farms in friendship and cooperation with each other. Most of these men and others right from the beginning were heavily involved with the Mingo Creek Presbyterian church built just a stone's throw north of the farms as well. These men had a thriving little community going for them and worked to keep it just the way they wanted it.

While John and Wilmer Happer managed their farm and coal interests, A. G. decided he was ready for, and needed gainful employment. There was a spot open for the office of Assessor of Internal Revenue. Based in Monongahela, Pennsylvania, and from 1866 until 1871, the Major tried his hand at being a bureaucrat. He figured that position would allow him to be of service yet accommodate his still lingering physical problems. He quickly realized that this was not for him, and only served one term. His father had warned him about being involved with a nest of vipers in the political world. He had found out firsthand what that was like. No, the business world was what he wanted, and to somehow use that to be able to help others.

The Major realized that to fulfill his dreams, he must branch out from the farm. He had to go live and work in town where there were opportunities for a budding entrepreneur. Instead of moving north to the big city of Pittsburgh, he wisely went just south to Washington, Pennsylvania. In Pittsburgh, he would be just another anonymous "go-getter" in a big crowded city. In Washington, however, he had family ties to the community, was closer to home with more support structure, and the much smaller city had more chances for him to start and grow a business.

The Last Stagecoach Between Washington and Pittsburgh.
Major Happer was on there somewhere.

In addition, Pittsburgh was only about 35 miles or so north, and while a stagecoach had run between the two towns, a railroad line was now under construction, so really, he had the best of both worlds. In fact, the Major being the Assessor of Internal Revenue was invited to be on the last ride of the stagecoach. On May 18, 1871, the "Queen of the Road" made its last run on the old Pittsburgh Pike. The next day, the first train from Pittsburgh steamed into Washington.

The Major's Offices at 55 South Main Street Washington PA. Today

A. G. Happer opened a small insurance office at 55 South Main Street, Washington, Pennsylvania, in 1871 where he pretty much just sold insurance at first. By happenstance, one of the events that helped him was the Great Chicago Fire that occurred on October 9th and 10th, of that year. Over three hundred people were killed and one hundred thousand were left homeless, about a third of Chicago's population at the time. This shocked the nation and brought to mind the good idea of having fire insurance for people all around the country. Interestingly, the Chicago fire wasn't the only, or largest fire that took place in the same few days. Three other major fires occurred around Lake Michigan. The Peshtigo fire destroyed the town of Peshtigo, Wisconsin, and about a dozen other small towns nearby. One and a half million acres were destroyed and upwards of 2500 people were killed, making it the deadliest fire in American history. East of Chicago, Holland, Michigan, and the surrounding area burned to the ground. Manistee, Michigan also burned and was afterward called The Great Michigan Fire. Port Huron, Michigan, and most of the "thumb" of Michigan's mitten burned. About one hundred and forty miles to the south, fire swept through Urbana, Illinois. Windsor, Ontario, Canada also burned on October 12, 1871.

Donations poured into Chicago from all over the country. In Washington County, Major Happer led the way and helped collect over two thousand dollars for the Chicago Relief Fund, along with food and clothing for the citizens of Chicago.

Miss Matilda Morgan Watson of Washington, Pennsylvania. She was born on April 21, 1849, in the Watson house on the south side of East Maiden Street, just east of the corner of Main Street in what was known as "Morgan Row." "Tilly," like most of the ladies of the upper crust, attended the public schools of Washington and then the Washington Seminary. She graduated with the class of 1867.

Right from the start she was interested in music and also took part in all the various philanthropies around Washington. While the Happers were prosperous, well known, and well-to-do, the Watsons were even more well known and were considered the same.

Andrew and Tilly Happer's First Home Today

The Watson pedigree is very impressive. Matilda was the daughter of James Watson, a very prominent attorney in Washington County. He was born in Canonsburg, Pennsylvania in 1809, and graduated from Canonsburg College. He practiced law with the Honorable Thomas McKennan of Washington. When McKennan was elected to Congress, Watson became senior partner and managed the firm. McKennan served four terms in Congress.

In 1835, Mr. Watson married Miss Maria Woodbridge Morgan, daughter of George Morgan and Elizabeth Aldrich Thompson. George Morgan was the son of Revolutionary War Colonel George Morgan of Princeton, New Jersey. After the war, Colonel Morgan came with his wife Mary Baynton Morgan and family to Washington County, where he took up farming in North Strabane until his death in 1810. The James Watson family moved into a stately brick house at 42 West Maiden Street in Washington.

Major Happer by this time, had grown his company into the largest insurance agency in the county. Matilda Watson knew an "up and comer" when she saw one, and they were married on November 7, 1877. They lived at the Watson house until the Major built a large house at 405 E. Maiden Street in Washington. It was a magnificent red brick home of 6,600 square feet, and had sixteen rooms. He also built two more homes next door that were sold. While this was happening, Major Happer also had built what was called "A magnificent house of Cleveland Stone." This one was built at 130 East Wheeling Street in Washington.

The Happer's "Magnificent House of Cleveland Stone" Today

It was a large, Queen Ann style home that was off the chart beautiful. Both these homes still stand today. The stately red brick house is now privately owned and the E. Wheeling St. home is now owned by Washington & Jefferson College.

By 1888, Happer began to build even larger real estate projects to enable the growing county. He teamed with friends E. F. Atcheson and James Kuntz Jr. to purchase the Wearer farm which they renamed West End. This development went so well that they continued on with several others. They bought some Morgan property adjacent to East Washington. The land was subdivided into lots where they constructed beautiful Queen Ann style homes, many of which are still standing today. The area then became it's own Borough known as East Washington.

It eventually had its own schools, and police department. So the Major was responsible for the formation and construction of an entire Borough.

And that's not all. The area was sorely in need of commercial development. A. G. Happer and his partners bought the 220 acre Gordon farm. They divided it into 1,500 lots and filed it with some of the top manufacturing companies in Pennsylvania. This made the local economy boom! The jobs were there and there were homes for the workers. This became a magnet for growth and opportunity in Washington County. This also made Major Happer the largest real estate and insurance company in Southwestern Pennsylvania.

Original Morganza Administration Building

The Pennsylvania House of Refuge had been in what was then Allegheny, Pa; right across the Allegheny River from Pittsburgh, since 1854. Created as a reform school, it had, by 1872, outgrown the surrounding area. The Major became interested in helping the children and young people that were there and soon to be displaced. Appealing to Pennsylvania Governor John Hartranft, and using some five hundred and three acres of what was a part of the old Colonel Morgan estate named "Morganza," Happer was able to move the school there. There was to be a main building, a girls department, a boys department, a church, workshops, and a lot more.

In July of 1873, the corner-stones were laid amid much ceremony which included a speech by the Governor. By fall 1876, four main buildings were completed and by December the institution was officially moved to Morganza, with Major A. G. Happer serving as President of the Board of Managers, a post he held until he retired in 1911.

Morganza During Major Happer's Management

In 1907, the Pennsylvania legislature made an appropriation to increase the size of the school. After seeing how well the school handled the education, training and social development of the children, Other Counties soon sent children to Morganza to take advantage of the excellent facilities available there, making it a statewide influence. According to the "History of Washington County" "The boys of the school have done a vast amount of work within the last few years, forming thereby habits of industry and learning, at the same time useful trades." During Happer's tenure there, the school had available an industrial department, stenography, typewriting, telegraphy, bricklaying, blacksmithing, mechanical and architectural drawing, woodworking, printing, and domestic science. It also provided religious instruction. A farm was established and the residents learned agrarian skills. They also had a band that marched in parades, sports teams and participated in pageants ad other social events. In the years following Major Happer's death, the school fell into decline and was eventually taken over by the state and its reputation suffered dramatically. Treatment became harsh and it was used for purposes other than what Major Happer had envisioned. Later, it was even used in the feature film "The Silence of the Lambs" and finally closed for good in the year 2000. The entire facility was raised in 2012. Even the hill upon which it stood has been leveled. All that is left today is a small and lonely cemetery holding vigil in a neglected patch of weeds.

Citizens National Bank

Citizens National Bank was organized by Major A. G. Happer and some of his business friends on September 12, 1885 in Washington Pennsylvania with an opening capitol stock of $100,000.00. Citizens was the third National Bank organized in the County. By October first, it had deposits of $25,864.34, and resources of $92,426.43. When the bank was organized, Washington was still a small town, but the bank quickly became a huge factor in the accommodation of both local merchants and the encouragement of manufacturing and industrial operations.

Soon after the bank opened, oil was discovered, and the town boomed with prosperity. Incidentally, Major Happer was heavily involved with that oil discovery and the development of what became the largest oil industry in the country until the Spindletop strike in Texas. Washington PA was the center of the world's oil industry for many years. Citizens Bank was instrumental in assisting the oil men in prospecting and building up the industry. Major Happer was the founder and served on the bank's Board of Directors for many years and was heavily involved with its operations. With sound management, by 1908 the bank boasted profits and surplus of over $1,000,000.00, and resources of over $4,225,848.20, making it at that time the largest financial institution in relationship of surplus to capitol, in Washington County, the eighth largest in the Commonwealth of Pennsylvania, and the eleventh largest in the United States of America. Citizens Bank prospered all through its existence, even during the Great Depression. Finally, it was purchased by banking giant Mellon Bank in 1948.

The Major wasn't finished there. He also founded the Washington Trust Company. Trust institutions are chartered by the Commonwealth of Pennsylvania and although they do operate a general banking business, they also act as trustees, administrators of estates, and executors and other fiduciary activities. The Washington Trust became the most suc-

The Washington Trust Building Then

cessful trust in the county and ranked among the largest in the entire state of Pennsylvania. The Board of Directors had some of the same people as did Citizens Bank, and that included, of course, Major Happer. At one time, Washington Trust owned the largest building in the county, at the corner of Main and Beau Streets.

Washington PA in the late 1870's was a hub of activity. The National Road ran right through town, linking the "other" Washington (DC) with Ohio and the West. One of the constant and major problems, however, was there was no major medical treatment to be had between Pittsburgh, some thirty-five miles to the north, and West Virginia. There simply was no viable medical care anywhere in

The Washington Trust Building Today

the area. One had to travel long distances to find a hospital of any size to provide treatment for serious and emergency needs.

There had been an attempt by several doctors to start a hospital in Washington, but they were only able to raise a few dollars and the effort soon fizzled out. Miss Nellie Reed who had aided the effort left their meager funds with Major Happer in case there was ever enough interest to revive the project.

In early 1897, three physicians renewed the call for a hospital. This time, however, the Major jumped on board with several others and wouldn't let the idea die. A charter was granted to Washington Hospital. There was to be a board of directors to run the hospital. The first order of business was to secure a building. The board had no money to either build or purchase one. It was decided to purchase the A. W. Acheson homestead on Acheson Avenue for $10,000. The Major used the money left in his care as seed money and he and several other men, advanced their personal funds to purchase the building. The property was deeded to A. G. Happer first as he had advanced practically all the money, also John Slater, Henry Schoenthal, Dr. George Kelly, Dr. J. Y. Scott, and J. B. Brittain as trustees until the debt could be paid off. Which it was, and in only two years, March of 1900.

The Washington Hospital opened in May of 1898. It was very small, with only twenty beds in all, with no real operating room. Surgery was performed in a spare room. Individuals and institutions were allowed to establish rooms for public use that they were responsible for maintenance and upkeep. They had their names painted on the door. There was a door with the name Happer.

Washington's First Hospital.

Founded by Major A. G. Happer

Major Happer was Board President for many years and oversaw the day-to-day operations of the hospital. During his tenure, the hospital prospered and successfully served the population of the entire region. Later, a larger building was built and the facility grew large enough to treat patients from all over Pennsylvania. The hospital has expanded through the years and is now known as Washington Health System and has become one of the largest and most advanced healthcare facilities in Pennsylvania.

Washington Hospital Today

They have several locations throughout the area. Nationally known for excellence in cardiac care, patients from across Pennsylvania and America come to Washington

Hospital for care. Without the forward thinking, initiative, funding, and sound management of Major A. G. Happer, Washington Hospital as we know it, would not be here today.

At about the same time, a traveling salesman from Washington named F. H. Dyer led the push for starting a local post of the Grand Army of the Republic. A previous attempt by others had failed. Twenty- eight veterans applied for a charter and Post 120 was organized on March 27, 1879. Conspicuous among the members was Major A. G. Happer. The post was named in honor of Captain William F. Templeton, of West Middleton, the second captain of Company A, of the famous One Hundredth Regiment, Pennsylvania Infantry, known as the "Roundheads," who was killed while leading his men in the charge on the railroad cut at the second battle of Bull Run, Virginia, August 29, 1862. The G.A.R. post held their meetings at the Odd Fellows Hall, located in the Young building on South Main Street. The locations of the meetings changed over the years as the veterans began to show their age and couldn't climb stairs as easily. Finally, the county donated space in the courthouse for these old heroes to meet until they were all gone. The Major was a member in good standing for the rest of his days.

In addition to this, the 10th Pennsylvania Infantry was organized in 1873, as the Pennsylvania National Guard. Two companies of the Regiment A and H were located in Washington County. Company A in Monongahela, and Company H in Washington. Major Happer served in Company H. And he served as its Adjutant from March 15, 1879, to September 28, 1880.

Throughout his life, The Major was interested in all things agriculture. He was a member of the "Washington Society for the Promotion of Agricultural and Domestic Manufacture in Washington County." This society was organized in 1847 but didn't hold any fairs until 1852. In 1855, they purchased land known for years as the "fairgrounds." They had their fair there until they went under in 1884. Major Happer was the Treasurer for many years. The fairgrounds were purchased by Washington and Jefferson College and became their athletic fields. Interestingly enough, the old grandstand built in 1855 was burned in the fall of 1906 by students celebrating the Washington and Jefferson victory in football over the University of Pittsburgh.

"The Fairgrounds"

The Major didn't give up on agriculture. The Western Pennsylvania Agricultural Association was formed in 1885, and the Major was instrumental in getting that one started and was a member for the entire length of its existence. They purchased grounds for their fair, and by all accounts were the best in the state. The fair was successful for years but became more of an annual horse racing event. As the founders aged, the fair went into decline and the last one was held in 1901.

By 1884, it was plain as day to the Major that Washington was growing and was ready to boom. In times past, the town had looked to the past, focusing on its rich colonial history. Now it was time to look to the future. Times were changing, and the area was suffering some growing pains. It needed to expand but with careful planning and an eye on the future. He hired his friend, Henry Hood, to run the day-to-day business in the insurance office, while Happer was venturing out into the field of real estate, trying to develop the vast areas of available land in the area. His first venture was known as Kalorama, which he purchased and platted. He sold the lots for a handsome profit and was already on to his next project called Woodland where he did the same thing. He continued successfully developing land in small sections.

In December of 1885, Happer, along with T. F. Birch, B. M. Clark, John R. Kuntz and Harry Chambers applied to the Governor for a charter for The Citizen's Water Company. The charter was granted in January 1886.

The Waterworks

The Major had no desire to manage the company, so he sold the franchise to Samuel Hazlett, of Washington, George H. Fox, James McCullough, Jr., W. Pollock, and V. Neubert of Kittanning, Pa. for $6,750. The owners in June 1887 signed a contract with B. E. Adams of Wheeling to lay a ten-inch main line down Main Street. They purchased land on Chartiers Creek for a pumping station and storage dams. They also bought condemned land on the hilltop opposite the cemetery for a reservoir, where a twelve-inch line was laid down to the pump station. Pipe was laid in the city, and on December 1, 1888, the lines were filled with water for the first time. Customers were signed up at a rate of $4.00 per year.

The Ganz Oil Well

Below the ground of Washington County lies a vast oil and natural gas field. In 1861, the Eureka Oil Company drilled the first well. There were other wells scattered around the county. Nothing much became of this until 1882 when the Morgan Oil Company drilled a well in South Strabane Township. Located on the farm of Alexander McGugin. They struck a huge pocket of natural gas at about 2200 feet that blew the tools through the top of the derrick. It was the biggest gas strike in the world at that time. The roar could be heard for miles and the people said that it seemed that one of nature's wonders had been uncorked.

Due to the high pressure and volume, the men could not get the well capped. Then it got worse. It somehow caught on fire. The reflected light at night could be seen for miles around and people flocked to see it. The fire burned for over two years, some say four, without letup. It became a tourist attraction and trains brought in people from all around the surrounding area. Finally, a new well was drilled nearby and they were able to starve the fire out and cap the well. The new well was piped out to Pittsburgh and supplied that city with gas for many years.

This was the real beginning of the great oil and gas boom in Washington County. In 1884, Citizen's Natural Gas Company drilled a well near the Pennsylvania Railroad station on Chestnut Street. They struck oil this time and the boom was on for real. It wasn't long before there were over one hundred oil wells in the area. Farmers were taking advantage of all this with oil and gas leases. Some became rich almost overnight.

In 1884, the Wheeling Oil Company was formed, and Major Happer was one of its directors. Already being in the real estate business made it a natural add-on for his company. He had the expertise and contacts to acquire oil leases throughout the area. There were oil wells on the Happer farm and other family members' properties.

Oil Derricks Dot the Landscape in Finleyville ca. 1903

In 1885, Washington and Jefferson College bought the old Agricultural Fairgrounds of which the Major had been the Treasurer for many years. The college had wells drilled on what became their athletic fields. It stands to reason that the Major would have been involved in that transaction. The fields eventually became Cameron Stadium.

While it lasted, Washington County was the epicenter of oil and natural gas exploration in the world and produced more oil and gas than anywhere else.

A Strike in Nearby Taylorstown

Oil was shipped all over the East, and most of it was bought by the Standard Oil Company, owned by John D. Rockefeller. The boom lasted about twenty years, and when the famous Lucas Gusher at the Spindletop strike happened in Texas on January 10, 1901, the oil boom moved west.

There was still much more to be done. The country was changing, modern times were here. It seemed that new inventions were popping up every day. That fellow Edison seemed to have a new idea every week. One new idea that interested the Major was Alexander Bell's new toy, the telephone. It was going great guns in most major cities and by 1883 Happer thought that Washington should have it too. Along with H. U. Seaman and Robert Wolfe, Major A. G. Happer pushed for an exchange to be opened in town. Finally, on October 1884, the first Central office was opened in the Briceland building on West Wheeling Street, and Jennie Rogers was the first operator. The Major of course was one of the first customers and his phone number was 26.

As we've seen, the Major was very active in com-munity affairs for many years. There is one that hasn't been mentioned, his church. When Happer moved to Washington, Pennsylvania for good in 1871, it was no accident that when he had achieved sufficient success, he built his "magnificent house of Cleveland stone" right next door to the First Presbyterian Church.

The Happers had been for generations heav-ily involved with the Mingo Creek Presbyterian Church. In fact, most of them are buried in the cemetery there, near Finleyville. The Major, how-

First Presbyterian Church

ever, threw in with the church next door. For over forty-five years he was a member there, forty years the leader of the choir, and a trustee for over twenty-five years. He would be absent from church services or choir practice only due to illness.

The new century brought little change for the Major. He continued with his real estate and insurance business. He continued to be involved with the improvements to the city and county. The only thing lacking in his life was the blessings of children. He and Tilly never had any children of their own.

The early 1900s were a time of change and optimism for the town of Washington. It was a busy town, and bustling with activity. The great oil boom was dying out, but the coal boom was still going strong. Washington County has massive coal reserves underlying most of the county, in fact, it's one of the largest in the world. For decades, the coal business was the largest industry in the county. The Happers had coal interests for many years. By the time of WWI, the two largest bituminous coal mines in the world were located in Washington County, Pennsylvania.

The Washington Centennial celebration in 1910 was a grand affair. The Major was getting a little older now, but he was still a vigorous man and kept busy every day. In 1911, at age 72, he retired as President of the board of directors of the Morganza Training School. He still served on the board of the Washington Hospital and was actively managing its affairs. He was still involved with the agricultural community as well. He still served on the boards of the Citizen's Bank and the Washington Trust Co. The GAR still counted him as a member in good standing.

In November 1914, the Major began having trouble with his vision. His doctors were unable to diagnose the problem. By the end of March 1915, he was nearly blind. In mid-April, he traveled to Pittsburgh's West Penn Hospital to see the specialists there. He returned home, and his condition worsened. Two weeks later, on April 27, 1915, at 12:30 a. m; Major Happer suffered a stroke and passed away at his home, with Tilly at his side. Apparently, he was suffering from a malignancy in his eyes, and on that night, according to the autopsy report, he had suffered a fatal stroke. He had lived 75 years, 8 months, and 12 days. If thought about, he had lived several lifetimes worth in that time span. The Major's life was a life well lived.

Washington Reporter

WASHINGTON, PA., TUESDAY, APRIL 27, 1915.   TEN PAGES   NO. 12066—ONE CENT

MAJOR HAPPER DIED EARLY THIS MORNING

Had Notable War Record. Was Active in Business And Philanthropy

Major Andrew Gardner Happer died at his residence in East Wheeling street at 12:30 o'clock this morning. He had been ill for about six months with an affliction of the eyes. He came home from the West Penn hospital, where he had undergone treatment by eminent eye specialists two weeks ago last Friday, and had since grown steadily worse.

The funeral services will be held at the late home, 171 East Wheeling street, at 1 o'clock Thursday afternoon.

A son of John Arrell Happer and Violet Gardner Happer, Major Happer was born in Union township, this county, on August 15, 1869. His family was

THE LATE A. G. HAPPER

Continued on page 8

LOCAL 'PHONE SERVICE IS TO BE IMPROVED

All Toll Lines Leading From Town Are Being Reconstructed

REBUILDING 70 LINES

Changes Also Made to Remove Causes of Complaint In Local Service

MEETS DEMANDS OF INCREASED BUSINESS

THE HOTTEST APRIL 26 IN 41 YEARS

PUSHING PLANS FOR GOOD ROADS DAY IN COUNTY

Let Every Citizen Do His Part

The passing of the Major was the end of an era for Washington, Pennsylvania. Gone was the friendly, smiling, kindly Major Happer, roaming about town on some business or other. Generous to a fault, in his will he bequeathed to his longtime friend and employee Henry G. Hood, fully one-half of his insurance and real estate business, still easily the largest in Southwestern Pennsylvania at that time. His beloved Tilly retained the other half until her death, then Henry was to receive that half. Henry was to continue to manage the business while Matilda received one-half of the proceeds. The only condition was that the name of the firm was to remain The A. G. Happer Agency. Henry G. Hood and Matilda Happer were the executors of the Major's estate. At least for a while. Henry G. Hood was removed as executor by the Orphan's Court, probably at his own request due to the fact that he was to inherit a significant part of the estate. His son, Henry H. Hood, who also worked as a salesman in the agency was chosen instead. The Major's wake was held in their home as was customary. He was then finally laid to rest in the Watson family plot in Washington Cemetery. The Major's passing was front-page news, of course. The Washington Reporter ran a large story with a photo above the fold, telling some of the highlights of the Major's life. Another article appeared elsewhere in the paper. I believe this piece summed up the man reasonably well.

"In the death of Major Andrew Gardner Happer, Washington loses one of its best known and most respected citizens. He was a man far above the average, and as a man who ever served, stood out clearly above the rank and file of those who were served... Some wise man once said," require all things of thyself, and nothing of others." Perhaps this was the unconscious motto of Major Happer's life. With him, service was the natural attitude. To it were subordinated the strife for personal gain, in either fame or fortune; by it were overcome all the petty mishaps of life that bewilder and sour the man or ordinary aims, ordinary ideals, ordinary character. From his youth Major Happer served. He was a boy in college when came the first call to public service. Fighting for the continuance of the union of the United States of America, he served his country for the entire four years of the great conflict of the

North and South. In the service of his country he endured not only the ordinary hardships of a soldier, but tortures which the man who was not born to serve could never have borne. At the close of the war, the same zeal and energy which for four years had been the sole property of his country became the common possession of his fellows. As he had strived to save his country in war, so he strove to save it in peace. In the years following the end of the war, he helped to re-establish system and order in the national government, having been appointed collector of internal revenue in Washington County. With Washington and Washington County his field, his chance for service was in a sense narrower but more centralized. For almost half a century he was a member of the First Presbyterian church and there he served in the strictest sense of the word. To all branches of the church life he gave unselfish and loyal aid. His wise judgment, his sincerity and genuine ability to foresee and plan made his service in the many educational, charitable, and business interests with which he was associated much more than merely valuable. It was a necessity. And so he passed. As he served, so he died; peacefully, hopefully, happily. His life and his death represent all that is best and noble, and the pity of it is that more of humankind have not learned and will never learn, the hard lesson of service."

Tilly was devastated by the Major's passing. Her family was a great help through this depressing time. Her nine brothers and sisters along with the rest of the enormous family, helped her cope with the loss. She never remarried and continued to live in the home the Major built for her for the next twenty years with her cook Mary Washington and her driver Leroy Lewis. She continued to receive half the proceeds from the insurance and real estate business, so she had no major financial problems to worry about, even during the great depression.

Tilly passed away at her home on February first, 1935 at the ripe old age of 86. She had been ill for two weeks then suffered a heart attack and the following day suffered another one. The obituary written in the Washington Observer perhaps says it best.

"Mrs. Happer's entire life was spent in Washington, where her inter-est in public and charitable organizations and work remained high throughout her long life. She was known for her many acts of charity and kindness, carried out in such a quiet way that the public never knew of them.

Her interest in her church, the First Presbyterian and its auxiliaries, Washington Hospital, Washington & Jefferson College, Y.W.C.A., and all local benevolent and charitable organizations remained with her up to the very last. Mrs. Happer's interest in music was well known and she had heard all of the noted singers of her day. She was deeply interested in young musicians and artists, and helped many of them."

She was a great-granddaughter of Revolutionary War figure Colonel George Morgan, and the daughter of prominent attorney James Watson. She had been very active in church affairs and other civic philanthropies. She was laid to rest beside her husband in the family plot in Washington Cemetery.

A G Happer and Matilda Graves Front Row

The Morgan\ Happer Resting Places in Washington Cemetery

Since the Happers had no children to leave their worldly goods to, Tilly bequeathed the estate out to a number of close family members, with two exceptions. She left her driver Leroy Lewis $200. It doesn't sound like much by today's standards, but in 1935 that was a lot of money. She also set up a trust fund at the Citizens National Bank in the amount of $2000.00 to be invested and the proceeds to be paid in the amount of $10.00 per week to her cook, Mary Washington every week for the rest of her life. Thus providing lifetime income for her longtime friend. Again, $40 a month was nice money back then when many folks were out of work and going hungry. The Happers had always been generous, even when no one was looking. Andrew and Tilly's beautiful Victorian home made of "Cleveland stone," became a funeral parlor. After that, it was a bed and breakfast for a while. The good news is, it survives today as the Admissions Office for Washington and Jefferson College. The interior has been by necessity divided into offices, however, they did everything possible to preserve the interior woodwork and embellishments of the typical Queen Anne home, including the magnificent winding oak staircase with its huge stained glass windows.

So, what happened to the Happer farm? The Major's father, John died in 1890 leaving the farm to his wife Violet to do with as she wished. If the Major's brother J. Wilmer Happer wished to continue farming the land, he was to pay rent of no more than $400 per year plus all taxes. Violet Happer passed away five years later in 1895 leaving no will. We don't know exactly what happened after John Happer died, or after Violet died. The Major and his brother J. Wilmer were their father's executors and would have handled any business or financial dealings that needed to be taken care of.

There is some good news, however. The farm had indeed remained in the Happer family all this time. Even after the Major died in 1915, the farm was still the Happer farm. Finally, in February 1925, it all came to an end. Matilda Happer, and Henry G. Hood as executors of the Major's estate, along with the surviving children of John Happer, sold the entire remaining 220 acres.

The land is still there today, probably still owned by the descendants of the family that bought it. It hasn't been paved over, or developed into neighborhoods of expensive houses or commercial buildings yet as have many of the old farms. The property was divided into lots for the now grown children and grand children of the buyers. There are still some farm fields there, along with a few deserted, broken-down outbuildings, the only remaining evidence of its storied past. The Happers owned that land from 1787 until 1925, 138 years. From the time of the Revolution, through the Whiskey Rebellion, the War of 1812, the Civil War, the war with Spain, and the World War, clear up until the roaring '20s and into the Great Depression, the Happers were able to own, work, cherish, and take care of the land. It appears that the current owners have at least tried to continue that tradition somewhat. I hope they understand just what history they have in their hands.

The news is somewhat better for the Major's insurance and real estate agency. He founded the company in 1871 in the little storefront office at 55 South Main Street. He built it into the largest insurance and real estate business in Southwestern Pennsylvania. Fairly early on he hired Henry G. Hood, who over time, became his right-hand man and lifelong friend. Henry pretty much ran the day-to-day business in the office, while the Major was in the field developing the area surrounding the town of Washington. Eventually, Henry's son, Henry H. Hood came to work as a salesman in the office. And later another son, Louis V. Hood was hired as well. With the Major's passing in 1915, half the agency became the property of Henry G. Hood, who continued as before under the same name, only now, the large development projects were gone with the Major. Henry G. Hood was also an officer in the Canton Land Company. Information about this company appears to be nonexistent as of this writing, but this was when the Major was still alive, so it's possible both of them were involved somehow.

When Tilly passed away in 1935, Henry G. Hood became the sole owner. He was then permitted under the terms of the Major's will to change the company name which he did, to Henry G. Hood & Sons. He kept the office at the same location. In 1972 it became the Hood Insurance Associates and in 1979 it moved to 620 North Main Street. In 1990 Richard Garlitz became president and the company moved to Washington Road, then to West Chestnut Street. Finally, the last listing found for the Major's old company was in 2004. Hood Insurance Associates was on Southpointe Blvd. It seems now to have disappeared after more than a century.

Even though the Major and Matilda Happer had no children of their own, they did have a very interesting family record. Their extended family is veritable Who's Who of not only Washington County, PA, but all of the state and in fact the United States in general.

I think it appropriate to mention a few of the more interesting and consequential family members that made their mark on the world that they lived in both then and now. From before the American Revolution right up until today, the Happer family is making their presence felt. You will see that the A. G. Happer legacy continues on even today.

David Thompson Watson was Matilda Happer's older brother. He was born in Washington, Pennsylvania on January 2, 1844. He was admitted to Washington College in 1858. He took time out to serve in the Union Army, mustering into Company C, 168th Pennsylvania Volunteer Infantry on October 16, 1862, as a private. His regiment saw no hostilities and was mustered out on July 23, 1863. He resumed his education and graduated in 1864. In early 1865, he enrolled at Harvard Law and completed his studies there in the fall of 1866.

D. T. Watson

He practiced law in Massachusetts for a short time before returning home to practice in his father's law office. He stayed there for only a short time before moving to Pittsburgh where he opened an office on Grant Street. Some of his more notable clients initially were the famous Arbuckle Coffee roasting company, Dravo Company, and the Second National Bank. As he became more successful, he attracted the attention of Andrew Carnegie. He served as counsel for both him and Henry Clay Frick. He also worked for the Vanderbilts. The cherry on top, however, was when he was asked to serve on the legal team that brokered the deal that finalized the purchase of Alaska by the United States from Russia.

In 1889, he married Margaret Walker, daughter of a Pittsburgh banker. They had a home in Allegheny, Pa; just across the Allegheny River from the city. Allegheny is now a part of Pittsburgh called North Side. Like many well-to-do families at that time, they purchased a summer home in the country. It was located a few miles down the Ohio River near Leetsdale and Sewickley. It was a large estate with woodlands and farm fields. They called it "Sunnyhill".

The Watsons were very interested in children, even though they were never blessed with any of their own. This led to discussions with a leading orthopedic surgeon, Dr. David Silver about starting a home for crippled children. David Watson never lived to see it. He passed away on February 24, 1916. He did however ensure that their dream would come true. His will spelled out the establishment of the D.T. Watson Home for Crippled Children, which opened in 1920. The home was very successful. Dr. Jonas Saulk conducted his first clinical trials for his Polio vaccine at home during the epidemic in the 1950s.

The home continued until 1984 when the people running the organization expanded the operation beyond what it was meant to be. They later realized their mistake and tried to return to the Watson's original mission. They renamed what was left, the Watson Institute, which by 2001, was gobbled up by a private school and a small hospital. Today, the old D. T. Watson Home does exist, but in name only.

John Happer was a nephew of Major A. G. Happer. He was from the branch of the family that went west early on. He was born in Scandia, Kansas in 1892, he went on to marry Mary Hannah Martin and they had five children. He later married Miss Anna Casey in 1929. They had moved to the Chicago area by 1930 when John worked as the controller for the Wilson Meat Packing Company.

John Happer

Wilson was starting a new venture in the sporting goods business. What was unusual is that John was a friend of famous Notre Dame football coach Knute Rockne.

On the morning of March 31, 1931, John Happer and Knute Rockne took off in a small plane, a Fokker F-10-A bound for Los Angles for a business meeting, along with six others. The plane lost a wing and crashed in a pasture near Bazaar, Kansas, killing all aboard. There is a monument standing at the crash site today with the names of all the victims engraved upon it. Knute K. Rockne, John Happer, Waldo B. Miller, H. J. Christen, Spencer Goldthwaite, C.A. Robrecht, Robert Fry, Herman J. Mathias.

On the seventy-fifth anniversary of the crash in 2006, the monument was re-dedicated. Among those in attendance was the now eighty-nine-year-old man who was one of the first to reach the crash in 1931, Easter Heathman, and nine Happer descendants. The Wilson Company went on to become the famous Wilson Sporting Goods Company that we know today.

Lydia Happer was the Major's, Grand Niece. While living in Washington, DC, she met and married a young Army, Second Lieutenant named Maxwell Davenport Taylor in 1925. Max Taylor had an astounding military career. Here are a very few of the highlights. He graduated from West Point in 1922. For the next twenty years, he worked his way up the ranks. In

Rockne Crash Site Memorial

1942 when he was promoted to Brigadier General, serving with the 82nd Airborne. Promoted to Major General in 1944 and given command of the 101st Airborne. He became the first allied General officer to land in France during the Normandy invasion when the 101st parachuted into France on June 5, 1944.

During the Battle of the Bulge, he was called back to Washington for a staff conference and was absent when the 101st was surrounded by the Germans at Bastogne. His second in command, Brigadier General Anthony C. McAuliffe, was the man who when asked by the German commander to surrender replied with the famous one-word answer, "Nuts." General Taylor commanded the 101st through the end of the war.

Lt. General Maxwell Taylor

From 1945 to 1949 he was superintendent of West Point, afterwards, he was the commander of Allied troops in Berlin from 1949 to 1951. He was Chief of Staff of the European Command in 1949. He was commander of the Eighth Army in Korea in 1953. Then he was Commander in Chief of the United Nations Command in 1955. From there he moved to Chief of Staff of the United States Army from 1955 to 1959, when he retired for the first time.

After the April 1961 failure of the Bay of Pigs invasion, Kennedy recalled Taylor and appointed him to head a task force to investigate the failure of the invasion. He was recalled again by President Kennedy in 1962 to serve as Chairman of the Joint Chiefs of Staff, which he held until 1964.

Both President Kennedy and his brother, Attorney General Robert F. Kennedy, had immense regard for Taylor, whom they saw as a man of unquestionable integrity, sincerity, intelligence, and diplomacy. In the course of their work together, Taylor developed a deep regard and a personal affection for Robert F. Kennedy, a friendship that was wholly mutual and which remained firm until Kennedy's assassination in 1968. Robert Kennedy named one of his sons after the general. Matthew Maxwell Taylor Kennedy.

Taylor retired once again, but was appointed the U S Ambassador to South Viet Nam by President Johnson, and served from 1964 to 1965. He then became Special Consultant to the President and Chairman of the Foreign Intelligence Advisory Board from 1965 until 1969, and President of the Institute of Defense Analysis as well. General Taylor during his career was awarded the following decorations for his service: Distinguished Service Cross, Silver Star, Distinguished Service Medal, Bronze Star, Legion of Merit, and the Purple Heart.

General Taylor died in Washington, D. C. on April 19, 1987. He was buried at Arlington National Cemetery. His wife, Lydia Happer Taylor, passed away on April 22, 1997, at the age of 95, in Washington, D. C. She had accompanied her husband to assignments in Germany, Vietnam, and Japan. She was the co-founder of the Army Distaff Foundation, which later became Knowllwood, a military retirement facility in Northwest Washington.

Lydia and the General had two sons. One of them, Thomas Happer Taylor is a military historian with at least seven books to his credit. He also served our country honorably in the Viet Nam war where he had volunteered for service. He was assigned to the 101st Airborne. Taylor saw plenty of combat and was wounded in action. He was awarded the Silver Star and two Bronze Stars for valor, and a Purple Heart.

Their other son, John M. Taylor, was born at West Point, New York. He graduated from Williams College and went on the earn his master's from George Washington University. He worked for the U. S. government at the CIA and State Department for many years. Mr. Taylor is a historian and distinguished author of eight books including, *Duty Faithfully Performed, Robert E. Lee and His Critics.*

Last but not least we end with Andrew Happer. No, not THAT Andrew Happer, but the son of Reverend Andrew Patton Happer, and the nephew of Major Happer. This one lived in China for years in various positions, but it just wasn't for him. He returned to the States with his wife. I don't have much info on them, but his story is interesting nonetheless.

He returned to China on a business trip. While there he was bitten by a dog and became very ill and died of rabies. He never got to see his newborn son Andrew III.

There are Happers scattered all over the world today, just not in or near Washington PA. From the mid-west to Hawaii, from Texas to China, if you look hard enough you will find the name Happer.

There are many stories of the Happers that are outside the scope of this book. It seems a shame to exclude them as there are many outstanding people and accomplishments that should be recognized. Maybe in another book, I can tell those tales that must be skipped over here. An odd thing is that in all the years I have researched the Happers, I have found only four pictures of Major Happer and none of Matilda.

Andrew Happer Jr

I spent a year tracing his estate down through the family (the Happers had no children) to try to find out what happened to all the letters, pictures, etc. I did find an itemized account of all the estate with a cousin of Tilly's. It sat in storage for many years in Washington, PA. After much frustration, I was able to find the last known descendant that is known to have the Major's estate.

She had no children and passed away in 1976. None of her nieces, uncles, etc have even heard of Major Happer, and know of no such estate their Great Aunt may have had. So, yet another dead end. However, I will keep searching for the major's letters and any photos that may remain. And somewhere out there in some hot, musty attic, or damp basement, is an engraved pocket watch with the name of Major A. G. Happer inscribed, and some of his letters home from the war, and maybe, just maybe, a few pictures of them.

Mrs Andrew Happer With Andrew III

As for Major Andrew Gardner Happer, I can say without reservation that of all the stories and writings of Civil War soldiers that I have seen and read over the years, no story compares

274

Washington Walk of Fame

Major Happer's Brick in the Walk of Fame

to Major Happer's. There are many examples of men who became politicians and captains of industry. There are many tales of great accomplishments. But none quite as compelling as the Majors. He led an exemplary life from beginning to end.

He felt a responsibility to continue on in his ancestor's desire to serve others. He survived hardships few others have. He continued to serve as best he could even with permanent injury.

His motives can never be questioned. The results speak for themselves. He served his fellow soldiers and citizens all his adult life without regard for fame or notoriety. Time after time, he made other people's lives better without taking credit and not giving that a second thought. He never once put his name on any of the entities he founded, even though he could have and in retrospect, maybe should have. He was a man who did the right thing when no one was looking.

The Author Standing on The Happer's Front Porch

If you visit Washington Pennsylvania today, you will find no obvious evidence that A. G. Happer ever lived there. There is no statue, no monument, and no building named after him. Few there have ever heard his name and have no idea who he was or what he accomplished there. It's actually quite shocking. Other men there have received great acclaim and are well known and represented everywhere you look around town. It's sad to see that when the great men of Washington County Pennsylvania are listed, the Major's name is somehow always absent.

However, that is now changing. As a result of my first book Born To Serve, The Major A. G. Happer Story, after four long years of hard work and effort by myself and many other people, the Major was at long last, awarded a Pennsylvania State Historical Marker. It will proudly stand outside his former home, in Washington PA now owned by Washington & Jefferson College. It will signify recognition of the man and his efforts to better the human condition and lead his city and county into the twentieth century.

Also, he has been elected into the Washington County Hall of Fame by the Washington County Historical Society. Both of these are great honors reserved for people who deserve to be recognized permanently for their selfless efforts and accomplishments to advance the betterment of the state, county, and city. The Major is also enshrined in the Washington Walk of Fame, located at the old train station. He has a brick installed there in recognition of his service.

I'm certain that the Major if he were here today would be embarrassed about all the attention, and would mention others he thought more deserving. That is just the kind of man he was. We shall always remember him.

Major Andrew Gardner Happer

Sarah Happer Parsons

John Isaac Parsons

Carrie Parsons

Leila Parsons

Isaac W. Parsons

John Howe Parsons

The Vault at The Washington Trust Co.

Mingo Creek Presbyterian Church Today

Many of the Happers are Buried Here

Margaret Happer

Lura A. Happer

Andrew F. Happer

Lincoln's Viewing Stand at
Harrisburg

EPILOGUE

How did we get to this point?

I chose this topic for my new book because as time has marched on, the soldiers who served during the Civil War have largely been forgotten. I mean the little guys. The common, private soldier not the Generals as much, not the big shots, but the regular guys who left home and family to answer the call. What these men did is fading away to nothing. The most significant event in American history is being wiped away by time and apathy. And what happened to them after the war has been ignored, until now.

I always want to know the rest of the story. I have to find out what happened later. Whatever became of them? What about their family? Where did they live, and what did they do for a living after the war? So, I set out on a journey to find out and answer those very questions, at least in one county in Southwestern Pennsylvania.

The stories selected for inclusion here were chosen for their relevance, interest, and the images associated with the people concerned. I researched over four hundred soldiers from Washington County Pennsylvania alone.

A good mix was decided upon as the project went forward, things changed along the way as they always will when attempting any writing project. Some soldiers had to be left out for now, others added. Some had their stories shortened to remain within the scope of the book. However, I did take liberties with that. That was difficult , as so many great images had to be omitted. Some really interesting and excellent tales had to be left out because of the time element. This project suffered long delays and was put on hold for months at a time. When the time was right, I restarted the work and by necessity, I had to again shorten the book to have it released in a reasonable amount of time and not have to wait until 2024.

So, what is the right thing to do? I decided to make this volume one and do another volume so I could tell those stories that deserve to be told, and find more images of the veterans in uniform if possible, and concentrate more on the veterans themselves. And those veterans, be they scamps, scoundrels, or heroes, will never be forgotten. We shall forever remember, all of them.

J. D.

About the Author

Who is this guy?

Jim Douglas resides with his family in Southwestern Pennsylvania. Jim is a Civil War Historian and a serious collector of Civil War artifacts. He provide advice on authenticity to various collectors, sellers and auctioneers, and others. He also hand-colorizes black and white Civil War (and other) images. Mr. and Mrs. Douglas collect antiques and especially Christmas and Halloween antique and vintage decorations.

Jim has been a speaker at many Civil War-related functions, and has appeared at various times in the Pittsburgh Tribune-Review commenting on Civil War topics and in the Washington PA Observer Reporter in connection with his books. He is very honored to be a member of and Historian and Council to Company G of the 11th Pennsylvania Volunteer Infantry reenactors.

Mr. Douglas is especially honored to receive on behalf of Major Andrew Gardner Happer, Washington County Historical Society's Hall of Fame Enshrinement in September of 2023. When the great men in the history of Washington County are listed, Major Andrew G. Happer will at long last, and forever be among them.

Jim was most proud to be the Sponsor of the successful effort to have a Pennsylvania State Historical Marker awarded to Major Happer. It was a very long and very difficult process, but he was able to make it happen...for the Major.

Jim will be the Master of Ceremonies and keynote speaker at the Major Andrew Gardner Happer Pennsylvania State Historical Marker dedication event in early 2024 in historic Washington Pennsylvania.

You can follow Jim at his website: www.jimdouglasauthor.com and on Instagram: @jimdouglas_author

For additional pictures of all the veterans and their families in this book, please check Jim's website and social media pages. There will be many more images, some in full color that we couldn't fit into this book.

All colorized images in this book were hand done by the author.

LOOK FOR OTHER BOOKS BY JIM DOUGLAS

Look for his other titles:

Born To Serve
The Major A. G. Happer Story

The Bloody Eleventh
A Regimental History

Available on Amazon and Barnes and Noble
and
Many Local Bookstores

Signed Copies Available on the Author's Website
www.jimdouglasauthor.com